Coasts

Coasts

Richard A. Davis, Jr.
University of South Florida

Prentice Hall
Upper Saddle River, New Jersey 07458

Library of Congress Cataloging-in-Publication Data

Davis, Richard A. (Richard Albert)
      Coasts / Richard A. Davis, Jr.
          p.   cm.
      Includes index.
      ISBN 0-13-359944-2
      1. Coasts.   I. Title.
GB451.2.D388   1996
551.4'57—dc20   95–21189
                                     CIP

Acquisitions editor: Robert McConnin
Editorial/production management: J. Carey Publishing Service
Cover director: Jayne Conte
Manufacturing buyer: Trudy Pisciotti

© 1996 by Prentice-Hall, Inc.
Simon & Schuster/A Viacom Company
Upper Saddle River, New Jersey 07458

Printed in the United States of America

10 9 8 7 6 5 4 3 2 1

ISBN 0-13-359944-2

Prentice-Hall International (UK) Limited, *London*
Prentice-Hall of Australia Pty. Limited, *Sydney*
Prentice-Hall Canada Inc., *Toronto*
Prentice-Hall Hispanoamericana, S.A., *Mexico*
Prentice-Hall of India Private Limited, *New Delhi*
Prentice-Hall of Japan, Inc., *Tokyo*
Simon & Schuster Asia Pte. Ltd., *Singapore*
Editora Prentice-Hall do Brasil, Ltda., *Rio de Janeiro*

Contents

3

Sea-Level Change and the Coast   39

4

Coastal Processes   64

5

River Deltas   104

6
Estuaries, Marshes, and Tidal Flats   131

7
Sandy Coasts   157

8
Rocky Coasts 205

9
Human Intervention in Coastal Environments 232

Index 271

Preface

Because coastal environments are there for all of us to see and appreciate, it is important that there be readily available information about the nature of these environments and how they operate on the earth's surface. Undergraduate students typically have considerable interest in the coast, and most have spent some time there for various reasons. This book provides the reader with a comprehensive but broad appreciation and understanding of coastal environments. It combines some of the basic features of the geology of the earth's crust with characteristics and processes of the ocean margins to provide the reader with the fundamental principles that govern the nature and development of coastal environments. Building upon this framework are chapters covering each one of the major building block environments that collectively emcompass the coast—deltas, estuaries, sandy coasts, and rocky coasts. The book closes with a chapter that considers the many ways in which human activity influences and alters the natural coastal environments.

The coast is where the land meets the sea, the most widespread boundary on the planet. Our knowledge of the solid earth is extensive and has been promulgated through various books and courses for well over a century. It is difficult to go anywhere on the earth's surface without experiencing some aspect of geology. More recently, essentially after World War II, our knowledge of the world ocean has greatly expanded. This has led to widespread research, and to numerous books and courses on the broad topic of oceanography. Even though few of us have an opportunity of directly experiencing the ocean environment, there is great interest in it.

The coastal zone covers little area on a global scale but this narrow strip extends through all climates, geologic provinces, and geographic locations. It includes all environments in which there is significant interaction between the domain of the land and that of the sea. Coasts are among our most precious natural resources because of their protection of upland areas, their role as sites of both residential and commercial development, their attraction as recreational and vacation venues, and their natural beauty. As a consequence, most people have some interest in, or experience with, the coast during their lifetime. Virtually everyone goes to the beach, and now that air travel is universal most of us fly over coastal areas. We commonly see coastal environments in the media surrounding circumstances of floods, earthquakes, hurricanes, or oil spills, and perhaps most importantly, most of us live within a two-hour drive of the coast. Thus, the bottom line is, whether we realize it or not, we all have a vested interest in the coast and its behavior. This book will provide the student with a broad perspective on coastal systems and their dynamics.

The book is designed as an undergraduate text for a general course on coasts or to be used as a supplement for a general oceanography course in which the instructor wants an expanded section on coasts. It also provides good reference information for related courses in physical geography, coastal engineering, and coastal management. Extensive illustrations are used to illustrate the many examples discussed in the text.

ACKNOWLEDGMENTS

Completion of this book has benefitted greatly from the many people who have hosted my coastal travels and studies, and from numerous colleagues that have provided photographs. I am also grateful for the comments of reviewers Robert Dolan of the University of Virginia, Duncan FitzGerald of Boston University, William Fox of Williams College, Jennifer Prouty of Texas A & M University-Corpus Christi, and Peter Rosen of Northeastern University. Editor Robert McConnin of Prentice Hall saw the book through the entire process and Jennifer Carey of J. Carey Publishing Service championed the production of the manuscript. All of these folks made very important contributions to the book.

Richard A. Davis, Jr.
Tampa, Florida

1

The Nature of Coasts

The coast is many things to many people, and our perspective of it ranges widely depending on where and how we live, work, and recreate. This narrow band of earth may be covered with water or not or may be covered only part of the time. The coast represents a broad spectrum of environments both for people and for the natural fauna and flora that inhabit it. Because it is typically very beautiful and interesting, many people live on or near the coast and many more visit it for the same reasons. It provides livelihood for a large number of people either directly or indirectly, with some having the task of protecting it from intruders or enemies.

HISTORY OF COASTAL OCCUPATION

The ancient civilizations of the Eastern Mediterranean Sea were largely associated with the coast, including the famous Greek, Roman, and Egyptian settlements and the fortifications of biblical times. Many of the great cities of the time were located on the natural harbors afforded by the geologic and physiographic conditions granted by the coast (Fig. 1.1). Very northern Viking settlements in the Scandinavian countries of Norway, Sweden, and Denmark were also typically located along the coast. Here great fjords provided shelter and fortification, and ready access to what was a primary food source, the main avenue of transportation, and battleground. During the same time period, the northern coast of Europe was also occupied for similar reasons but in a very different coastal setting of lowlands and barrier islands.

Cities in the New World such as Boston, New York, Baltimore and San

FIGURE 1.1
Eastern Mediterranean area showing locations of several important ancient coastal cities
in the modern countries of Italy, Egypt, Greece, and Turkey.

Francisco owe their location to the presence of a protected harbor. In their early
states nearly all major civilizations of the world were either directly on the coast
or had important interaction with it. The few exceptions were the Incan, Mayan,
and some other civilizations of Central and South America and large portions of
the Middle East and China.

Early reasons for this extensive occupation of coastal areas were strictly
pragmatic. Coasts were essential for harboring ships, which were the primary
means of transporting goods, one of the major activities of the times. The adjacent sea was also a primary source of food. This pattern of coastal occupation and
utilization continued until the latter part of the nineteenth century by which
time the interior areas of the United States had been settled and large cities were
scattered all over the country (Fig. 1.2). However, many of these cities are near
water as well, either on the Great Lakes (Chicago, Detroit, Cleveland, and Buf-
falo) or on the banks of large rivers (St. Louis, Memphis, Cincinnati, and Pitts-
burgh). All were settled on the water because their location fostered commerce
that depended on water transportation.

Since ancient times, the coast has been a strategic setting for military activity. At first it was the cities housing military installations. Later it became impor-

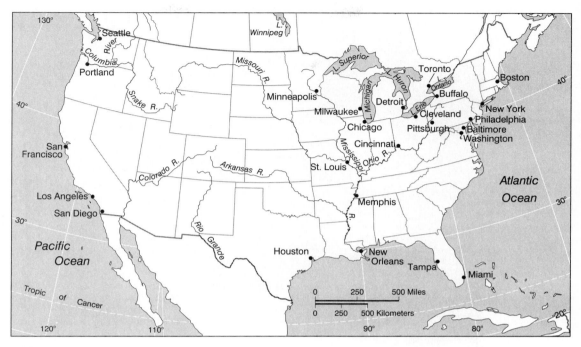

FIGURE 1.2

Outline map of the United States with major cities located along the water; marine coasts, Great Lakes coasts, and rivers. Most of the large cities in the United States fall into one of these three categories.

tant as a staging ground for large-scale invasions; examples include the British conquest of France in the early fifteenth century and during the twentieth century when Allied troops landed on the beaches of the Pacific (Fig. 1.3) and Normandy during World War II. Thus for thousands of years the coast was considered desirable for occupation that would support transportation of goods and military activities as well as feed the population.

Only at the end of nineteenth century did coastal activities expand into broad-based recreational use with related support industries. As the result of the Industrial Revolution, and overall prosperity, both in North America and to a lesser extent in Europe, people began to look to the coast as a place to take family holidays. Nearly 50 percent of the present world population lives on or within a two-hour drive of the coast.

This being the case, it is to our advantage to have a good understanding of the coast—its diverse environments, its inhabitants, and the dynamics of change that characterizes it. We must also know how human activity affects coastal areas, sometimes with major deleterious effects.

FIGURE 1.3
Troops landing on a Pacific Island coast during World War II.
(AP/Wide World Photos)

HISTORICAL RESEARCH TRENDS

Only recently have scientists undertaken comprehensive investigations of the coast. Some nineteenth-century publications considered the origin of barrier islands, the development of coral reef coasts (including those by Sir Charles Darwin on his famous voyage with the H.M.S. *Beagle*), and characteristics of the cliffed coasts of Brittany and the British Isles.

The first systematic efforts at studying the coast in the early twentieth century were made by geomorphologists, those who are interested in the morphology or landforms of the earth. Geomorphologists also investigate mountains, deserts, rivers, and other earth features. Their studies produced various classifications, maps, and reports on coastal features. Some scientists focused on the evolution of coasts and the processes responsible for molding them. For example, in 1919 Douglas W. Johnson wrote a classic and pioneering book entitled *Shore Processes and Shoreline Development,* an effort that is still commonly referenced.

Engineers also gave special attention to the coast going back several centuries. Their interest was directed toward construction efforts of harbors, docks, wharves, and bridges, on one hand, and stabilization of the open coast on the other (Fig. 1.4). Although both groups of professionals directed their efforts toward different aspects of the coast, in many ways their interests overlapped.

Ancient peoples recognized that the coast is continually changing and that

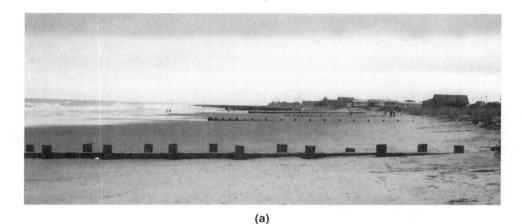

(a)

(b)

FIGURE 1.4
Examples of structures used to protect coasts from erosion include a) groins and b) seawalls.

the open zone that faces the ocean is extremely dynamic. Erosion was a big problem (Fig. 1.5), and settlements were lost or threatened as the shoreline retreated. Dikes have been constructed along the North Sea coast of Holland and Germany for centuries, both for protection (Fig. 1.6) and for land reclamation. In most other areas, however, construction on the open coast was designed to slow or prevent erosion. As a result, various types of structures were emplaced at critical locations along densely inhabited coastal areas.

For decades these activities represented the major efforts of science and technology to understand, and in some respects, to control, the response of the coast to natural processes. World War II was also an important period for furthering our understanding of the coast. Major war efforts took place along the coast—the landing of troops, supplies, and equipment both on the European mainland and on Pacific islands. All branches of the military were involved in studying coastal geomorphology; coastal processes including waves, tides, and currents; and the analysis of coastal weather patterns. During this period much of the world's coast was mapped in detail. The Beach Erosion Board, a research branch of the U.S. Army affiliated with the Corps of Engineers, made many very important contributions to our knowledge of coasts, conducting extensive research on beaches, waves, erosion, and other important aspects of the coast,

FIGURE 1.5
Wave induced erosion along a beach/dune area on the east coast of Florida near St. Augustine.

FIGURE 1.6
Photo of a dike along The Netherlands coast on the North Sea. Like many of the dikes, this one supports a roadway.

using both their own staff and academic researchers from many of the best universities. Francis P. Shepard and Douglas L. Inman of the Scripps Institution of Oceanography (Fig. 1.7) were prominent contributors to the research programs of this group, and later became among the most prominent coastal researchers in the world.

This coastal research effort continued after the war, but with a distinctly engineering emphasis. The name of the Beach Erosion Board was changed to Coastal Engineering Research Center. Originally housed at Ft. Belvoir, Virginia, it is now located in Vicksburg, Mississippi. At about this time the Office of Naval Research (ONR) became heavily involved in basic coastal research. Their first major efforts in this endeavor were through the Coastal Studies Institute of Louisiana State University. Although this organization conducted a variety of coastal research projects, its major effort was a global study of river deltas, beginning near home with the Mississippi Delta. As time passed, the ONR expanded its coastal research to emphasize beaches, inlets, and deltas, places where military activities could potentially take place. During the 1960s and 1970s this agency, through the leadership of Dr. Evelyn Pruitt, supported most of the research on modern open coastal environments and thus began the modern era of coastal research, which emphasized the process-response systems. In other words, it was no longer enough to observe coastal features or environments and

FIGURE 1.7
The old Scripps Pier at Scripps Institution of Oceanography at La Jolla, California. Considerable data on nearshore processes have been collected from this structure over several decades. It has now been replaced by a new version.
(Courtesy of Scripps Institution of Oceanography)

to describe them. The focus now included the origin and development of these features, which necessitated studying the physical and biological processes at work on the coast and then integrating these data with the resulting features. Thus, the process-response approach to coastal research. In reality therefore, coastal research of this type is only a few decades old.

COASTAL ELEMENTS

This book considers the factors that determine what type of coast develops. The processes that develop and maintain coastal environments, and in some cases, those that destroy the coast, will be discussed in order to convey the dynamic nature of all coastal elements. Each of the major coastal systems—deltas, estuaries, strandplain coasts, barrier islands, and rocky coasts—will be considered in light of these controlling factors and processes. Lastly, we will address the strong influence of human activity on coastal environments.

Most of the emphasis will be directed toward geologic and physical attributes of the coast, although organisms will not be overlooked. There are many excellent books that focus on the fauna and flora of coastal environments; only a superficial treatment is included here.

Open coasts can be divided into two general categories: dominantly erosional and primarily depositional (Fig. 1.8) over geologically significant periods of time, that is, thousands of years. Erosional coasts are extensive and have considerable variety and typically include some beaches and other local depositional features. Although they are among the most beautiful and spectacular of all coastal types, there is less variation in this rocky, erosional type of coast than in those characterized by deposition. Depositional coasts include deltas, barrier island systems, and strandplain coasts, each with their own numerous distinct environments. The variety of morphological features and the complex interaction of depositional coasts deserves extensive attention and thus receives emphasis in this book.

Rivers carry tremendous quantities of sediment to their mouths at which point they deposit it. Although much is entrained by waves and currents, commonly there is a net accumulation of sediment at the river mouth known as a delta (Fig. 1.9). In fact, most of the sediment along all types of depositional coasts owes its presence, at least indirectly, to a river. Deltas range widely in size and shape. Most are dominated by mud and sand but some have abundant gravel. The primary conditions for delta formation are a supply of sediment, a place for it to accumulate, and the inability of the open water processes to remove all of the sediment from the river mouth. Deltas may form on the open coast or in embayments.

In many high-latitude areas the sediment comprising coastal environments has been reworked from glacial deposits, a situation that dominates the Alaskan and New England coasts.

Sea level has risen considerably over the past several thousand years due to glacial melting and other factors, flooding many parts of the land and developing extensive and numerous coastal bays. Streams, some large and some small, feed most of these bays called *estuaries* (Fig. 1.10) that are commonly surrounded by some combination of wetlands (usually either salt marshes or mangrove swamps) and tidal flats. Another common type of coastal bay is one that tends to parallel the coast and that is protected from the open ocean by a barrier island. These elongate water bodies have little influx of fresh water or tidal exchange and are called *lagoons*. Tidal flats and marshes are uncommon along this type of bay. Not all coastal bays are estuaries or lagoons. Tectonic activity or other geologic attributes create other bays. They may have no streams emptying into them and there is open tidal circulation. No special designation is applied; they are simply coastal bays.

The above-mentioned barrier islands are another important part of the scheme of coastal complexes. Barrier islands are, as the name implies, a protection in front of the mainland, typically fronting lagoons and/or estuaries. These barriers include beaches, adjacent dunes, and other environments. Wetlands, especially salt marshes, are widespread on the landward side of barrier islands. Tidal inlets dissect

(a)

(b)

FIGURE 1.8
Examples of (a) a rocky erosional coast in southern Maine, and (b) a barrier-island, depositional coast in Massachusetts.

(a - Courtesy of U.S. National Park Service; b - Courtesy of Miles O. Hayes)

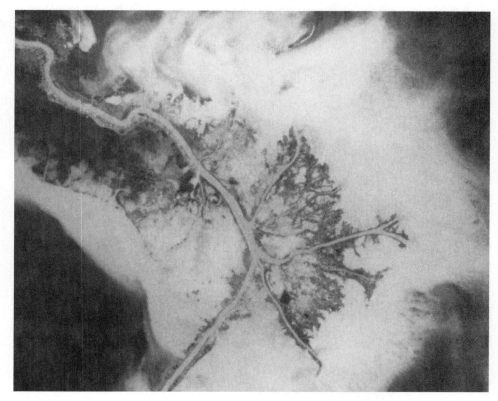

FIGURE 1.9
Satellite photo of the Mississippi Delta showing considerable suspended sediment being discharged through numerous distributaries.
(Image from EROS Data Center)

barrier islands and are among the most dynamic of all coastal environments; not only do they separate adjacent barrier islands, they also provide for the exchange of water and nutrients between the open ocean and estuarine systems.

Strandplain coasts have beaches and dunes but lack the coastal bay; they are directly attached to the mainland, essentially as if the seaward half of a barrier island were plastered against the mainland.

The presence of rocky or headland coasts can occur as short isolated sections within extensive sandy depositonal coasts such as along parts of the east coast of Australia or some parts of New England. Other geomorphically similar coasts may have their origin in glacial deposits. In both cases, the coast is characterized as erosional and may provide sediments for nearby depositional beaches.

FIGURE 1.10
Headland on the Oregon coast with an associated barrier spit protecting the small estuary.
(Courtesy of W.T. Fox)

GENERAL COASTAL SETTINGS

Varied geologic conditions provide different settings for the coast and give distinct variety and beauty to that part of the earth's surface. Thus, some coasts are quite rugged with bedrock cliffs and irregular shorelines whereas others are low-lying, almost featureless areas with long, smooth shorelines. To be sure, with time, any coast may change extensively but some important relationships continue through geologically significant periods of time, up to several million years.

Changes at a given part of the coast are typically slow and continuous but can be sporadic and rapid. Consider an area along the Pacific coast in Oregon or Washington, both places where sandy beaches interrupt rugged cliffs. This coast results from a particular regional geologic setting that includes varied rock types with considerable folds, faults, and intrusive and extrusive igneous rocks. These, along with the regional climate of abundant rainfall, give rise to an irregular topography in the western parts of both states, the Coast Ranges. For millions of years the ocean surface has met the edge of this rugged mountainous area intermittently. This position of intersection has, however, been essentially at its present location for at most only a few thousand years. In these few thousand years the waves, wind, and currents have been able to wear some of the rock away and have deposited the debris as beaches that are discontinuous with bedrock headlands interrupting them. Some of the erosional debris has been carried to the deeper waters of the adjacent continental shelf, and some of the original rock was dissolved by chemical weathering.

Overprinted on this combination of slow processes of change is the fluctuation in sea level. Though the coast has been located at its present position along the Coast Ranges for a few thousand years, in actual fact, sea level has been changing very slowly throughout that time, about 1 to 2 millimeters per year. In the geologic past this rate was both much faster and a bit slower. The point is, as coastal processes work to shape the substrate and the adjacent land, the position of the shoreline changes as well. This translates the processes and their effects across the shallow continental shelf and the adjacent coastal zone, producing long and slow but relatively steady coastal change.

We can hypothetically apply the contrasting condition of sporadic but rapid change to the same area. The Northwestern part of the United States is one of tectonic activity. Numerous earthquakes have occurred throughout history all the way from California up through parts of Alaska. The spectacular eruption of the Mount Saint Helens volcano in 1980 is testimony to the scale that a single event can achieve.

Suppose, for example, that an earthquake of considerable magnitude took place in the general area of the coast and locally shifted the earth's crust significantly up or down. Regardless of which relative motion took place, the shoreline would either be elevated markedly above its former position or submerged. Even a change of only a meter or so either way would dramatically change the shoreline and the coastal geomorphology. This presents a new set of coastal conditions that could elevate the beach and expose a formerly submerged wave-cut terrace or drown the coast and create a steep cliffed shoreline. Thus, the rate of change is of interest to scientists studying coastal development. Change can take place over thousands of years or in only a day.

The geography and geology of the coast provide spatial variation in the coastal setting. The size of the coastal reach that we are considering is important. Characteristics of the coastal zone may change over various scales ranging in extent from subglobal to only meters. The Pacific coasts of North and South America have many features in common because of a similar plate tectonic setting. The next chapter will discuss this subject in detail. A smaller but still large-scale element would be the Outer Banks of North Carolina or the Mississippi Delta. Each extends for a hundred or more kilometers, and each has a common set of characteristics. A given barrier island, a tidal inlet, or an estuary represents a smaller but important coastal element. Small pocket beaches, individual rocky headlands, or a sand bar are important but small coastal elements.

Each specific coastal setting, regardless of scale, is unique but with quite similar characteristics to other coastal settings of the same type. Although each delta is different, a common set of features characterizes them all. The general approach of this book is to consider the general attributes of each of the various types of coastal settings. Numerous examples of each coastal setting will then provide some idea of the range available for each. Finally, the overprint of time will demonstrate the dynamic nature of all these coastal elements.

2
Plate Tectonics and the Coast

Global-scale patterns of coastal types may at first glance appear to have no special organization. It has long been recognized that some regions, such as the Atlantic and Gulf coasts of the United States, are characterized by fairly broad, low-relief coastal plains adjacent to a coast characterized by barrier islands that front extensive estuary complexes. Even in our school geography classes we learn that these areas have been sites of sediment deposition for millions of years (Fig. 2.1a). By contrast, the Pacific coast of the United States is rugged with beautifully sculptured cliffs and local pocket beaches (Fig. 2.1b) where waves are typically much larger than the Gulf or Atlantic coasts. We have learned that these are erosional coasts.

Rationale for this set of coastal circumstances includes the aforementioned wave energy, the size of the adjacent water body (the Gulf of Mexico is quite small compared to the Pacific Ocean), the nature of the adjacent continental margin, and the geology of the coastal area itself. To be sure, all of these factors are good reasons for the differences in the composition and appearance of the coasts under discussion. Similar relationships exist throughout the rest of the earth's surface. The major question to be answered, however, is how these circumstances came into being on a global scale. Why is the Pacific Ocean margin so different from the Atlantic? Can we relate coastal patterns to some grand scheme on the earth's surface? The development and acceptance of the modern theory of plate tectonics provides a rationale for these general differences and the general patterns that we see on the earth's surface. More specifically, this theory helps us to understand the different broad types of coasts.

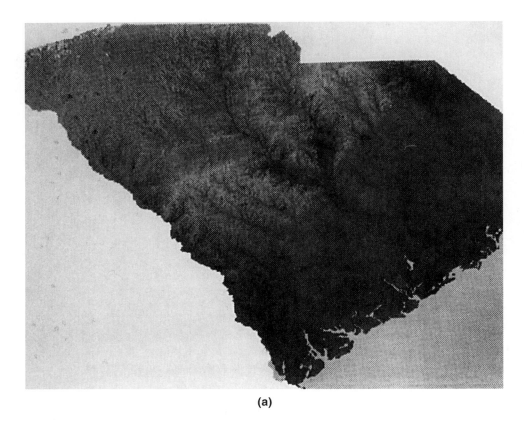

(a)

FIGURE 2.1
Physiography of a) the Atlantic coastal plain and adjacent coast in South Carolina, and b)
The Coast Range and adjacent coast of Oregon, two contrasting geomorphic provinces.
(Images from NOAA Maps)

HISTORY OF THE CONTINENTAL DRIFT IDEA

The distribution of land masses and water bodies on the earth's surface has long
been a subject of interest and speculation. One of the first global-scale relationships to be considered was the apparent fit between the coasts of the land masses
on either side of the Atlantic Ocean first recognized by Sir Francis Bacon in the
early 1620s when he noted an obvious similarity between the outline of eastern
South America and western Africa (Fig. 2.2). In 1858, Antonio Snider suggested
that the continents of South America and Africa had actually broken apart and
moved over the surface of the earth to form the Atlantic Ocean (Fig. 2.3)—the
concept that later became known as the theory of continental drift.

A variety of people presented ideas about the interesting shapes of land

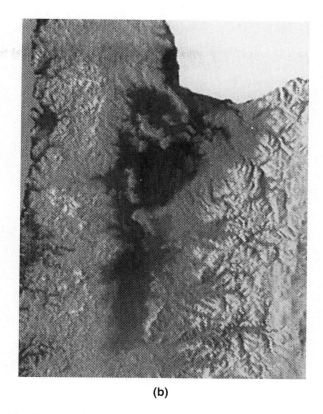

(b)

FIGURE 2.1 *(Cont.)*

masses and their distribution on a global scale. Virtually all of the evidence for possible connection of now distant land masses came from the geologic community. Similarities of rock types, fossils, and structural elements were found across oceans. Fossils in Paleozoic rocks of the Appalachian area, about 400 million years old, were more like those of similar age rocks in the British Isles than they were to fossils of the same age in the western part of the United States. In the Southern Hemisphere there were many unexplained similarities between fossils and glacial deposits in southern South America, southern Africa, Australia, and India, places very distant from one another.

At about the beginning of the twentieth century, there was much interest in the subject of continental drift, both for and against. It became a very emotional issue among mostly geologists but physicists and scientists of other disciplines were also involved. The physicists were especially interested in the possible mechanisms for, and the theoretical feasibility of, large-scale movement of the rigid continental crust. The first sophisticated and widely disseminated theory was presented by Alfred Wegener, a German scientist from the University of

FIGURE 2.2
Cross-Atlantic geologic
connections that give support to
the idea of continental drift.

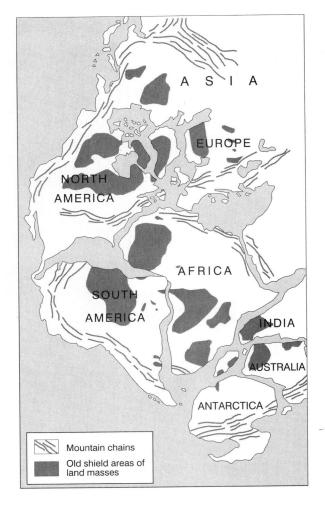

Marburg. His primary areas of specialization were in astronomy and meteorology but Werner's interests were quite broad. His first public presentations of ideas on continental drift were to scientific societies in Frankfurt and in Marburg in 1912. Shortly thereafter Werner's classic book *Die Entstehung der Kontinente und Ozeane* (The origin of continents and oceans) was published. It has been reprinted many times and is still available in English translation. Wegener died a fairly young man in an accident while on a rescue expedition in Greenland in 1930.

Wegener's ideas were based on substantial information. He envisioned a supercontinent, Pangaea, which had a shallow seaway, Tethys, across the middle of much of its eastern portion (Fig. 2.4). This seaway separated Gondwanaland, the southern portion of the supercontinent, from Laurasia, the northern part. He

FIGURE 2.3
Snider's early pre-drift reconstruction of the
continents.

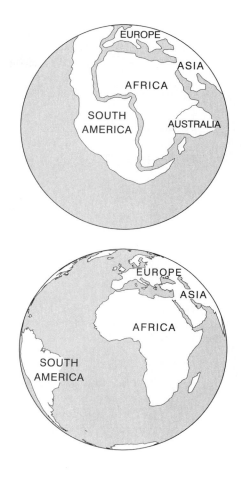

believed that the folded mountain ranges of the earth resulted from collisions between continents and used the Himalayas, which he attributed to the collision
between India and Asia, as an example. Wegener mapped many types of geologic features to show continuity between now-separated land masses. His theory included a mechanism for drift—differences in gravitational forces from place
to place. This was the weak link in the argument, and it puzzled the scientific
community as a whole.

There were some outrageous suggestions for a drift mechanism. Included
was a proposal by Howard Baker, an American paleontologist, who suggested
that a celestial body passed close to the earth and the strong gravitational forces
pulled a piece of the crust away, resulting in the Pacific Ocean. The removed
crust was thought to be our present moon.

Through the first half of the twentieth century much of the scientific world

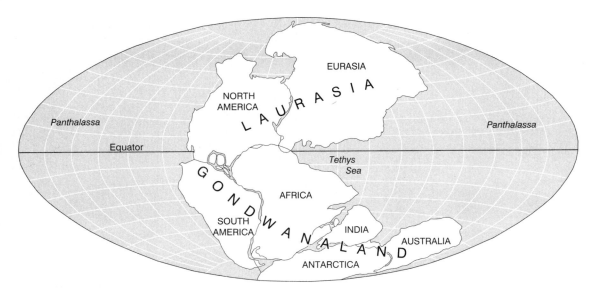

FIGURE 2.4
Wegener's protocontinent, Pangea, showing its northern and southern sections separated by the sea called Tethys.

eventually cast the idea of continental drift aside. The only places in which it received widespread support during that time were in southern Africa and Australia, especially Tasmania. Prominent geologists at the University of Cape Town and the University of Tasmania maintained their support for the idea and hosted various global conferences on the topic.

In the early 1950s there was a bit of a revival of the concept and the Society of Economic Paleontologists and Mineralogists held a research symposium on continental drift at their annual meeting in 1954. This symposium produced a volume of papers on various aspects of the topic with emphasis on new evidence for the concept; there was little about mechanisms for drift. Much new data was forthcoming shortly thereafter, and the concept was thus revitalized.

CONCEPT OF PLATE TECTONICS

A major problem with early efforts to document the phenomenon of continental drift was that virtually all of the data available came from the continental land masses; little information came from the oceans. If some of the oceans were in fact formed by the drift process, it is reasonable to expect a record of it or evidence for it in the ocean basins. Before World War II very little was known about the ocean basins; we didn't even have good maps of the ocean floor. Much oceanographic information was gathered as part of wartime naval operations, especially associated with submarine activities. This included bathymetry, oceanic currents, and tempertaure/salinity profiles. Many top-level scientists including geologists, physicists, chemists, and meteorologists, were involved either as naval officers or as consultants. After the war ended, the time was available to scientifically assess much of the data that had been collected years before. In addition, governments throughout the globe were providing a high level of support for oceanographic research. These activities helped formulate the modern concept of plate tectonics and replaced the older ideas of continental drift through the availability and understanding of new information. Not only were the data to support this phenomenon available from the land masses, there was also important evidence present on the ocean floor and beneath. The old problem of a mechanism for the dynamic crust of the earth was also answered.

Oceanic Data

The geologic support for the concept of moving land masses was pretty well substantiated in the early years as noted previously. However, the data from the ocean floors were new and were not synthesized and interpreted until the 1950s and 1960s. Maps of the ocean showed that there was an almost continuous submarine, volcanic, mountain range, the ocean ridge system (Fig. 2.5), that extended for about 80,000 kilometers around the globe. Included in this system are the Mid-Atlantic Ridge that divides the Atlantic Ocean, and the East Pacific Rise that extends from the Gulf of California down the southeastern part of the Pacific Ocean. Maps also showed that this ridge system was fractured and dislocated at numerous places along its course. These *transform faults*, as they are called, had evidence for both lateral and vertical motion. Associated with the new geologic maps of the oceans was the mapping of the earthquake activity on a global scale. It was long known that most of the severe seismic activity on the earth was located around the Pacific Ocean. This comprehensive map of earthquake epicenters showed distinct global patterns (Fig. 2.6). Highest concentratons are in the so-called Ring of Fire around the Pacific (now called the Circum-Pacific Belt) and secondary levels of activity are located along the oceanic ridge system. Additional areas of high seismic activity are in the eastern Mediterranean and in the Himalayas. There is a very noticeable correspondence between earthquake activity and the distribution of oceanic trenches.

Other important information gleaned from the oceans includes paleomagnetic data, age of oceanic islands, and the age of marine sediments taken from cores of the ocean basins. The paleomagnetic data are based on the fact that when magnetic minerals such as iron oxide (magnetite) crystallize, they do so in keeping with the earth's magnetic field at the time of crystallization. This includes not only the orientation of the field but also the pole designations. The earth's magnetic field reverses about once or twice every million years. Much of the ocean

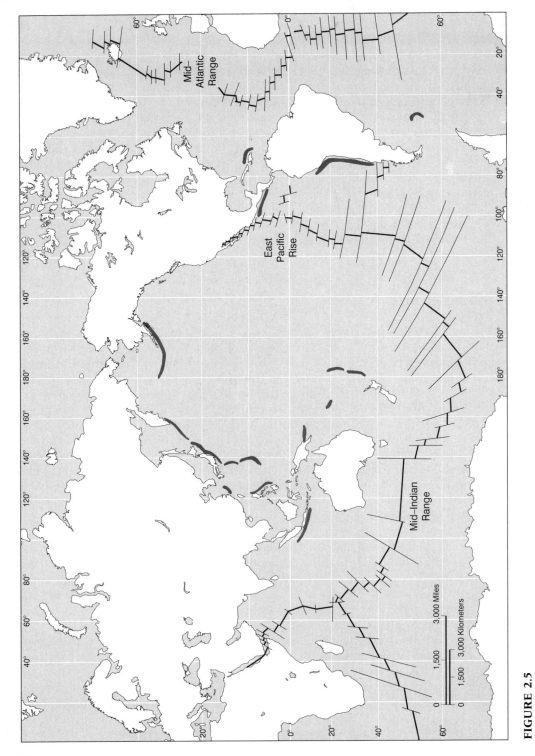

FIGURE 2.5
Global map showing the distribution of oceanic ridges and deep-sea trenches.

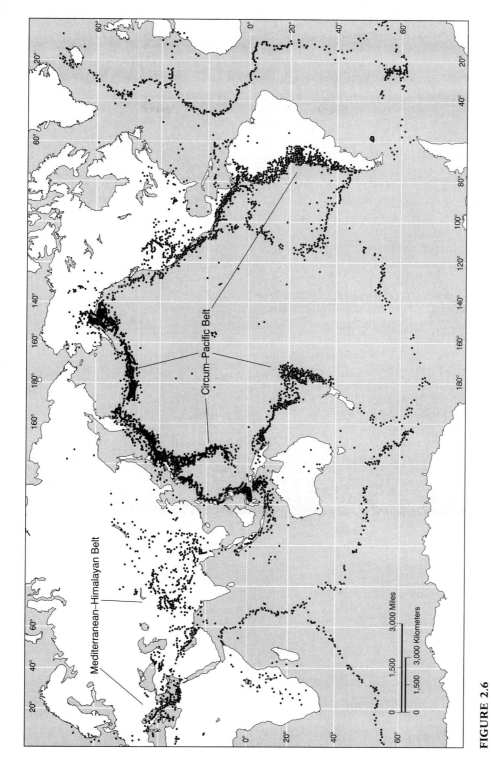

FIGURE 2.6
Global map showing the distribution of earthquake epicenters.

floor is volcanic in origin, and this type of rock includes a significant amount of magnetic minerals. Therefore, by studying the magnetic character of these rocks, it is possible to understand something about the magnetic field of the earth at the time of their formation. Maps of the paleomagnetism recorded on the ocean floor show a distinct pattern of stripes that develop as the magnetic field reverses and that parallel the ocean ridge system (Fig. 2.7). Dating of these rocks shows that the magnetic stripes increase in age the further away they are from the oceanic ridge and that they are distinctly mirrored on either side of the ridge.

Other dating of oceanic materials also shows a pattern of increasing age away from the oceanic ridges. The oceanic islands, that is, those composed of oceanic crust, show this phenomenon. Islands on or adjacent to the ridge such as Iceland, are quite young, Bermuda on the other hand is about midway between the ridge and North America. It shows an age about three times that of Iceland. This pattern is well-documented throughout the islands of the Atlantic Ocean. Additionally, the ages of the oldest deep sea sediments at any position on the ocean basins show a similar pattern. These sediments increase in age as they go from the ridge system toward the land masses. The oldest sediments under the western Atlantic Ocean are found near the New Jersey coast. In the Pacific the oldest sediments are near Japan whereas the oceanic ridges system is in the southeastern Pacific off South America (Fig. 2.8). The oldest known sediments from any of the ocean basins are Triassic in age, about 180 million years old. This age is in marked contrast with the oldest rocks on the continents, which are just over 4 billion years old.

The density of the oceanic sediment also changes systematically. It is less dense in the younger rocks and increases in density in the older ones because the

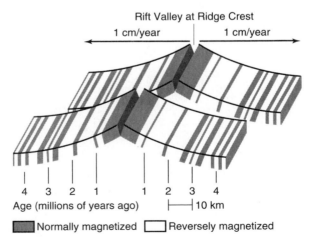

FIGURE 2.7
Diagram showing magnetic stripes and transform faults associated with oceanic ridges.

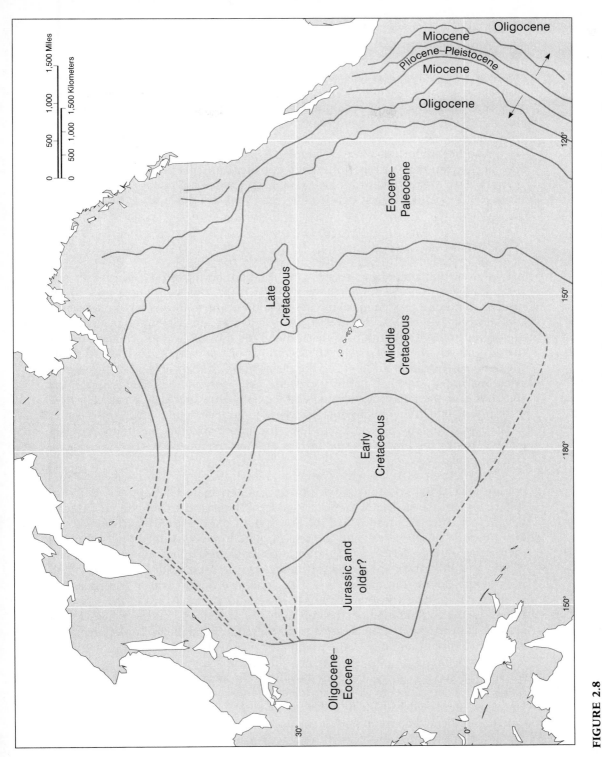

FIGURE 2.8

Age of sediments across the Pacific Ocean showing increasing age away from the East Pacific Rise with the oldest being near Japan in the northwest part of the basin. (Map courtesy of the DSDP)

25

younger rocks contain considerable water, which is gradually lost over time, and also because rocks become compacted over time. All of these patterns indicate two important things—the stratigraphic record in the ocean basins is young relative to the age of the earth, and there is a distinct pattern of increasing age away from the oceanic ridges.

Another important piece of data from the ocean floor has implications for the mechanism that causes the movement of continents and for formation of ocean basins. Measurements of heat flow from the sea floor show that it is highest over the oceanic ridge system and decreases toward the land masses.

Mechanisms

Although virtually all of the geologic information, both from the continents and from the ocean basins, supports the concept of moving continents and young oceans, none of these data provide information on how all this takes place, only that it probably did. Detailed analysis of seismic data, especially that in the island arc/oceanic trench systems, provides some of the most critical information necessary to unravel the mysteries of the dynamics of the earth's crust. By studying the deep earthquakes and plotting the distribution of their epicenters, it became apparent that a distinct pattern existed. The epicenters descend under the trenches and the adjacent volcanic complexes. Using the early ideas of a rigid lithosphere, which is equivalent to the crust and upper rigid mantle, and a somewhat plastic underlying asthenosphere, the upper mantle, this then provides good evidence for how the crust moves and what happens to it in the overall scheme of plate tectonics.

The oceanic ridge system represents the oceanic lithosphere's locus of formation (Fig. 2.9). Volcanic activity brings molten material from the asthenosphere toward the surface where it crystallizes. The island arc and oceanic trench systems are the places into which the lithospheric plate descends (subducts) back into the asthenosphere causing the crustal plate to be consumed by the hot asthenosphere (Fig. 2.10). These are called *subduction zones* and as the plate subducts, it downwarps the edge of the adjacent crustal plate forming a trench such as the Puerto Rican Trench in the Caribbean or the Tonga Trench in the western Pacific. The volcanic activity of the island arc landward of the trench is caused by the combination of stress on the plate margin and on the availability of molten material below. Back-arc spreading, creating shallow coastal seas between a continent and a volcanic island area, results from this same molten material. The China Sea is a good example of such a shallow sea. Thus we have a conveyor-belt type of system whereby lithospheric material is formed at the ridges and moves away to eventually descend into a subduction zone at a trench. The movement is driven in part by gravity; the denser plate descends into the trench and the less dense material rises at the ridges.

Much of the motion of the lithospheric plates is a relatively simple spread-

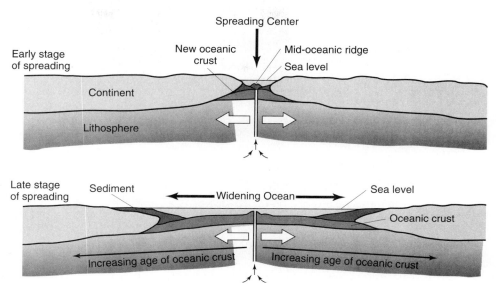

FIGURE 2.9
Diagram showing the spliting of crust and movement of plates.

ing at the oceanic ridge and then a convergence at the trenches. Because the rigid lithospheric plates are curved and are moving over a spherical surface, some spatial problems need to be resolved. The presence of the numerous transform faults along the oceanic ridge system is a partial answer to this question. These faults represent places where the stress of the plate is relieved and the crust slides laterally, enabling movement within a curved plate but still "fitting" the globe. A look at the dozen crustal plates that comprise the lithosphere shows a wide range in size and shape (Fig. 2.11).

There is a wide range of calculated and observed rates of plate movement. The slowest are about 1 centimeter per year but range up to as much as 10 centimeters per year. Most of these data are calculated from the known ages and positions of marine sediments and magnetic minerals. The dynamics of these lithospheric plates (plate tectonics) form the basis for explaining the arrangement of the major features on the earth's surface, including the continents.

PLATE TECTONICS AND COASTAL DEVELOPMENT

The coast has not yet been mentioned in the context of plate tectonics; it is, however, very important to an understanding of the global-scale patterns we see in coastal development and coastal types. As mentioned earlier, there has always been descriptive information about certain coastal regions being quite different

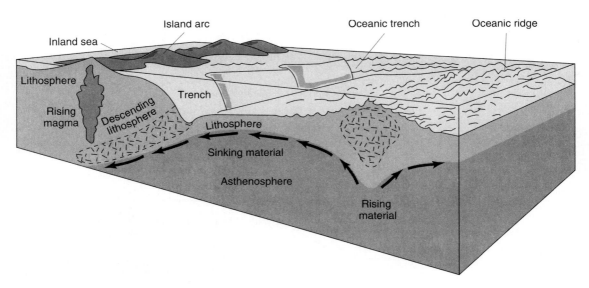

FIGURE 2.10
Island arc and trench system showing descending plate as subduction of the crust occurs.

from the others. This has led to numerous classifications of coasts; most are descriptive and replete with terminology. Some are based on genesis but have little convincing data on origin. Others represent a combination of the two types. None have been widely accepted.

The formulation and confirmation of the plate tectonics concept provided the necessary information to develop a broadly based genetic coastal classification that could be substantiated. The comprehensive organization of the interrelationships between plate tectonics and coastal types was presented by Douglas L. Inman of Scripps Institution of Oceanography and one of his colleagues, C. E. Nordstrom (Fig. 2.12). Their synthesis, published in 1971, came shortly after publication of the landmark papers on plate tectonics. The result is a relatively simple but useful classification of coastal types in a plate tectonic setting.

The basis for the classification lies in three major types of continental coasts: (1) those associated with the leading edge of a plate, (2) those associated with the trailing edge of a plate, and (3) those coasts that are fronted by marginal seas such as those that are formed between a landmass and a volcanic island arc at the plate boundary. Island coasts are not considered.

The broad character of the coasts themselves is tied directly to the nature of the adjacent continental margin and the landward continent (Fig. 2.13). This is the largest component of the coastal classification—the first-order feature. Inman and Nordstrom also include two additional levels within their classification. Second-order features are on the scale of the processes that mold the coast, that

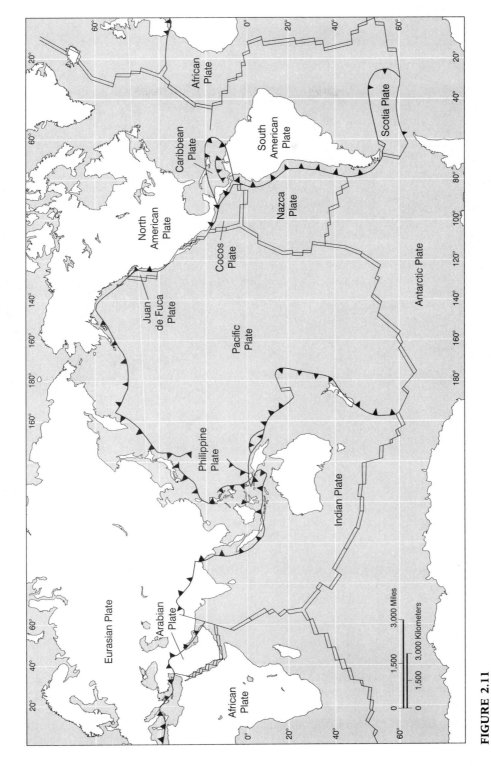

FIGURE 2.11
Global map showing major crustal plates and their names.

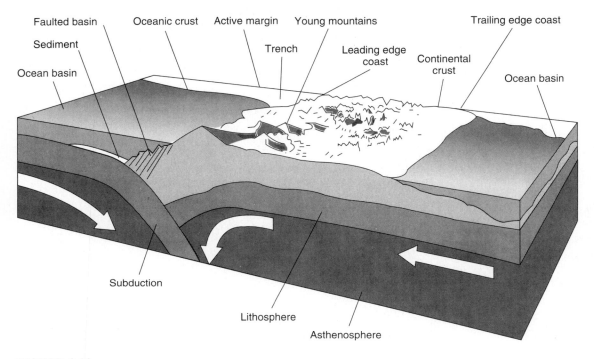

FIGURE 2.12
Schematic diagram of collision and trailing edge coasts.
(From Inman, D. L. and Nordstrom, C. E., 1971, On the tectonic classifications of coasts, *Jour. Geol,* 79, p. 4, Fig. 2)

is, a distance over which wave or tidal climate would be similar. Third-order features are local and short-term features of deposition, typically caused by wave action, such as a pocket beach. The first-order features are geographically extensive, typically over 1000 kilometers in length and including the entire coastal zone with all its variety of specific environments. Second-order features may extend tens to hundreds of kilometers, and third-order features typically extend no more than a few kilometers.

Leading Edge Coasts

Collision between the two plates may result in leading edge coasts when the continental edge of one plate collides with the oceanic edge of another. When two continental edges collide mountains are formed—such as the Himalayas that resulted from the collision of the Indian Plate with the Eurasian Plate. By contrast, when two oceanic plates collide they produce island arcs and oceanic

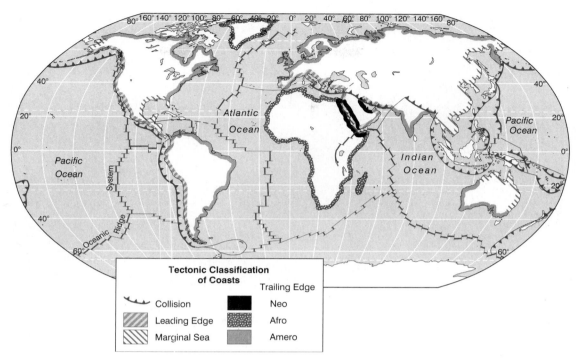

FIGURE 2.13
Global map of tectonic coastal types.
(From Inman and Nordstrom, 1971, p. 10, Fig. 4)

trenches such as along the boundary of the Indian and Pacific plates in the Philippines and Indonesia.

Leading edge coasts are tectonically active and structurally complex. They are characterized by rugged, high-relief topography in both the landward and seaward direction (Fig. 2.14). The major occurrence of leading edge coasts is along the Pacific coast of North and South America. In both places the plate boundaries essentially coincide with the edges of the landmasses. In the case of South America, it is a rather straightforward relationship between two converging plates, the Nazca Plate and the South American Plate. The North American situation is a bit more complicated because of the numerous transform faults that exist along the boundary between the Pacific and North American plates. For example, the Gulf of California rests over the plate boundary as does the well-known San Andreas Fault system of California. Part of southern California can be considered to be on the Pacific Plate.

The geology of this part of California is complex, both on the land and beneath the adjacent ocean. The continental margin here is considered a continen-

FIGURE 2.14
Example of rugged, high-energy, leading edge coast from Oregon.

tal borderland rather than the typical continental shelf-slope system. This borderland is a complex of small basins produced by fractures and crustal movement along steep surfaces called *faults*. A similar geology is present on the adjacent coastal area and is representative of collision or leading edge coasts.

This type of coastal area is set near mountainous terrain, a high-relief region producing streams that erode downward and carry much sand and gravel. The streams do not have extensive drainage basins; high relief produces closely spaced drainage divides. Most of the sediment that is transported by these streams is carried directly to the coast. Here it may be trapped in estuaries or may empty directly on the open coast. Even though a large amount of sediment may be dumped on a collision coast, river deltas are rare because of the general absence of a broad continental shelf that could accommodate the sediment and because of the high wave energy on the Pacific Coast, which tends to disperse the sediment. None of the twenty-five largest deltas in the world occurs on a collision type coast.

Submarine canyons are large, deep, and steep-sided valleys that are cut into the continental margin by strong currents that were prevalent during times of low sea level. These canyons tend to have their heads quite near the shoreline on a continental borderland–type of continental margin. This permits river-borne sediment to empty directly into a canyon that serves as a conduit directly to deep water (Fig. 2.15). In some areas fluvial sediment is dumped at the open coast and

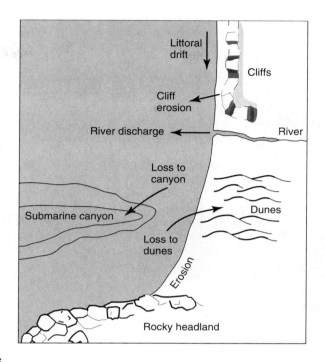

FIGURE 2.15
Sketch showing sediment budget on a leading edge coast with streams, beach, littoral drift, and capture by submarine canyon.
(Modified after Komar, P. D., 1976, *Beach Processes and Sedimentation*, Prentice-Hall, Inc., Englewood Cliffs, New Jersey, p. 242, Fig. 9-8)

then carried alongshore until it is interrupted by the head of a submarine canyon and carried to deep water.

The net result is that collision coasts have poorly developed drainage systems, and the sediment that is delivered to this type of coast is eventually transported out of the coastal system and into deep water. This general lack of coastal sediment has been exacerbated by human activity in the form of numerous dams along the drainage systems. These dams not only trap the water but also trap the sediment being carried by the streams. As a consequence, the reservoirs tend to be efficient sediment traps and cause the naturally depleted beaches to be further reduced in size and extent.

The only areas of significant sediment accumulation on collision coasts are associated with estuaries that form as the result of a variety of circumstances. Some are due to sea level and subsequent flooding of stream valleys while others are caused by faulting and the resulting displacement of the crust. Much of the estuarine development of the San Francisco Bay area is of a structural origin associated with its position on the San Andreas Fault zone.

Trailing Edge Coasts

By far the most diverse of the first-order coastal types are those that form on the trailing edge of crustal plates. Because of their diversity and the range of tectonic settings in which they occur, Inman and Nordstrom have split this type into three categories: (1) neo-trailing edge coasts, (2) Afro-trailing edge coasts, and (3) Amero-trailing edge coasts. The first of these categories represents the earliest stages of coastal development, which take place at active spreading centers. The Red Sea and the Gulf of Aden, where the Arabian and African plates are separating (Fig. 2.16), and the aforementioned Gulf of California, where the

FIGURE 2.16
Satellite (space shuttle) image of the Red Sea—a neo-trailing edge system.
(Courtesy of NASA)

Pacific and American plates are diverging, serve as good examples. Both of these regions have long and narrow water bodies representing very early stages of separation where a continental margin has yet to be developed. These conditions produce coasts that are varied in nature; some may mimic collision coasts with high relief. Generally there is little sediment available due to an absence of drainage systems.

The Afro-trailing edge coast is developed on continental areas where both coasts are of the trailing edge variety. An obvious example is the African continent, which lacks any collision area except at its northernmost part along the Mediterranean Sea. Greenland also falls into this category. In an overall scheme of geologic and geomorphic maturity of the coastal regime, this type falls in the middle between the juvenile, neo-trailing edge type and the mature Amero-trailing edge types.

Afro-trailing edge coasts do not have the benefit of high relief and extensive erosion in the hinterland to provide abundant sediment for the coast. Nevertheless, there are substantial rivers and deltas developed along this coastal type. Examples are the Niger and Congo Rivers in Africa; climate prevents this phenomenon in Greenland.

Amero-trailing edge coasts (Fig. 2.17), as the name implies, are characterized by the east coasts of North and South America. Both are on tectonically stable portions of the continents that have been this way for at least tens of millions of years. The resulting coastal plains are broad with little relief and well-developed drainage systems. South America is perhaps the best example with the continental divide in the Andes Mountains along the western portion of the continent and the remainder of the continent serving the Atlantic side. The Amazon River system has by far the largest drainage area in the world, and there are other large rivers in South America as well. The subcontinent of India has a somewhat similar condition with drainage coming from the highlands of the Himalayas. Two of the greatest discharge rivers in the world—the Ganges–Brahmaputra and the Indus—have their headwaters here and empty on the Indian coast.

This type of geologic and geomorphic setting provided great quantities of sediment to the trailing edge side of the continents shortly after the plates separated about 190 million years ago in the Triassic. As a consequence, they have a wide, stable continental margin that supports a wide coastal zone characterized by deposition. The Amero-trailing edge coast is the most mature of the three types of trailing edge coastal types. In addition to the east coasts of North and South America, similar coastal types are present on the north coasts of Europe and Asia on the Eurasian Plate and throughout most of Australia, which is on the Indian Plate. Amero-trailing edge coasts also extend across the north margin of North America. Because of the rigorous conditions here, there is a lack of human development and research. As a result, we know little about this area except for the north slope of Alaska, recently studied in conjunction with oil exploration and production.

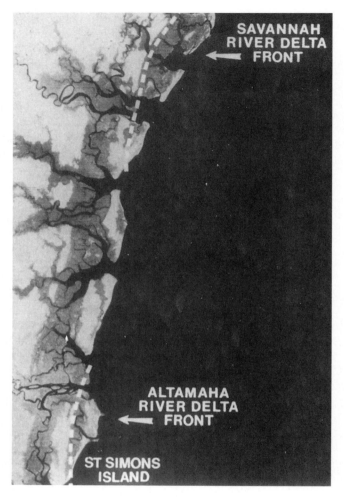

FIGURE 2.17
The coastal plain of Georgia, an example of a trailing edge coast that displays a broad, flat coastal plain and numerous barrier islands.
(Courtesy of M. O. Hayes)

Marginal Sea Coasts

Two extensive and important parts of the earth's coast are fronted by marginal seas that are, in turn, bounded oceanward by island arc–oceanic trench systems. Examples are the east coast of Asia and the coast of the Gulf of Mexico in North America; they are similar yet very different. The Asian example represents the classic example of Inman and Nordstrom's classification, whereas the Gulf of Mexico is a modification of that classification in that much of it is surrounded by land. This coastal type is located near a converging plate margin but is not tectonically active in the sense of leading edge coastal types. Relief is low and drainage systems are quite well developed. Consider, for example, that the Gulf of Mexico is served by the Mississippi River system and that southeast Asia has four rivers that rank in the top ten in the world for sediment load delivered to the coast—the Yangtze, Huang Ho, Mekong, and Irrawaddy. Another important factor in the coastal development of marginal seas is the relatively low wave energy they experience due to limited size of the water body. The combination of the large rivers with huge sediment loads and the relatively low wave energy allows marginal sea coasts and their adjacent basins to rapidly accumulate large amounts of sediment.

The fortuitous circumstances of climate are also a major contributor to the extensive accumulation of sediment along both of the marginal sea areas. The Gulf Coast and the Mississippi River drainage system are in a temperate climate with abundant rainfall, and the river has the third largest drainage area in the world. The Southeast Asia climate is temperate to subtropical with much rainfall and high rates of weathering. These conditions produce both tremendous quantities of sediment and cause high levels of discharge. All of these factors benefit coastal accumulation by forming deltas and adjacent depositional areas.

COMMENTS AND SUMMARY

Although there is considerable internal cohesiveness to this tectonic classification of coasts, there may be some misleading aspects as well. One must remember that the categories apply only to the big picture—the global approach. It considers only the first-order scale. This means that just because there may be high cliffs experiencing erosion, this is not an indication of a leading edge tectonic setting. Much of the southern coast of Australia in the states of Victoria and South Australia is bounded by near vertical cliffs of eroding sandstone and limestone. This coast is not in a tectonically active area nor is it near a plate boundary. The present coastal morphology is simply the result of high wave energy from the Southern Ocean coupled with little sediment supply from rivers—a combination that produces an eroding coast.

The opposite situation is prevalent along portions of the southern coast of Alaska, which is on the margin of the North American Plate as it collides with the Pacific Plate. Here the coast is characterized by abundant sediment accumulation in the form of extensive tidal flats, marshes, and barrier islands. Not what one would expect to find in a tectonically active area at a collision plate margin. The reason for this condition is the glaciation that has taken place along this coast during the Quaternary. As glaciers have melted during the past several thousand years, they have provided tremendous volumes of sediment of all particle sizes. Even though this part of the Alaskan coast is subjected to intense wave energy, the large supply of sediment, including abundant gravel, has resulted in net sediment accumulation.

These two examples serve to point out that we must consider the coast at the first-order scale of thousands of kilometers in order to apply a tectonic classification to the coast. The next level of coastal classification is regional in extent and involves morphology that can be superimposed upon virtually any tectonic setting. This morphological and sedimentologic type of classification relies on the interactions of localized situations of wave and tidal energy, rock types and structural fabric of the rocks, sediment supply, and climate.

Rivers and glaciers may be involved, and each can cause either deposition or erosion although deposition is the most prevalent coastal feature of both. Large and frequent waves cause erosion, and small waves typically result in deposition of sediment. Another aspect of this level of coastal classification is related to both plant and animal organisms. The most prominent of these are the coral reefs that front extensive coastal areas on many tectonic settings. They are actually most widespread along the neo-trailing edge coasts, the best example being the Red Sea where the African and Arabian plates are separating. Most of the coast on both sides is of various types of coral reef. Marginal seas such as the Gulf of Mexico also have important reaches of coast bordered by reefs, such as that which is along most of the coast of Mexico and Belize. Many low latitude areas that include collision coasts also have coral reef coasts such as in the Caribbean, western Pacific, and eastern Indian oceans. Marshy and mangrove coasts may also extend for hundreds of kilometers, typically in marginal seas. The reason for this type of setting is the generally low wave energy conditions that prevail here. Vegetated communities on the open coasts cannot tolerate even moderate wave conditions. Parts of Florida and Southeast Asia display such vegetated open coasts.

The tectonic classification is fundamental in considering the global organization of coastal settings. As we consider various coastal types in the following chapters, it is important to put them in the context of the global perspective. As the earth's lithosphere changes through geologic time these coastal types will change in a like fashion. It is in this way that many different coastal settings and specific environments become incorporated in the geologic record of the earth's history. We can recognize the coastal setting in rocks extending well back into Precambrian time, at least a billion years ago. In many of these ancient coastal depositional environments it is possible to decipher the tectonic setting in which these environments were accumulated.

3
Sea-Level Change
and the Coast

Fluctuations in sea level may cause the coast to respond, sometimes in extreme fashion. These changes in sea level may be either slow and subtle or rapid and dramatic. Global sea level is in a slow but constant state of flux due to many factors, including climate and plate tectonics. In only a few moments, an earthquake can abruptly lower sea level by uplifting a shore or by causing the adjacent sea floor to sink, either of which produces a relative change in the position of sea level. More subtly, sea level regularly rises and falls with the cyclic shifts in wind patterns and ocean currents. It might gradually rise over centuries to flood a coastal plain. Thousands of years may go by as continental areas previously covered with the great weight of glaciers are allowed to rebound after the ice has melted. As a consequence, old shorelines may rise many meters above sea level.

These types of sea-level change—tectonic upheavals, climatic fluctuations, land subsidence, and rebound from retreating glaciers—are all relative changes that have a limited geographic range, generally hundreds of kilometers. Of greater importance are the global, or eustatic, changes in sea level that occur when the total volume of water in the world ocean is changed. We may be in a period of accelerating sea-level rise today due to the advance of global warming caused by the greenhouse effect.

This chapter considers each type of sea-level change, its causes, and its effects on the coasts. Although the periodic rise and fall of sea level associated with astronomical tides does affect the coast, it has no effect on the net local sea level. Tides will be discussed in Chapter 4 where coastal processes are considered.

TECTONIC CAUSES FOR SEA-LEVEL CHANGE

Seismic activity along an unstable portion of the earth's crust may cause a sudden shift in relative sea level by sinking or uplifting the shore. This may be in the form of a volcanic eruption, an earthquake or any other seismic event, typically along or in the vicinity of a plate boundary.

On March 27, 1964, a severe earthquake along the oceanic and continental collision boundary of the Pacific and North American crustal plates brought spectacular changes to the southern coast of Alaska (Fig. 3.1). The quake registered about 8.3 on the Richter scale, in the epicenter area on the north shore of Prince William Sound between Anchorage and Valdez. This level is one of the highest ever recorded in North America. Up and down the coast, blocks of land were uplifted or subsided by as much as a few meters. At one fishing port, bedrock rose more than 6 meters above sea level, trapping fishing boats on land and leaving the dock pilings high and dry. Offshore, nearby islands were uplifted more than 12 meters, and on the adjacent continental shelf, a section of the sea floor dropped more than 15 meters—all of this in a matter of minutes.

FIGURE 3.1
Photograph of coast in the Anchorage, Alaska area showing uplift and property damage associated with the earthquake of March 27, 1964.
(Official U.S. Navy photograph)

Severe earthquakes that permanently change local sea level are fairly common along convergent plate boundaries where land masses are present. This is most likely to occur along the leading edge West coasts of North and South America and along the eastern Mediterranean and continuing through to the Middle East.

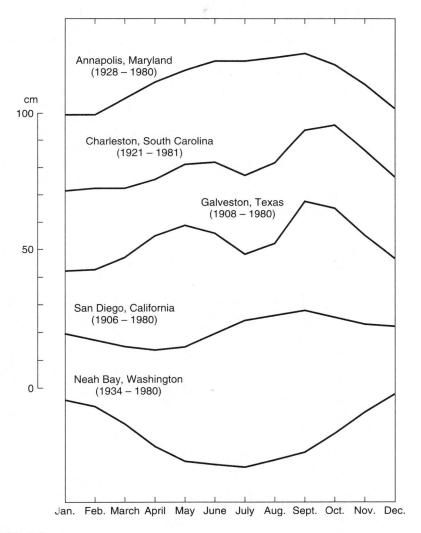

FIGURE 3.2
Examples of annual cycles of sea-level changes as obtained from smoothing of tide gauge records.
(From Komar, P. D. and Enfield, 1987, Short-term sea-level changes and coastal erosion, *IN SEPM Spec. Publ.* No. 41, Tulsa, Oklahoma, p. 18)

CLIMATIC CHANGES AND SEA-LEVEL CHANGE

Sea level is also affected by seasonal and other cyclical fluctuations in climate. Globally, mean sea level typically shows a seasonal difference of about 10 to 30 centimeters depending upon location (Fig. 3.2). Sea level is generally lowest in the spring and highest in the fall, alternating back and forth between the Northern and Southern Hemispheres. Closer to the equator, where the seasons are more subtle, the mean sea level also shows less seasonal change than in the mid-latitudes.

The simplest and most easily predictable of this type of seasonal sea-level fluctuation is produced by changes in weather patterns as the sun and the earth shift in their positions relative to each other (Fig. 3.3). As the sun moves through the latitudes with the seasons, water temperatures change, and the wind patterns and intensities change as a consequence. Sea level experiences a modest change in response to these seasonal wind differences. This response is essentially the result of water being pushed in different directions from seasonal changes in atmospheric pressure and therefore wind direction.

Although the overall pattern of seasonal sea-level change is predictable, it is interesting to note that wide differences occur from one area to another. In the

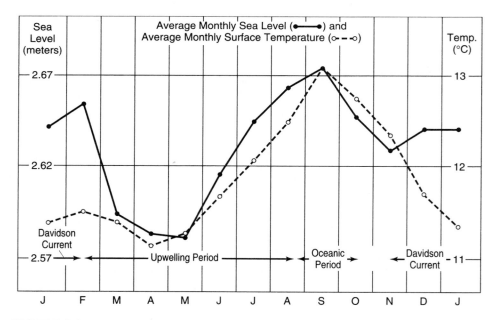

FIGURE 3.3
Annual cycle of both sea-level and water temperature showing their coincidence and their relationship to the dominant oceanic conditions of the time.
(From Komar and Enfield, 1987, p. 19)

Bay of Bengal, for example, an extreme mean sea-level variation of about 100 centimeters reflects the seasonal extremes of dry winters and monsoon-drenched summers combined with the changes in wind patterns. In other bodies of water, such as large bays or estuaries, local wave and current patterns produce variations from the expected seasonal patterns.

The change in volume of water caused by differences in temperature also causes seasonal changes in sea level. On the East Coast of the United States, sea level is highest in the summertime because it is then that the warm, expansive Gulf Stream flows close by. Across the country on the coast of Washington, sea level in the summertime is at its lowest because of the cold, narrow California Current that flows down from the north at that time. Moreover, as the California Current veers west, out to the Pacific Ocean, the colder subsurface waters upwell to replace it, contributing further to the unusually low sea level. The highest mean sea level on the Washington coast occurs in winter, when frigid Arctic winds generate coastal storms that blow onshore and pile up water.

The sea-level cycle on the southern California coast has been monitored for several decades. Data show a strong correlation between the seasonal fluctuations in sea level and the pattern of coastal erosion. High sea level and high energy conditions during the winter months were, as expected, coincident with the greatest rates of coastal erosion—a good example of how some commonly overlooked cyclic changes in sea level can significantly influence coastal erosion.

Another anomalous weather-related sea-level cycle occurs every four to seven years over most of the South Pacific Ocean in response to the appearance of El Niño—the warm current off the western coast of South America. Because the phenomenon of El Niño tends to appear in late December, fishermen have named the current "the child," signifying the birth of Christ. During this part of the summer in the Southern Hemisphere, the cold Peru Current normally moves northward along the coast, accompanied by a wind-driven upwelling of even colder, nutrient-rich deep water as the Peru Current veers west into the Pacific due to the Coriolis effect (explained in Chapter 4). This upwelling of fertile waters supports one of the world's most important fishing grounds. The pathway of the Peru Current is almost a mirror image of the summertime California Current that moves to the west as it flows south.

At these irregular four- to seven-year intervals, the west-to-east trade winds diminish, allowing a warm current to move south and drive the Peru Current into the Pacific prematurely. This warmer current is the El Niño. When it enters South American coastal waters, its thick surface layer of warm water acts as a barrier to the upwelling of the cold nutrient-laden waters below. It may stay to the south for a year or more causing fish populations to either migrate to other feeding grounds or die, thereby disrupting the economics of the adjacent coastal areas. The warmer sea warms the air above causing more air evaporation. This moisture-laden air mass moves landward, bringing torrential storms that produce flooding and coastal erosion and cause changes in other wind and current patterns.

The sea level rises all along the western South American coast not only from El Niño's climatic effects but also because its warm water takes up more space than does the colder Peru Current. While the El Niño is active, the changes in wind and current patterns produce very long waves that move across the entire Pacific Ocean. As in all onshore wind conditions, trade winds normally cause a pileup of water along coastal areas. El Niño, however, produces changes in the strength and direction of the trade winds, which releases the piled-up water in the form of a very long wave moving on the surface of the ocean. The movement of one of these waves that developed during the 1982–1983 El Niño has been traced by collecting and collating sea-level data from tide gauge records from coastal stations throughout the Pacific Ocean (Fig. 3.4). Calculations show that the wave traveled at a speed of about 75 kilometers per day and maintained a height of 30 to 40 centimeters from its point of origin to its arrival at the western North American coast. There was unusually high erosion along the California and Oregon coasts that winter. Although severe storms during that time caused some of the damage, some must also be attributed to the high sea level brought about by the El Niño wave (Fig. 3.5). The El Niño condition also caused anomalous weather conditions including storms throughout the South Pacific on both the South American and the Australasian side of the basin.

SUBSIDENCE DUE TO COMPACTION AND FLUID WITHDRAWAL

In parts of the coastal zone along East Texas or near the Mississippi Delta in Louisiana, sea level is rising locally because the land itself is sinking, or subsiding. Thus the local sea-level rise is much greater than the global rise. The highest rates of local sea-level rise in the United States are in the Mississippi River Delta area, where it is rising 9 to 10 millimeters per year, approximately three times the global average. About 6 to 7 millimeters of that rise is due to subsidence caused by both compaction of delta sediments and the withdrawal of fluids from the coastal zone.

In the lower Mississippi River Delta, huge quantities of fine sediment are carried by the river, as much as 1.6 metric tons per day at the active lobe, and deposited at its mouth. Because this sediment accumulates so rapidly, it traps much water as it settles. The resulting mud, at places up to 90 percent water, piles up through the active delta region. As the weight of the mud compresses the underlying sediments, the land surface subsides and a relative rise in sea level is thus produced.

While the natural process of compaction has occurred for many millions of years, subsidence along a significant part of the northern coast of the Gulf of Mexico, caused by the withdrawal of large volumes of fluid, is a direct result of recent human activities. Nearly 100,000 wells have produced huge volumes of oil and natural gas from the Mississippi Delta and from the adjacent coastal zone of the Gulf of Mexico. Large quantities of water have also been taken for domestic and industrial use. Because of these activities some of the land near Galveston, Texas, has sunk nearly 2 meters in this century (Fig. 3.6). To lessen the threat of further subsidence, the region is shifting to use of surface water sources, and water is now being pumped back into the ground. Another human impact on the coastal zone is not as easily remedied. Building weighty, high-rise office towers on unstable sediments has caused seawater incursions and the land to sink in parts of the inland port cities of Houston and New Orleans.

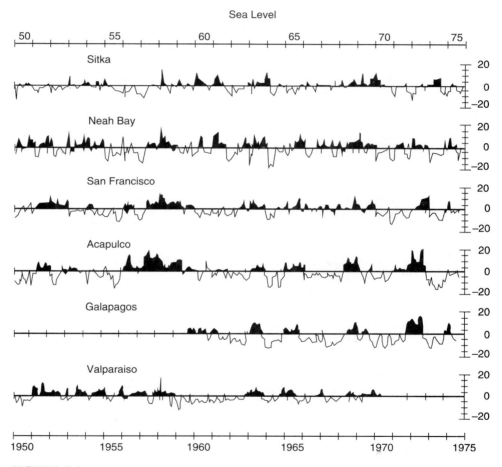

FIGURE 3.4
Sea-level variations from throughout the Pacific Ocean over a 25-year period showing anomalies that have been attributed to an El Nino effect.

(From Enfield, D. B. and Allen, J. S., 1980, On the structure and dynamics of monthly mean sea level anomalies along the Pacific coast of North and South America. *Jour. Phys. Oceanog.*, 10, pp. 557–578. Reprinted by permission of the American Meteorological Society.)

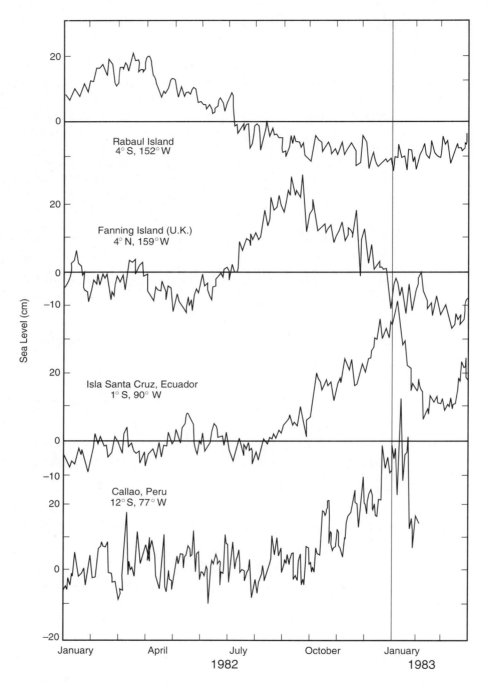

FIGURE 3.5
Water level records from Pacific locations during the 1982–1983 El Nino period showing the migration of the trapped sea-level "wave."
(From Komar and Enfield, 1987, p. 24, Fig. 7)

FIGURE 3.6
Photograph of flooding in southeast Texas near Galveston Bay that is, in part, due to a
rise in sea level resulting from withdrawal of oil and gas in this area.
(Courtesy of Orrin H. Pilkey)

If local sea level in the lower Mississippi Delta continues to rise at a rate of 9
to 10 millimeters per year, and if this rate is sustained for 50 years, it could
amount to 0.5 meter of sea level rise, enough to submerge large areas of coastal
wetlands. This figure combines a 3-millimeter global rise, another 1 to 2 millimeters from fluid withdrawal, and the 5 to 6 millimeters resulting from natural sediment compaction. Compaction can take place in any large and rapidly growing
delta. The Amazon River Delta, for example, is receiving great quantities of sediment, and the rate is increasing as the rain forests disappear, increasing erosion
of landscape. Some subsidence is also present here but the remoteness of the
area limits the available information on subsidence rates.

Compaction is not only an important contributor to the land subsidence in
delta regions throughout the world, it also affects peat bogs, marshes, and other
organic-rich sediment accumulations that hold large volumes of water. However,
its influence here would be quite small because these deposits are not thick
enough to cause compaction on their own.

ISOSTASY

The Mississippi River Delta is one example of regional subsidence, but broad regions of the continental lithosphere itself can also sink under a heavy load. Over
a period of several thousand years, the weight of a huge ice sheet can cause the
continental lithosphere to become depressed by as much as 100 meters, depend-

ing on the thickness and density of both the ice mass and the underlying lithosphere. The vertical movements of the lithosphere are accommodated by the lateral movement of semi-plastic material in the upper asthenosphere. Glaciers can be thousands of meters thick but their growth and decay are achieved slowly. As the glacier melts, removing the weight of the ice from the landmass, the lithosphere rises, or rebounds. These shifts in the presence and absence of large ice masses have taken place numerous times as glaciers advance and retreat over the continents. Such adjustments to the relative position of the lithospheric crust are called *isostatic adjustments;* isostasy is the condition of equilibrium of the earth's crust that is achieved by a constant rebalancing of the forces that tend to elevate the lithosphere against those that tend to depress it.

The loading and subsequent rebounding of the lithosphere is only one kind of isostasy. A change in density of the lithosphere will cause isostatic crustal movement and produce accompanying changes in sea level. Young, hot lithospheric material that is produced at the rift zone of the oceanic ridge system is relatively low in density. As this lithosphere cools over a period of several millions of years, it contracts, becomes denser, and slowly subsides over the asthenosphere. Because most of this activity takes place in the ocean basin, the resulting rise in sea level over the subsiding sea floor is imperceptible. At the few regions on earth where coastlines are close to diverging plates, the local subsidence of the lithosphere can produce a rise in sea level and a slow inundation of land. The coasts of both the Red Sea and the narrow Gulf of California are on such diverging oceanic plates and thus are candidates for this type of local sea-level rise.

Another aspect of isostatic adjustment of the earth's crust is associated with the thick accumulation of sediments and volcanic rocks in the lithosphere. This can take place in sedimentary basins or along thick prograding coastal plains such as the Gulf and Atlantic coasts of the United States. In both cases, thousands of meters of sediment accumulates over tens of millions of years causing crustal subsidence and related sea-level rise. The same phenomenon is associated with the thick accumulations of volcanic crust such as exists in the volcanic islands in the Pacific Ocean. One of the best examples of this phenomenon is the Hawaiian Islands.

CHANGES IN THE VOLUME OF THE WORLD OCEAN

A global or eustatic change in sea level can come about in two ways—by adding or reducing the amount of water in the entire world ocean, or more subtly, by changing the temperature of the world ocean so that its volume increases or decreases as water expands or contracts. In either case, when the volume of water changes it causes an absolute, or eustatic, change in sea level. A worldwide and long-term change in climate can bring about both of these conditions simultaneously. A cold climate forms ice sheets and thereby traps much water in the glaciers while at the same time it lowers the temperature of the ocean. Both conditions cause a reduction in the volume of the world ocean. A warm climate melts the glaciers and returns the water to the oceans and at the same time raises the ocean's temperature leading to an increase in ocean volume and thus in sea level (Fig. 3.7).

Drastic temperature changes are not required to produce drastic changes in sea level. A rise or fall in the mean annual temperature of only one or two degrees Celsius has a profound effect on both the volume of ice retained on the surface of the earth and the volume of the water in the world ocean. During the last ice age, thick ice sheets covered much of the Northern Hemisphere. The ocean receded, its waters were bound up in ice or became contracted with the cold, leading to the exposure of nearly all of the continental shelf. These conditions were produced with a mean annual temperature difference of only about two to three degrees Celsius lower than it is today. If the trend toward a warmer global climate continues and the mean temperature increases by only a few degrees, the entire process will reverse—the ice sheets will melt and the ocean will encroach upon the continents until many of the port cities are at least partly under water.

Insufficient data have made it difficult, however, to assess the pace and direction of global climate and sea-level changes over the short term. Accurate records of sea level have been kept for only a little more than a century and our weather records in most parts of the world do not reliably extend back even that

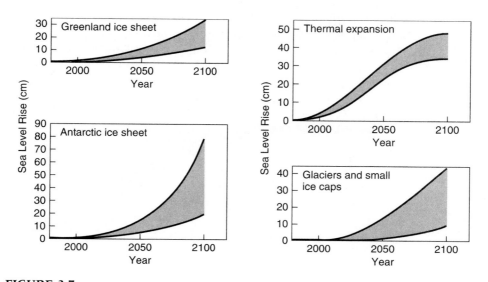

FIGURE 3.7
Contributions to sea-level rise during the next century.
(From Ince, M. (ed), 1990, *The Rising Seas*, Proc. of Cities on Water Conf., Venice, Italy)

far. The great sea-level changes of the past, as recorded in the advance and re-treat of the glaciers, occurred in cycles of tens of thousands of years or more. Our hundred-year-old records, therefore, cannot be superimposed on past changes to make any sort of valid prediction. Nevertheless, the recent rise in global temper-atures has forced us to consider a possible human-generated cause for the world-wide rise in sea level taking place today. The still-accelerating release into the at-mosphere of carbon dioxide and other greenhouse gases has some climatologists projecting a global warming of three degrees Celsius by the year 2030 (Fig. 3.8). Such a rise in mean annual temperature could melt enough of the ice cover in Greenland and Antarctica to raise the global sea level up to 5 meters in a rela-tively short time. Even here, however, we may be trying to superpose a short-term data base on periods of cyclicity. The current increase in carbon dioxide might just be part of a longer cycle that predates civilization and will decline by itself. But it is hard to discount the obvious contribution to global warming being made by our current high levels of combustion and our destruction of photosyn-thesizing plants. It is prudent for us to take careful note of the warming and melting patterns of the past and their effects on the global sea level to help us in-terpret the global warming pattern and sea level changes in our century.

ADVANCE AND RETREAT OF ICE SHEETS

During the Quaternary Period, which began about two million years ago and continues today, as best as we can tell, eustatic sea level seems to have changed quickly compared to most times in the earth's history. The driving force behind these sea-level changes has been the advance and retreat of continental ice sheets and the polar ice caps—Antarctica and Greenland. Up until about 18,000

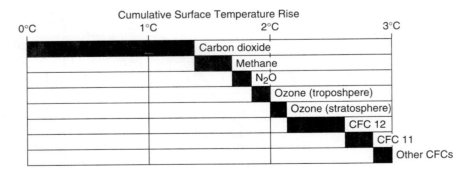

FIGURE 3.8
Sources of global warming as projected for the year 2030 by the United Nations Environment Program.
(From Ince, 1990)

years ago, when the Pleistocene Epoch of the Quaternary Period came to a close, thick ice sheets repeatedly covered and then withdrew from most of Europe, northern Asia, and North America down to the Missouri and Ohio River valleys (Fig. 3.9). Their incursions in the Southern Hemisphere, except for Antarctica, were limited due to the paucity of land in the high latitudes.

The record of the Pleistocene Epoch that is preserved on the continental landmasses has been interpreted to include four ice ages during which glaciation alternated with interglacial melting. Each of these glacial and interglacial periods lasted at least tens of thousands of years. In North America these periods of glacial advance are named, from oldest to youngest, the Nebraskan, Kansan, Illinoisan, and Wisconsinan for the states in which the ice sheets deposited considerable sediment. Europe and other parts of the world have their own terminology. There is land-based evidence that the glacial stages culminated 630,000 B.P. (Nebraskan), 430,000 B.P. (Kansan), 150,000 B.P. (Illinoisan) and 20,000 B.P. (Wisconsinan).

For the first half of the twentieth century this interpretation was accepted and taught throughout not only North America but the rest of the world as well. As more and more information was obtained from the ocean floor through sediment cores, it became apparent that many more Pleistocene glacial events probably took place; their traces have been masked on land by deposits of larger glacial incursions.

This discovery primarily results from new techniques for investigating ancient climatic conditions on the earth. Foremost among these is the use of oxygen isotopes, that is, variations in the atomic makeup of oxygen. Typical oxygen has an atomic weight of 16 but there is also a heavier isotope, oxygen 18. Both isotopes behave the same chemically and both are incorporated in the skeletons of organisms as part of the compound, calcium carbonate ($CaCO_3$). In 1947 a theory was developed at the University of Chicago stating that the relative concentration of the two oxygen isotopes taken into the skeletons of organisms depended on the temperature of the ocean water in which they were living. From this it was reasoned that the temperature of the water during the time that the organism was living could be determined using a mass spectrometer to analyze the $^{16}O/^{18}O$ content of the calcium carbonate forming the skeleton. A few years later, in 1955, the skeletons of planktonic foraminifer from several deep-sea cores were analyzed using these techniques. These floating, single-celled protozoa have calcium carbonate skeletons and are numerous in the cores. Samples analyzed from these cores provided data that demonstrated that there were numerous periods of significant temperature fluctuation in ocean waters in only 300,000 years. These changes were assumed to be in response to climatic changes associated with glacial activity and were in marked contrast to the Pleistocene glacial history of land-based studies.

Furthermore, the cycles shown by the isotopic data in these sediment cores matched well a periodicity that had been predicted many years earlier by Mulitin Milankovitch, a Yugoslavian astronomer. His theory of climatic changes was

FIGURE 3.9
Map of the North America showing the distribution of glacial ice sheets during the peak condition of the
Pleistocene glaciation.
(From Skinner, B. J. and Porter, S. C., 1987, *Physical Geology,* John Wiley & Sons, New York, p. 365, Fig. 13.37)

based upon cycles of radiation received by the earth as it tilts relative to the sun. There are three astronomical cycles associated with this variation in tilting and its effect on climate: (1) variation in acentricity of the earth's orbit around the sun with a periodicity of 90,000 to 100,000 years, (2) changes in the obliquity of the earth's plane of orbit and the angle that it makes with the plane of the ecliptic having a period of 41,000 years, and (3) the precession or wobbling of the earth's axis with a period of 21,000 years. During the period prior to about 700,000 B.P. Milankovitch's cycles had a periodicity of 41,000 years and after that it was 100,000 years. The differences are interpreted to reflect changes in major oceanic circulation patterns having a corresponding periodicity. This interpretation is made because the major ocean currents have a strong influence on our climate. We are all aware of the warming effect the Gulf Stream has, not only on northeastern North America but also on western Europe and the British Isles. A change in the mean temperature of this current only a few degrees in magnitude or a shift in its path relative to the continents can produce a marked change in the climate of the adjacent landmasses.

Thus far, more has been learned about the climatic conditions during the Pleistocene Epoch from examining and analyzing the record preserved in the ocean basins. It is also important to understand how long-term astronomical relationships have influenced our climates and that patterns result from these cyclic changes.

It is the most recent of these cycles that has produced the glaciation that has molded the shoreline of our present coast. The last of the great advances of glaciers, the Wisconsinan Ice Age, began about 120,000 years ago and persisted for over 100,000 years. Since then we have been in the Holocene (formerly called the Recent) Epoch characterized by glacial melting. The Antarctic and Greenland ice sheets of today are remnants of the last Wisconsinan advance. This period of overall melting and related warming has been interrupted by a few "Little Ice Ages," extended periods of abnormally cold weather, some of which have occurred during recorded history. The most prominent was chronicled in Europe between about 1450 and 1850.

By calculating the difference in volume between the Wisconsinan ice sheets and those remaining today, we can determine how much ice melted and how this has affected global sea level. We can then extrapolate what would happen to sea level and what the consequence would be to our planet if our present rate of global warming continued until the remaining ice sheets melted.

To make this calculation, we must first estimate the surface area and depth of these previously existing ice sheets. The surface area covered by the Antarctic ice sheet during the Wisconsinan advance was nearly 14 million square kilometers; today, it is about 12.5 million, not much smaller. The North American Laurentide ice sheet east of the Canadian Rockies, lower in latitude and therefore subject to more melting that the Antarctic, once covered more than 13 million square kilometers of land and now covers only 147,000. There was also considerable ice covering Greenland, Europe and Asia. The total surface covered by ice

12,000 years ago was more that 44 million square kilometers, and it is not just under 15 million, one-third of its former extent.

It is more difficult to determine the volume of the Wisconsinan ice sheet than it is to determine its surface area. Perhaps the best way to approach the problem is to use the Greenland ice sheet as a model. The Antarctic ice is more than 2 kilometers thick in some places but it rests on rugged topography and its thickness varies too much to make generalizations about its volume; moreover, much of it is unexplored. The Greenland ice sheet, on the other hand, is well-known because of extensive petroleum exploration surveys and scientific and military studies. Glaciologists have estimated that the Greenland ice sheet holds about 2.5 million cubic kilometers of ice. By extrapolating surface areas and estimating average thicknesses based on latitude, we can conclude that 75 million cubic kilometers of ice were contained in the vast glaciers of the Wisconsinan Ice Age. We can further conclude that about 50 million cubic kilometers of ice have melted since the Wisconsinan Ice Age—roughly equivalent to 20 meltings of today's Greenland ice cap. Allowing for a 10 percent decrease in volume when ice turns to water, 45 million cubic kilometers of water were returned to the ocean. The mammoth shift of weight and mass from the continent to the ocean had—and is still having—tremendous repercussions.

As the mass of the ice sheets was gradually removed from the backs of the continents through melting, the continental lithosphere beneath the load began to rise up, or rebound, in an isostatic adjustment. If, as is likely, some regions were covered with ice 3000 meters thick at the peak of the ice age, the rebound when the ice melted would have reached about 1000 meters. This is produced by the isostatic adjustment of removing 3000 meters of ice at a density of 0.9 grams per cubic centimeter, about one-third the density of the continental lithosphere, equivalent to about 1000 meters of lithospheric crust. The pace of the rebound has been slow and uneven, and in some places it is still ongoing (Fig. 3.10).

Meanwhile, in the world ocean, the added mass pouring in from the continents caused a sinking of the ocean floor, which has a much younger and thinner crust than the continents. But the tremendous increase in the volume of water raised sea level despite the sinking floor of the ocean. Taking into account the uplift of the continents, the subsidence of the ocean floor, and the increase in the volume of ocean water, the long-term net rise in global sea level may have been about 150 meters, with local variations due to differences in continental rebound.

CONTINENTAL REBOUND

Because the Wisconsinan glacial ice melted gradually, the continental rebound was also slow. Most of the isostatic adjustment of the underlying crust was accomplished before the melt was actually over because the weight of the remaining ice was no longer sufficient to cause significant subsidence. In some places

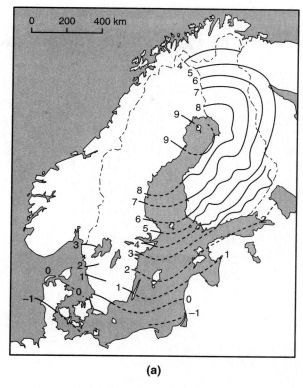

(a)

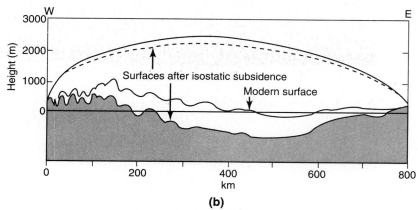

(b)

FIGURE 3.10

Map (a) and cross-section (b) showing the subsidence and rebound associated with glacial development and melting across the northern part of Norway and Finland. Contours are rates of sea-level rise in mm/yr.

(From Bloom, A. L., 1978, *Geomorphology*, Prentice-Hall, Inc., Englewood Cliffs, New Jersey, p. 405)

though, where the ice was thickest and the crust is thin, the rebound is still on-going. Significant uplift of continental mass is taking place today in Scandinavia, in the Hudson Bay area of Canada, and in Argentina and lower Chile.

Along the Scandinavian coast, the mean annual sea level drops about 6 to 7 millimeters a year, indicating an uplift of continental crust. Adding the annual global sea level rise of 2 to 3 millimeters, the rate uplift is about 9 millimeters a year. This extrapolates to a local relative lowering of sea level of 30 to 35 meters given that glaciers receded from Scandinavia 5000 years ago. The total rebound in the Hudson Bay area of Canada is even greater. In aerial photographs of the northern Scandinavian coast, and of other coasts of active uplift, one can see a parallel series of ridges marking the old shorelines and abandoned beaches as the sea level dropped and the ocean receded from the land (Fig. 3.11).

The rate of active continental uplift diminishes in a southward direction in the Northern Hemisphere because the ice was thinner and melted more rapidly in the south. This is seen in the profile along the New England coast; the land slopes downward from Maine to New York. The position of relative sea level reflects the uplift; it drops several millimeters a year in Maine but holds steady in New York. The Great Lakes, which owe their origin to glaciers, show even

FIGURE 3.11
Photograph of beach ridges around Hudson Bay, Canada providing evidence for isostatic rebound after glaciation.
(Courtesy of A. Hequette)

clearer signs of a north-to-south tilt; the ancient shorelines on the northern sides of the lakes are several meters higher than the same age shorelines on the south sides. Lake Michigan is gradually getting shallower at the north end and deeper in the south. If the present rate of rebound persists, in about 3000 years the lake will drain into the Mississippi River system rather than through the other lakes into the St. Lawrence Seaway as it does now.

Wherever the northern landmass is still rebounding from a melting ice sheet, coastal uplift leaves shoreline after shoreline high and dry (Fig. 3.11), abandoned by the receding water level. But eventually the rebound will slow and the water level will rise again.

THE HOLOCENE RISE IN SEA LEVEL

The Holocene Epoch is characterized by the melting of the last Pleistocene ice sheet, the Wisconsinan, and the subsequent rise in global sea level. What we would most like to determine is when the rise began, how fast has it proceeded, how long will it last, and how long will it go before it reverses. In other words, we wish to study the sea-level curve and extrapolate the next segment of the curve. Unfortunately, geologists, oceanographers, and climatologists who study sea-level fluctuations cannot agree among themselves about what the projection should look like, which is understandable given the complexity of the problem.

It is generally agreed that sea level was at its lowest position about 17,000 to 18,000 years ago, when the ice sheets of the Wisconsinan Ice Age had reached their maximum development. The lowest level, called the *lowstand,* is deduced by uncovering evidence of the oldest drowned shoreline on the continental shelf. This evidence might take the form of beach sand, marsh deposits, drowned wave eroded platforms, drowned deltas, or almost any indicator of an old shoreline such as coastal fossil plant or animal remains that are in place, not transported. Other factors such as tectonic uplift and subsidence must also be taken into account before the vertical position of the lowstand is determined. Most researchers have placed the lowstand depth between 130 and 150 meters below present sea level and agree that sea level rose rapidly and at a fairly uniform rate until about 6000 to 7000 years before present (B.P.) (Fig. 3.12). The annual rise during this period was near 10 millimeters a year, fast enough for the sea to cover many coastal cities in a century.

During this period of rapidly rising sea level, the shoreline moved so rapidly that the sand bars and barrier islands that protect so many of our coasts today had no time to build vertically. The lack of a stable shoreline for any length of time coupled with moderate to high tidal ranges produced tide-dominated coasts with widespread estuaries and tidal flats. Some areas such as Australia and New Zealand saw relative sea level reach its present position about 6500 to 7000 years ago, at the end of this period of rapid rise. In most landmasses of the world, sea-level rise continued but at a much reduced rate due to centuries of slowing in

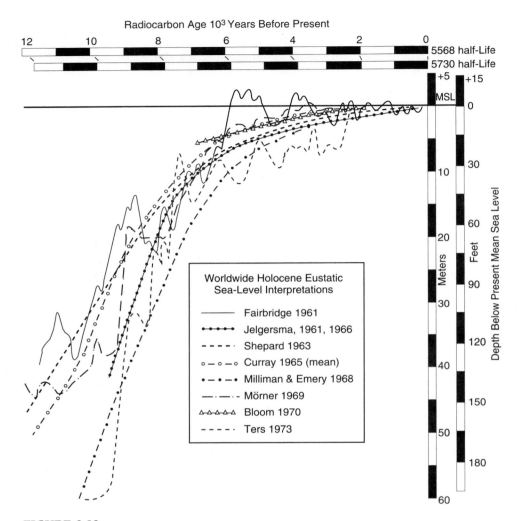

FIGURE 3.12
Diagram showing numerous sea-level curves from the past 10,000 years for different parts of the world as determined by various authors.
(Belknap, D. F. and Kraft, J. C., 1977, Holocene relative sea-level changes and coastal stratigraphic units on the northwest flank of the Baltimore Canyon trough geosyncline, *Jour. Sed. Petrology,* 47, pp. 610–629)

glacial melting. This slower rate of relative rise resulted in more stable shorelines and permitted waves to become the dominant coastal process forming beaches and barrier islands.

There is disagreement about the position of sea level in much of North America during the past 3000 years. Some researchers believe it has been stable at the present position, some believe it has moved above and below its present position, and many think relative sea level has been gradually rising during the period, over only about 3 meters (Fig. 3.13).

CURRENT AND FUTURE SEA-LEVEL CHANGES

The impact of an ever-increasing global population coupled with the depletion of the ozone layer of the earth's atmosphere, which has led to apparent global warming, have had noticeable effects on the sea level of the global ocean. Recent data from tide gauges around the world indicate that eustatic sea level is rising at an increasing rate. Several criteria are considered when determining the reliability of such data. Good records come from tide gauges that are mounted on a stable surface, preferably bedrock. Pier pilings, for example, are not very reliable because they can settle or may shift position due to tidal or wave scour. The overall tectonic stability of an area must also be considered to determine eustatic sea-level change accurately. Given these criteria, we have, on average, approximately 100 years of reliable data on sea level.

Much of our knowledge of recent trends in sea level is due to the National Ocean Survey (NOS). Personnel of this agency have studied and interpreted data from hundreds of tide stations, some of which have been in operation for more than a century. Examples from their studies of various parts of North America serve to illustrate the nature of these data and the trends that are present (Fig. 3.14). Data from the East Coast of the United States show overall increase with

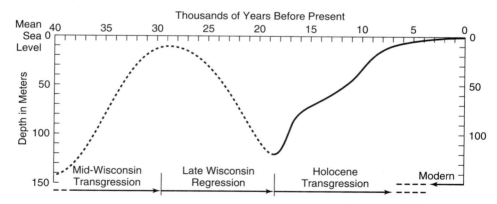

FIGURE 3.13

Simplified sea-level curve for the Holocene which is fairly representative of the Gulf and much of the Atlantic coasts of the United States.

(From Curray, J. R., 1965, In Wright, N. E. and Frey, D. G. (eds), *Quaternary of the United States,* Princeton University Press, p. 725, Fig. 2)

FIGURE 3.14
Tide gauge records for the past several decades as compiled by Hicks and colleagues. These show well the differences around the United States based largely on tectonic conditions; Alaskan sea level is subsiding locally but it is stable in other areas, as is Oregon. The east coast is showing a rise of about 2 mm per year.
(Adapted from Hicks, S. D., 1972, *Shore and Beach*, 40, p. 20)

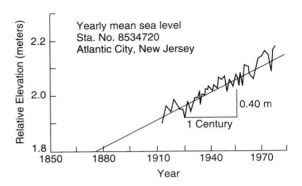

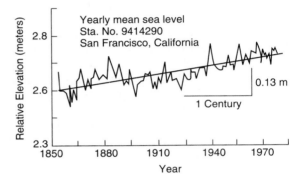

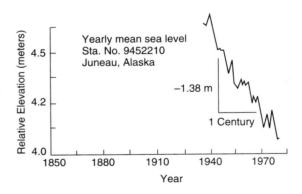

considerable short-term ups and downs. In New England this pattern is displayed with a greater than average range in the average rate of rise. Similar data from the West Coast of the United States indicate more variation by location but little overall increase in sea level for the period of record. The data from both coasts are influenced by their tectonic settings. The more stable East Coast has experienced a rise in sea level but that ranges from relatively slow rises in the north where isostatic rebound is still going on to more rapid rises in the south where this phenomenon is absent. The West Coast, a crustal plate collision area, experiences great variety in sea-level conditions. Low rates of local sea-level rise characterize the western states and in Alaska, where the situation is generally reversed; many locations show a decrease in sea level due to tectonic conditions of uplift, up to 10 mm per year (Fig. 3.15).

On a global scale, the last century has experienced a distinct but variable increase in sea level everywhere except for the Pacific Ocean (Fig. 3.16). The variable increase is due to a combination of tectonic conditions, regional subsidence, and climatic changes of up to several years duration. The coasts of the Pacific Ocean are mostly collision coasts where tectonic conditions override eustatic changes in sea level.

It should be noted, however, that one century of data for sea-level changes is insufficient to accurately predict long-term sea-level trends. During the past several thousand years, perturbations in sea level have occurred as climatic conditions varied within the long-term warming and melting trend. These small deviations were sometimes a century or more in length. A good example of this took place a few hundred years ago in what is known as the *Little Ice Age*. During that time a marked change in climate took place, the existing ice sheets appeared

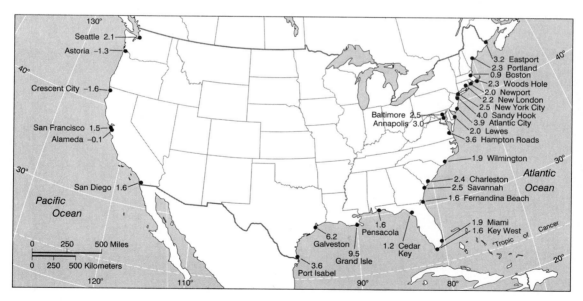

FIGURE 3.15
Rates of sea-level rise around the continental United States as shown from tide gauges. Compare the East Coast, Mississippi Delta area, and the West Coast.
(From National Academy of Sciences, 1987, *Responding to Sea Level*, National Academy Press, Washington, D.C., p. 10, Fig. 1-1)

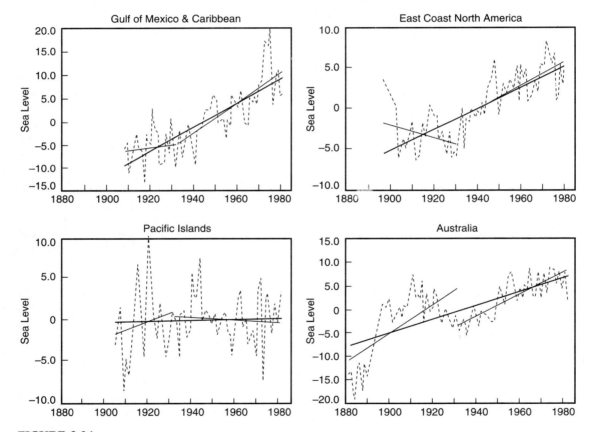

FIGURE 3.16
Summary of sea-level curves for the past century from around the world. Note that the only place where a noticeable increase has not occurred is the Pacific Ocean.
(From Gornitz, V. and Lebedeff, S., 1987, Global sea-level changes during the past century, In *SEPM Spec. Publ. No. 41*, p. 10, Fig. 7)

to increase in size, and there was a slight reversal of the rise in sea level. This reversal of a long-term trend was best documented in Europe and in China where an extensive population was present to record the events associated with it. Similar but smaller scale perturbations have been recorded in recent times through careful observation of individual glaciers and correlation of these observations with weather records. It has been shown that glaciers advance and retreat in accordance with weather records and that the periodicity ranges from years to decades. Factors that contribute to these perturbations include variations in sun spots, shifting oceanic currents, and slight changes in earth–sun positions.

Implications for Coastal Environments

The coast as we know it today represents one of the youngest elements of the earth's history. Most of the coast we see now dates back only a few thousand years in the total earth history of about five billion years. The coast represents one of the fastest changing parts of the earth's surface and as a result, its equilibrium is very fragile.

Changes in sea level either directly or indirectly affect virtually all of the sediment accumulations and landforms in the coastal zone. As the shoreline moves, it either exposes or inundates the coastal areas and in so doing, causes the coast to change. Additionally, the position of the shoreline strongly influences various coastal processes, such as waves, tides, and currents, that act to shape the coastal environments.

During the period of significant human occupation on earth, eustatic sea level has changed by less than 3 meters. As result, we are often unaware of the fragile nature of the coast and we have come to take its relative stability for granted. We must recognize, however, that the nature of the sea is dynamic, not static. A rise in sea level on the order of 3 to 4 mm per year for a century or more will cause significant problems for many highly populated parts of the world. To see the damage that can result from rising sea levels, we need only to look at the Mississippi River Delta region, where an annual rise of 9 millimeters causes a loss of over 40 acres of coastal land each month.

4

Coastal Processes

Previous chapters have covered the large-scale and long-term aspects of the coastal system. Plate tectonics provides a global setting upon which the geological framework of the coastal zone is placed. Typically from tens to more than a hundred million years are required for plate margins to fully develop depending upon location. Sea-level fluctuations combine both local and global considerations in their distribution, and their effects take place over hundreds to thousands of years. Now it is appropriate to take a close look at the short-term, day-to-day processes that are quite local in their extent and that give each kilometer of the coast a character of its own.

There are three quite different types of processes that influence the coast—physical, biological, and chemical. Physical processes—and the waves, tides, and the currents that they generate—overwhelm the effects of the other two. The physical processes are obvious, take place rather quickly, and give each coastal area its primary characteristics. By contrast, the chemical and biological processes are generally slower and more subtle in their influence on the coast.

Physical processes are of two basic types: those generated by the wind, which include waves and wave-generated currents, and those that are tidal, both the change in water level and the currents produced by this rise and fall of sea level. The primary periods of these physical processes range from seconds, in the case of waves, to daily for the basic tidal cycle. Organisms that inhabit the coast interact with the sediments, the bedrock, and other organisms. In so doing, they produce important effects on the coast. Chemical processes result from both the weathering and precipitation of materials in the coastal zone and may have an important influence on it.

PHYSICAL PROCESSES

The underlying force in the spectrum of physical processes that molds the coastal zone into its complex association of different environments is gravity. Sir Isaac Newton's Law of Universal Gravitation provides the primary framework for causing tides. That is, waves are produced by wind, a sun-based phenomenon, and tides result from the attraction of the earth and its hydrosphere by the sun and moon. Their magnitude is controlled by the relative position of the earth, moon, and sun. Thus, the rotation of the earth, the movement of the moon relative to the earth, and the seasonal change in the position of the earth relative to the sun all have an influence on tidal conditions. Winds produced by variations in heating or cooling of the atmosphere control development of waves that in turn can also generate currents. Tidal fluctuations produce currents that erode, transport, and deposit materials in the coastal zone. The cumulative effects of these processes give us the morphology or the appearance of the coast at any given location.

Astronomic Tides

Newton's equation for the Law of Universal Gravitation states that

$$F = \frac{Gm_1m_2}{R_2}$$

(4.1)

The gravitational force (F) is proportional to the mass of the two bodies (m_1 and m_2) and is inversely related to the square of the distance between them (R^2). G is the universal gravitational constant. It is this relationship that explains why the sun, which has a mass 27×10^6 times that of the moon, has less than one-half of the moon's influence on the tides (Fig. 4.1). Because the sun is also nearly 400 times farther away from the earth than the moon, its influence is less.

There is also a centrifugal force operating within the earth–moon system, and this force balances the gravitational attraction between these celestial bodies to produce an equilibrium condition. Whereas the centrifugal force is the same at all locations on the earth's surface, the gravitational force differs by location due to the difference in distance between the near and far side of the earth. The combined effect of these two forces is the tide-producing force that is the cause of the regular changes in sea level that the earth experiences.

The cyclic movements of both the earth and the moon produce predictable tidal cycles as well. The moon revolves around the earth once every 27.3 days, a lunar month. As this is taking place, the earth is rotating on its axis with a period of 24 hours. This relationship causes the period of the earth's rotation relative to the movement of the moon to be 24 hours 50 minutes, a lunar day or a diurnal

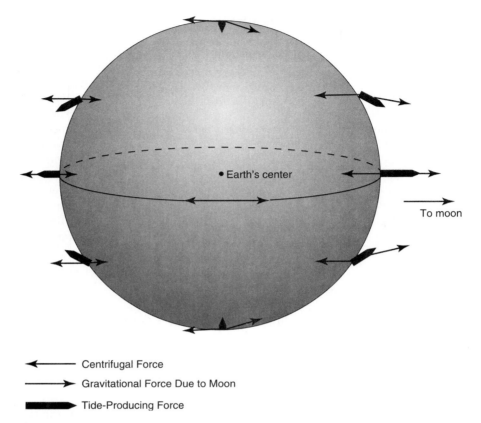

Centrifugal Force

Gravitational Force Due to Moon

Tide-Producing Force

FIGURE 4.1
Diagram of the earth showing the tide-producing force.

cycle. It is this lunar day that forms the basis for the tidal cycles. The actual periodicity of the tidal cycle is half of that value or 12 hours 25 minutes, a semidiurnal cycle, due to the double tidal bulge created by tide-producing forces.

If the moon were moving in the plane of the earth's equator, tidal effects would be equally distributed at a given location on the globe. Because the moon's path is actually at a 25-degree angle to the equator, the semidiurnal or twice-daily tidal ranges are unequal, especially in the mid-latitudes (Fig. 4.2).

The path taken by the moon's orbit around the earth–moon system is elliptical, which means that the moon is closer to the earth at some times than at others. Up to a 40 percent difference in the tide-producing effects can occur between *perigee*, the minimum distance between the two celestial bodies, and *apogee*, the maximum distance.

As the moon moves in its path around the earth, there are conditions during which the earth, moon, and the sun are aligned. These occur during new

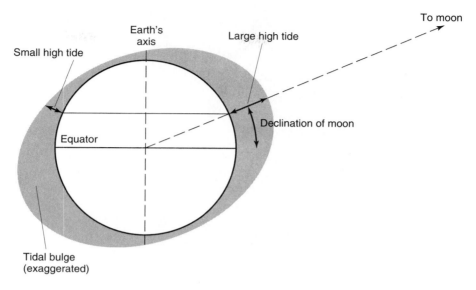

FIGURE 4.2

Diagram of the earth showing the relationships of the tidal bulges to the moon and the earth's latitude.

moon and full moon stages, producing maximum tidal range because the three celestial bodies are aligned. Such conditions produce spring tides unrelated to the season. The converse condition of the earth, moon, and sun being at right angles, produces minimum tidal range or neap tides during the first and third quarter conditions of the moon, at the time that the moon's image appears to be one-half its full size (Fig. 4.3). Spring and neap conditions occur at two-week intervals, twice a lunar month.

If the earth were a featureless sphere, we would expect that the tidal bulges would move rather uniformly as the earth rotates. The great complications caused by the presence of irregularities such as oddly shaped land masses and ocean basins, produce a system of oceanic bulges in the form of tidal waves (these are not tsunamis or seismic sea waves). In fact, the cyclic changes of sea level result from a forced wave moving from place to place in an orderly fashion in a given ocean basin. These tidal waves are not to be confused with the seismic sea waves of catastrophic proportions called tsunamis.

Objects that move over a rotating sphere (the earth) are subjected to apparent deflections in their path, a phenomenon known as the *Coriolis effect*. The combination of the specific ocean basin or portion of an ocean basin with the Coriolis effect results in what are called *amphidromic systems* (Fig. 4.4). These tidal circulation systems result from the combination of the Coriolis effect with land masses. As the earth rotates and the tidal wave propagates, Coriolis deflects the

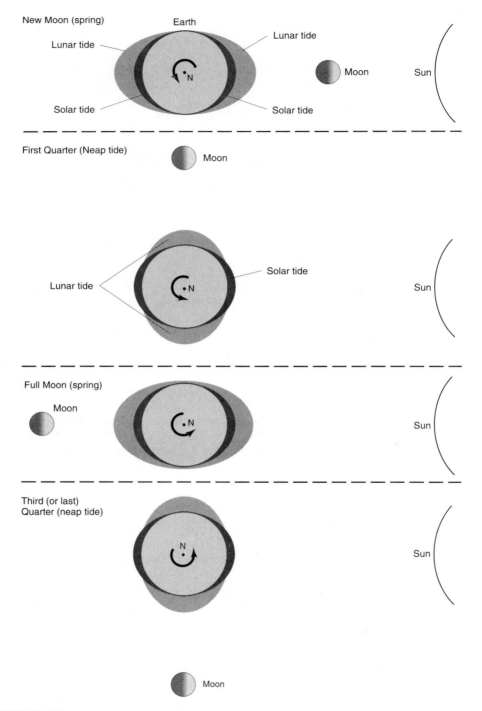

FIGURE 4.3
Lunar cycle showing the sun, moon, and earth relationships during spring and neap tides.

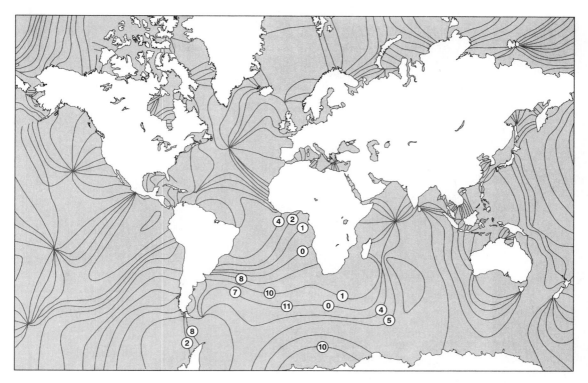

FIGURE 4.4
Global map showing amphidromic systems and the related tidal range associated with each one.

tidal bulge from the North to the West and from the South to the East, resulting in a rotation of the tidal bulge around a central area in which minimal water level change takes place. In these wheel-like spoked amphidromic systems the tidal wave moves about an amphidromic point, essentially the hub on this spoked wheel (Fig. 4.4). Movement is counterclockwise in the Northern Hemisphere and clockwise in the Southern Hemisphere. These amphidromic systems explain why high tide occurs at different times along a given reach of coast regardless of its orientation; high tide is, in effect, a wave moving along the shoreline. The tidal range at the amphidromic point is zero, increasing outward from it. Some islands, such as Madagascar and New Zealand, include the amphidromic point near their center with the amphidromic system moving around it. The amphidromic system is shown by cotidal lines that display the position of the tidal crest (high tide) at any given hour in the tidal cycle. By definition then, lines constructed at right angles to these co-tidal lines indicate locations of equal tidal range, the distance between high and low tide.

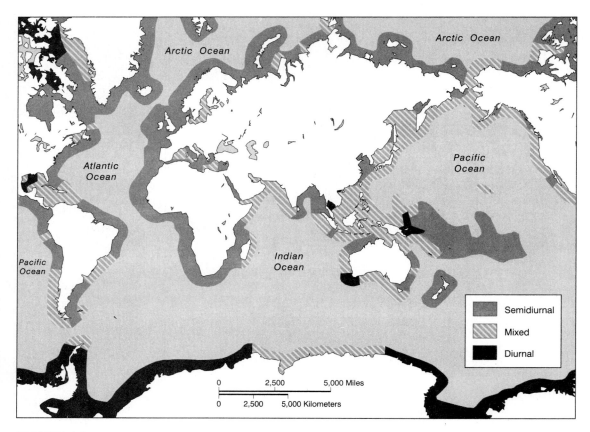

FIGURE 4.5
Global distribution of diurnal, semi-diurnal, and mixed tides.
(From Davies, J. L., 1980, *Geographical Variation in Coastal Development,* 2nd edition, Longman, New York, p. 49, Fig. 32)

Types of Tides Tidal cycles at a given location tend to take on one of three styles: diurnal, semidiurnal, or mixed. The diurnal tide has a period of one lunar day, therefore it includes a single high and a low tide in each cycle; the tidal wave has a period of 24 hours and 50 minutes. The semidiurnal tide includes two highs and two lows each lunar day; a period of 12 hours and 25 minutes. A mixed tide includes both diurnal and semidiurnal cycles during the lunar month. Diurnal tides are due mainly to the moon's declination whereas semidiurnal tides are caused by relative positions of the sun and moon. On a global basis, diurnal tides are most widespread around the Antarctic continent and nearby Indian Ocean. Semidiurnal tides are the most common type; they occur around the Atlantic and Arctic oceans as well as scattered around the Indian and Pacific (Fig. 4.5). They may have nearly equal highs and lows during the daily cycle or they may have distinctly different ones. In some books this phenomenon is mistakenly called mixed tides. Mixed tides that include both diurnal and semidiur-

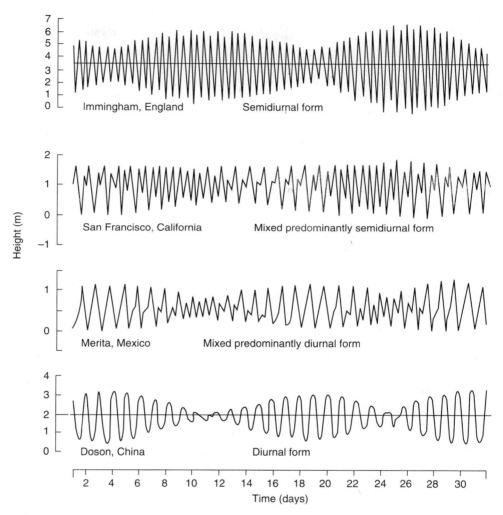

FIGURE 4.6
Examples of tidal curves showing each of the major patterns: equal semi-diurnal (Immingham, England), unequal semi-diurnal (San Francisco), mixed (Merita, Mexico), and diurnal (DoSon, China).

nal conditions during the lunar cycle also occur in many areas of the Indian and Pacific oceans and throughout the Gulf of Mexico.

The tidal conditions at any given coastal location are therefore rather complicated but are also predictable. They are complicated and influenced by multiple conditions at any one time: (1) the lunar condition, which produces neap and spring cycles and (2) the latitude and inclination of the moon, which produces the daily inequality. The resulting tidal curves for any location reflect these differences. Some tidal curves, such as those along much of the east coast and Europe, are dominated by a semidiurnal pattern (Fig. 4.6) and have a distinct spring and neap cycle. They differ from many locations in that there is little diurnal inequality between successive highs or lows. In San Francisco and most of the West coast of the United States, the tidal curve is also semidiurnal but shows a markedly different pattern. Here there is also a noticeable spring and neap cycle but there is a great range in the diurnal inequality. During some days there is little difference while during others it is extreme.

Mixed tides in the Gulf of Mexico produce a tidal curve that also shows distinct spring and neap periods that are overprinted by a shift from a diurnal to a semidiurnal type of tide. Consequently, there are times during a lunar month when the tides are diurnal and other times semidiurnal but with a distinct inequality.

Tidal Range   The amount of water-level change caused by tidal fluctuation is different from one location to another. This difference in the range between high and low tide, coupled with the specific nature of the tidal curve described previously, gives tides at any single location a fingerprint quality—every one is different! This difference takes place along the shoreline of the open ocean and also from the open ocean into coastal embayments, deltas, and other landward extensions of tidal influence.

Tidal range is lower in the open ocean than on the coast, especially as you approach an amphidromic point. As the tidal wave moves through the ocean it is traveling at about 700 km per hour, about the cruising speed of a commercial jet. The wave is slowed by about 75 percent and steepened at the continental margin. Here the gradual shallowing of the depth continues until the wave reaches the coast where it travels a few tens of kilometers per hour. It is this slowing and steepening of the tidal wave by the shallow water that produces the noticeable tidal ranges along the coast where easy reference is possible. Further increase in tidal range is caused by embayments, especially those that have a funnel shape. The result is that tidal range extends from less than 0.5 meters to 15.6 meters. Very high tidal ranges typically occur in embayments where the tidal wave piles up.

Global tidal ranges have been classified by John Davies, an Australian physical geographer who has studied all aspects of the earth's coasts. His relatively simple classification includes three categories: (1) microtidal coasts with a range of less than 2 meters, (2) mesotidal coasts having a range of 2 to 4 meters, and (3) macrotidal coasts that have a greater than 4 meter tidal range (Fig. 4.7). This organization is simply convenient, not based upon any recognized relationships, but it has become somewhat of a standard.

There is a terminology associated with tidal range and elevations that needs some explanation. We generally subdivide the vertical position of any coastal location into three categories: subtidal, intertidal, and supratidal. Subtidal environments are always covered with water, and supratidal environments are generally exposed to the atmosphere, except during storms when the lower supratidal area is flooded by storm or wind tides. Between these two is the intertidal area, which includes a number of different zones.

During spring-tide conditions, the tidal range covers a greater vertical distance than during neap conditions. The intertidal zone is typically considered to include everything between spring high-tide level and spring low-tide level. We therefore, speak of spring low tide or neap low tide as a specific elevation. A similar pair of terms is applied to neap tidal conditions. Mean tide level is also an important datum and is not the same as mean sea level on coastal charts. The reason is that in 1929 a vertical datum, the National Geodetic Vertical Datum (NGVD), was established in the United States for purposes of navigating coastal charts. It was sea level at the time it was established. The position of NGVD has changed in a range of amounts at all locations around the globe due to changes in relative sea level—eustatic, tectonic, or a combination. As a result, mean sea level as defined by NGVD is below present sea level and below mean tide level as it now exists except for locations where there has been significant tectonic uplift.

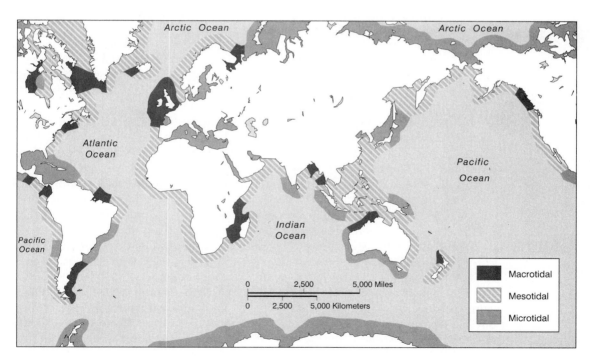

FIGURE 4.7
Global distribution of tidal range categories: microtidal, mesotidal, and macrotidal.
(From Davies, 1980, p. 51, Fig. 33)

Meteorologic Tides

In addition to the regular and predictable tides caused by astronomical conditions, there are also unpredictable but quite important tides caused by special conditions of the weather. These tides may greatly exceed the astronomical tides at some locations and because they are unpredictable they can cause great damage. Such tides are the result of severe to extreme conditions of atmospheric pressure and the related wind conditions that they produce, in other words, storms or near-storm conditions. In actuality, the high or low atmospheric pressure alone would cause a change in water level but these conditions are usually accompanied by strong winds.

Wind in contact with water produces a great deal of friction. The transfer of this wind energy to the sea surface not only produces waves, but also pushes the water in the direction of the wind. These interactions generate storm tides, or storm surges, as they are commonly called. This phenomenon produces both positive storm and negative storm tides depending upon wind direction relative to the coast or to the specific part of a coastal embayment. It is the positive storm tides that are feared by coastal residents because they can increase water level up to several meters. The negative storm tide is typically not as great in magnitude and does not have a destructive effect on the coast.

The spectrum of storm tides is great and these tides are recorded on the tide gauges as water-level fluctuations along with the astronomical tides. It is generally easy to separate the two simply by subtracting the predicted tide from the observed one. The difference can be attributed to meteorologic conditions, that is, the storm surge. Actually, this term is a bit misleading in that storm conditions are not required to produce either positive or negative meteorologic tides. The term *wind tide* is probably more appropriate. One of the most commonly occurring examples of wind tide is produced by the passage of frontal systems in the mid-latitudes. The coast of the Gulf of Mexico provides a good example.

Both the Texas and Florida coasts can be considered. As the front approaches the Texas coast from the north there is a modest wind with an onshore component. This condition generates a small positive wind tide (Fig. 4.8). As the front passes, there is strong offshore wind that produces a quite noticeable negative wind tide at the shoreline. This condition is relieved as the wind subsides. This same front crosses the Gulf of Mexico and approaches the west coast of the Florida peninsula with a fairly strong onshore wind component. A modest positive wind tide is recorded on the tide gauge before the front passes. The wind becomes stronger and blows nearly parallel to the shore with no noticeable wind tide on the open coast. As the wind direction shifts to the NNE there is a small but important offshore component, causing considerable water to be blown out and thus abnormally low tides.

The most important wind tides are the storm surges that are associated with hurricanes or other extreme storm conditions. A cyclonic storm system with very low barometric pressure combined with wind speeds of over 100 knots moving toward a coast at a speed of only 5 or so knots can produce a storm surge in excess of 5 meters. Hurricane Hugo, which hit the South Carolina coast in October 1989, produced a maximum storm surge of near 11 meters in the landward portions of some estuaries. It is this aspect of hurricanes that causes the most devastation to people and property (Fig. 4.9).

A combination of circumstances is needed to produce storm surges of this magnitude. First, strong onshore winds are necessary. The portion of the cyclonic storm in which winds blow offshore shows markedly less storm surge than when it blows onshore. Second, the speed of the storm is important. Rapidly moving hurricanes do not produce high storm surges but the slowly moving storms may cause very high tides. An additional condition that influences the amount of storm surge is the width and gradient of the continental shelf adjacent to the coast in question. A broad and gently sloping shelf provides a setting that permits

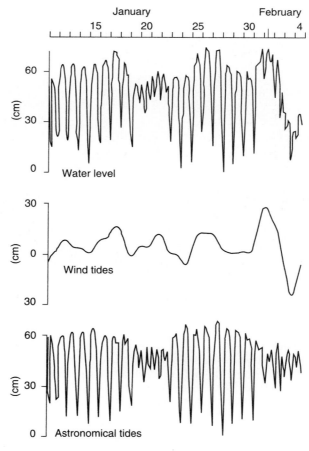

FIGURE 4.8
Tide gauge record from the Texas coast showing the predicted lunar tide and the subtracted meteorological tide.

(a)

(b)

FIGURE 4.9
Photographs showing indications of the extreme storm surge and erosion that occurred
during Hurricane Hugo, October, 1989 on the South Carolina coast.
(Courtesy of Donald Stauble, CERC)

onshore winds to achieve maximum elevation of sea level whereas along a narrow and steep coast there will be a minimal storm tide. Thus, plate tectonics
plays a role in hurricane influence. Leading edge or tectonically active coasts experience little storm tide as compared to a trailing edge or passive margin coast,
all other factors being equal. This explains why the Gulf and Atlantic coasts of

the U.S. experience higher storm surges than the Pacific coast of Central America, which also experiences hurricanes.

We need to remember that the storm tide is added onto the astronomical tide, which is completely unaffected by any level of storm. The timing of the storm tide relative to the astronomical tide is critical insofar as potential destruction along the coast is concerned. The worst scenario is for the most intense part of the storm to coincide with spring high tide, which superimposes an already high water level on the storm tide. In terms of damage, the best possible situation would be the opposite circumstance. Because of the storm's movement, it is common for significant variation in intensity to take place in only a few hours.

A comparison between Hurricane Carla on the Texas coast in September 1961 and Hurricane Hugo in South Carolina is illustrative. The tidal range on the Texas coast is less than 1 meter during spring conditions so the storm tide of over 3 meters during this hundred-year storm was just slightly influenced by either lunar or diurnal tidal conditions at the time of landfall. The South Carolina coast experiences tides of greater than 2 meters spring range, which is at its maximum during the month of October. These conditions coupled with the coincidence of landfall with high tide caused the tremendously high water as Hurricane Hugo moved across this coast.

There have been situations during passage of hurricanes when the primary storm tide was negative. As Hurricane Donna passed from the Gulf of Mexico across the Florida peninsula in 1960, the wind direction over Tampa Bay was primarily offshore. This was caused by a cyclone with its counterclockwise circulation passing to the south of this area. It also coincided with a low tide and caused water level to drop more than a meter below normal low tide. Many fish were left stranded by falling waters.

Tidal Currents

The rise and fall of water level along the coast involves a substantial flux of water, which produces currents as water flows from one place to another. These currents typically go unnoticed along the open coast beaches but are quite rapid in tidal inlets, estuaries, and other constricted places along the coast through which large volumes of water flow.

Like water level, tidal currents in the deep ocean are nearly imperceptible. As the tidal wave reaches the outer part of the continental margin it is decreased in speed with rates of only a few centimeters per second at the outer part of the continental shelf. Even at the open coast along the beach only weak tidal currents exist. In this part of the coast the waves and wave-generated currents overwhelm tidal currents.

The first environment in a landward direction in which tidal currents are strong is the tidal inlet. Here large volumes of water are forced through narrow constrictions during every tidal cycle. The larger the coastal bay serviced by the tidal inlet or the larger the tidal range, the more water must pass through the tidal inlet. Speeds in excess of 100 centimeters per second are quite common and some may be over 200 centimeters per second. Estuaries may also experience strong tidal currents, especially in tidal creeks that drain tidal flats, marshes, and other shallow or intertidal areas.

Strong tidal currents are commonly quite local in many places, particularly when they are channelized. These currents also vary greatly with time, particularly in the ebb or the flood stage of the tidal cycle. Because of this the tidal current at any given location over the duration of a tidal cycle shows an asymmetrical configuration. While the water level is changing in a symmetrical pattern as the tide floods and ebbs, the speed of the tidal current shows numerous variations. These variations are caused by the numerous sediment bodies and channel configurations that influence the direction and velocity of tidal currents. This phenomenon is referred to as *time–velocity asymmetry*. Figure 4.10 shows that the plot of the tidal current over a tidal cycle is quite different in both the speed and the distribution of the current over time in adjacent channels. This type of distribution is typical for estuaries, tidal inlets, river mouths, and any other coastal area where tidal currents are present. Time–velocity asymmetry is an important factor in the erosion, transportation, and deposition of sediment by tidal currents and therefore in the coastal system as a whole.

Waves

Waves can be considered a surface disturbance of a fluid in which energy is propagated. In this case, we are concerned with the interface between the ocean and the atmosphere but waves also occur within different liquid masses and within different gaseous masses. They occur within the atmosphere and within the

FIGURE 4.10
An example of time–velocity curves showing the asymmetry that is typical of adjacent tide-dominated environments.
(From Hayes, M. O. and Kana, T. E., (eds), 1976, Terrigenous clastic depositional environments. Tech. Rept. No. 11-CRC, Univ. of South Carolina, Columbia)

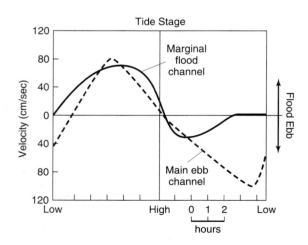

water column of the ocean. When the surface of the fluid is disturbed this disturbance is transferred from one location to another but the medium itself, in this
case water, does not move with the propagating disturbance.

The wave that influences the coast most is the progressive, surface wave
produced by wind. In this type of wave, energy travels across and through the
water in the direction of the propagation of the wave form. The movement of
these waves is due to restoring forces that cause an oscillatory motion that is basically sinusoidal in form. Both gravity and surface tension are important restoring forces that maintain waves as they propagate. Surface tension is important in
capillary waves that are less than 1.7 cm in length. The larger waves are called
gravity waves because their primary restoring force is gravity.

Each wave has several important components that are important in describing both it and its motion (Fig. 4.11). The wave length (L) is the horizontal
distance between two like locations on the wave form, crest to crest, trough to
trough, and so forth. The wave height (H) is the vertical distance between the
base of the trough and the crest; it is twice the amplitude. The steepness of the
wave is the ratio of the height to the length (H/L). Another important characteristic of gravity waves is the time (T), measured in seconds, required for a complete wave length to pass a reference point. Another way of measuring wave
propagation is by the frequency (f), the number of wave lengths passing per second. Normal gravity waves on the ocean surface have periods that commonly
range from a few seconds up to about 15.

The actual transfer of energy from the wind to the water surface is complicated and not completely understood. It is well-known, however, that wave size
depends on multiple factors: (1) wind speed, (2) length of time the wind blows,
and (3) the fetch, the distance over which the wind blows. Although the wave
form and its components are discussed in relatively simplistic terms, the actual
wave conditions in nature are extremely complicated. Typically there are multiple types of different sized waves (Fig. 4.12) moving in different directions all superimposed at a given location in the sea (Fig. 4.13). These waves combine to
produce a wave field that can be recorded and analyzed. Data produced are in
the form of a wave spectrum that can be separated into its component wave
forms, each with its own period and height. One of the most important aspects of
the spectral analysis of a wave field is the determination of the significant wave

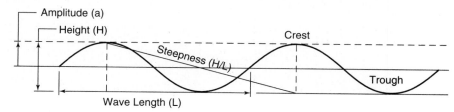

FIGURE 4.11
Diagram of a wave form showing each of the major components.

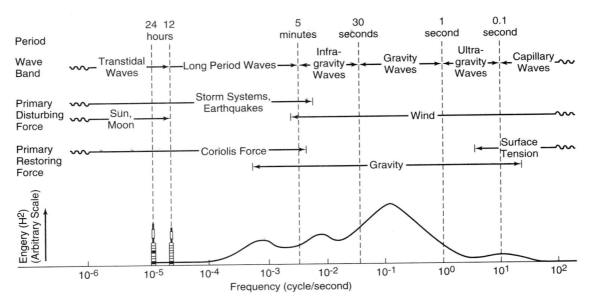

FIGURE 4.12
Schematic diagram showing various types of waves and their respective frequencies.
(Adapted from Kinsman, B., 1965, *Wind Waves*, Prentice-Hall, Inc., Englewood Cliffs, New Jersey, p. 23, Fig. 1.2-1)

FIGURE 4.13
Photograph of a complicated sea state in the North Sea caused by multiple wave forms superimposed.

height, the average height of the highest one-third of the waves occurring in the time period being analyzed. It is the significant wave height that is commonly used as an index of the wave energy.

Water Motion and Wave Propagation   It was stated previously that only the wave form is propagated in gravity waves, not the water itself. That being the case, we need to consider the motion of the water within gravity waves. Water does move in this wave type, but in an orbital path with the circulation in each orbit being in the direction of wave propagation (Fig. 4.14a). The surface water is moving landward on the crest of the wave and seaward in the

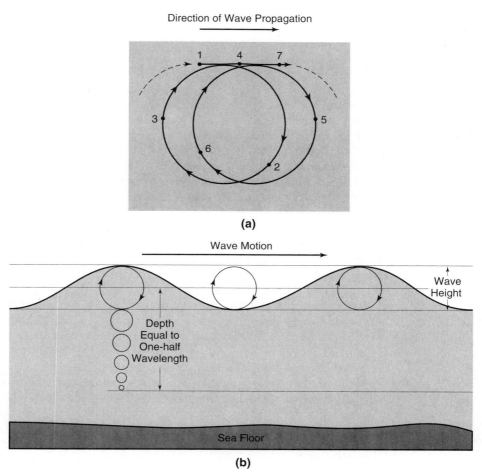

FIGURE 4.14
a) Motion of water particles in an orbit showing slight progression and b) diagram of overall water motion in a complete wave from the surface downward.

trough to accommodate this orbital motion. The diameter of the orbit at the surface is equal to the wave height, and this diameter decreases with depth. At a
depth of approximately one-half the wave length of the surface wave, the orbital
motion is very slow, and the orbits are very small and no longer able to move
sediment on the bottom (Fig. 4.14b). Because this orbital motion is forward on
the crest, backward on the trough with vertical motion halfway between, a fishing float or a ball appears to actually move up and down as the waves pass but
without progressing significantly itself, just like the water motion. Where wind is
present, close inspection of the actual path of water particles shows slight net
movement of water in the direction of propagation due to friction between the
wind and the water surface (Fig. 4.14a).

When the water depth is greater than half the wave length of the surface
wave, the wave is not influenced by the ocean floor as it propagates. As the wave
moves into increasingly shallow water during its approach to the coast, it begins
to interact with, or "feel" the bottom. This occurs as the orbital motion below the
surface comes in contact with the ocean floor. This interference causes the orbits
of water particles to become deformed and to slow down. This condition pro-
gresses as the wave moves into increasingly shallow water.

As the wave slows down it becomes steepened at the water surface at the
same time as bottom friction causes the wave to travel faster at the surface than at
the bottom. These conditions cause the wave to eventually become so steep that it
is no longer stable and its shape collapses. This is the breaking of waves that we
see in the surf along the coast. Restoring forces cause the wave to reform and to
continue its progression, perhaps to break again before reaching the shoreline.

Wind Wave Types   Although the theoretical and simplistic wave form is
one of a sinusoidal curve, in reality that form is not common. The shape taken
by a wave depends on the conditions of the wind, water depth, and its own progression. Whereas wind is responsible for the production of most gravity waves,
it is common for the waves to travel well beyond the area where the wind blows,
or the wind may stop and the waves may continue. Those waves that are directly
under the influence of wind are called *sea waves* (Fig. 4.15a). They tend to have a
relatively peaked crest and broad troughs. In natural conditions, sea waves tend
to be complicated by small waves superimposed on their surface. Whitecaps
occur when the wind blows off the tops of sea waves.

A common wave type is the swell wave that develops after the wind stops
or when the wave travels beyond the area of wind. The profile of a swell wave
approximates a sinusoidal shape with an undulating symmetrical form (Fig.
4.15b). Typically swell waves have a long wave length and small wave height.
They are much less steep than sea waves.

The breaking of waves as they enter shallow water takes on different characteristics depending upon the type of deep water wave and the breaking conditions. For example, swell waves are long and low, thus they begin to feel the bottom in relatively deep water. They gradually slow and steepen until they break

(a)

FIGURE 4.15
Photographs of a) sea waves and b) swell waves.

as plunging breakers with a large curling motion characterized by a sudden loss of energy (Fig. 4.16a). It is typical of gently sloping nearshore zones.

The other common type of breaking wave is the spilling breaker (Fig. 4.16b). This is most common as sea waves enter shallow water. This type of breaker looks a bit like water as it spills out of a container. As a result, the breaking and loss of energy takes place over some distance and up to several seconds and contrasts strongly with the plunging breakers. Surging breakers (Fig. 4.16c) and collapsing breakers are the other commonly described types of breaking waves and may be hard to distinguish from spilling breakers, especially the collapsing type. Collapsing breakers tend to form from swell waves that break on fairly steep beaches. As the wave steepens it breaks with the steep leading face collapsing rather quickly. This produces a wave that develops much like a plunging wave but its appearance as it breaks is a bit more like the spilling wave. A surging breaker develops on the

(b)

FIGURE 4.15   (*Cont.*)

steep beach face as the wave runs up to the shoreline. It steepens and just as the wave begins to break, it surges up the beach.

Wave Behavior   As waves move into shallow water and are influenced by the bottom and by various natural features or structures made by humans, they may experience changes in their energy distribution and/or direction. Basically three phenomena occur: refraction, diffraction, and reflection. In this way, waves act much like light.

It is rare that gravity waves approach the coast with the wave crest parallel to the shoreline; it is typically at some acute angle. As the wave enters shallow water it begins to be slowed by interference with the bottom that takes place at different times along the wave's progression. Thus the wave is bent or refracted as it passes through shallow water on its way to the shoreline (Fig. 4.17). Wave energy can be represented by orthogonals, which are lines constructed perpendicular to the wave crests. As the result of refraction, wave energy is concentrated at headland areas along the coast and is dissipated in embayments. This combination of conditions causes headlands to erode and embayments to accumulate sediment (Fig. 4.18).

(a)

(b)

FIGURE 4.16
Photographs showing the various types of breaking waves: a) plunging breaker,
b) spilling breaker, and c) surging breaker.

(c)

FIGURE 4.16   (*Cont.*)

The diffraction, or spreading of wave energy behind obstacles, occurs as part of the wave strikes an impermeable feature such as an island, a spit, or a breakwater and the rest of it passes by (Fig. 4.19). As the wave passes the obstacle, energy is transferred laterally to the sheltered areas behind the obstacle. In this way waves gradually reform behind the obstruction although they will have smaller height. This is the reason that boats behind breakwaters or other shelters still feel waves.

Reflection of wave energy is extremely important along the coast (Fig. 4.20). The amount and direction of the reflection depends, respectively, upon the amount of energy absorbed and the angle of approach. If a wave approaches a vertical and impermeable structure without any interference by the bottom, it will be reflected with 100 percent of its energy. The direction of this reflected energy is in accordance with the law of reflection; the angle of reflection is equal to the angle of incidence. In other words, waves approaching a vertical sea wall act just like light rays on a mirror. Incident waves on a rocky coast may experience just this sort of condition.

The more common situation is for a portion of the wave energy to be reflected, and the remainder to be dissipated during the shallowing of the water and the final surge up the beach. The amount of reflection is generally related to the steepness of the bottom and the beach; the steeper the beach the more

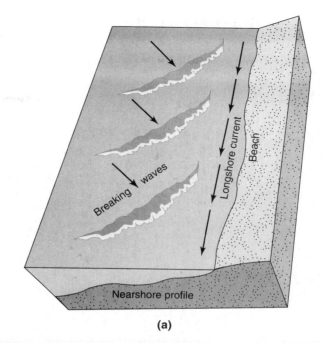

(a)

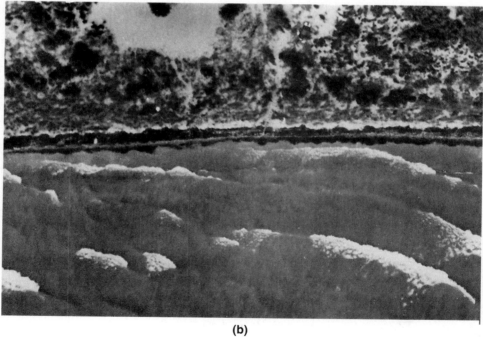

(b)

FIGURE 4.17
Diagram a) and photograph b) showing the refraction of waves as they enter shallow water and are differently slowed in their shoreward movement.

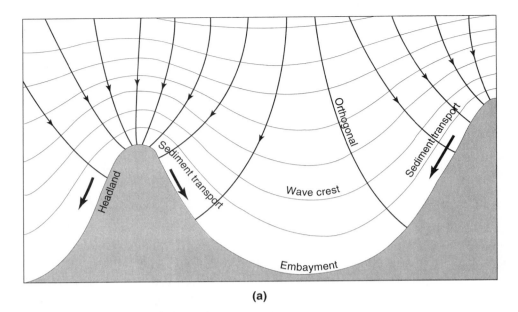

(a)

(b)

FIGURE 4.18
Diagram of refracted wave crests and corresponding orthogonals: a) showing concentration of wave energy at headlands and dissipation in embayments and photograph b) showing refraction.

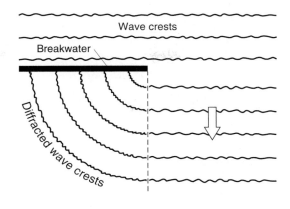

FIGURE 4.19
Wave diffraction showing lateral spreading of wave energy as an obstruction is passed.

reflection. Typically, greater than 20 percent of incident wave energy will be reflected at a beach.

Other Types of Waves   The word *tsunami* is Japanese for very long harbor wave because it is in harbors where much of the damage occurs. The term is typically used in conjunction with waves caused by seismic or other ocean floor disturbances that cause perturbations of the sea surface. Such a wave is commonly referred to as seismic sea wave. Earthquakes, volcanic eruptions, landslides, and possibly even large turbidity currents may trigger tsunamis. The wave length is generally up to hundreds of kilometers, wave height may be about a meter in deep water, and the wave travels at hundreds of kilometers per hour. Because of the great wave length, a tsunami will begin to be affected by the sea floor at great depth. This causes a slowing and steepening, the result being a wave several meters in height at the coast.

Many catastrophic tsunamis have influenced various coastal areas of the world. Not only do these huge waves destroy property and erode the beaches, several have caused a high loss of life (Fig. 4.21). Among the recorded disasters of this type were the tsunamis of 1692 in Jamaica, 1755 in Portugal, 1896 in Japan, and 1946 in Hawaii. The eruption of Krakatoa in the southwest Pacific in 1883 produced a tsunami that carried a large ship 3 kilometers inland to an elevation of 9 meters above sea level. The aforementioned 1964 earthquake in Alaska produced a tsunami that caused severe damage to Crescent City, California. The establishment of a network of seismic monitoring stations (Fig. 4.22) around the entire Pacific Ocean in the 1950s and 1960s has reduced greatly the threat to life. It is now possible to predict the development, movement, landfall, and size of tsunamis. This does not make them less dangerous, it only provides proper warning for hasty evacuation of coastal areas. Because of the speed at which these waves travel, the warning may be only minutes.

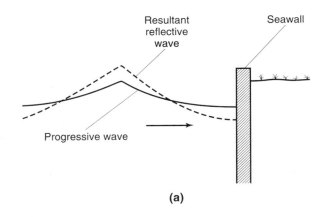

(a)

(b)

FIGURE 4.20
Diagram a) and photograph b) showing wave reflection at a vertical and impermeable structure where all energy is reflected.

FIGURE 4.21
Photograph of destruction along the coast of Colombia caused by a tsunami.
(Courtesy of the American Association for the Advancement of Science)

All of the previously discussed wave types are progressive, that is, the wave form moves forward. Special conditions do exist whereby standing waves that do not propagate are developed that can influence the coast. Standing waves are trapped in a container or a restricted water body such as an embayment, harbor, or lake. The wave length is equivalent to the diameter or length of the water body in which the wave develops. There is a node in the middle about which there is no motion and an alternating up and down motion at each end of the water body. Most common and most noticeable among these standing waves is the seiche. This is essentially a rhythmic sloshing of water level, like what one would see in a cup of coffee as it is carried up the steps or the regular sloshing back and forth that occurs in a bathtub. Seiches are most commonly due to weather conditions that cause rapid changes in barometric pressure and/or wind conditions. Water is commonly piled up on one side of the basin and is then released as the wind stops quickly or when the barometric pressure rises quickly.

The Great Lakes tend to experience the most dramatic seiches where changes in lake level of over a meter have occurred numerous times. Seiche waves have swept people from the beach and drowned them on Lake Michigan. Lake Erie is the most susceptible due to its shallow nature and orientation along the dominant wind direction. It has experienced seiches of over 2 meters.

The most influential type of standing wave on the coast is the one most difficult to recognize, the standing edge wave. Edge waves are produced by water

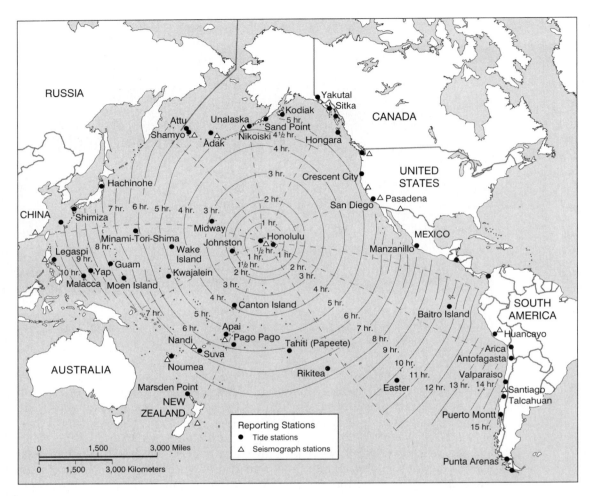

FIGURE 4.22
Map of the Pacific Ocean showing the tsunami warning network.
(Courtesy of the National Oceanographic and Atmospheric Administration)

that is trapped against the shore by wave refraction of the incoming gravity waves. These waves have the same period as the incoming gravity waves but their wave length is essentially perpendicular to the incoming gravity waves (Fig. 4.23). The wave height of edge waves is quite low in relation to the incoming waves and the wave is, therefore, not directly observable. Their maximum height is at the shore and this rapidly decreases offshore. It has been demonstrated that edge waves are not only present but are important factors in shaping the open ocean coast.

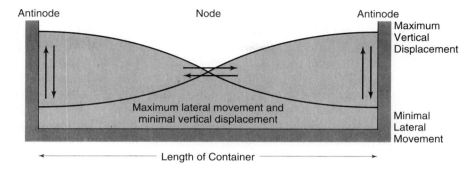

FIGURE 4.23
Diagram of a standing wave.

The best way to consider the nature and influence of standing edge waves is to look at the combination of this wave type with the incoming gravity wave. We can assume that the gravity wave approaches the shoreline with a uniform height at any given water depth. At that same water depth and position relative to the shoreline there is also a standing edge wave present. This wave is oriented perpendicular to the incoming wave and it is in a standing mode, not progressive. As a result, there are positions of nodes, where no motion takes place, and antinodes, positions of maximum motion but in a vertical manner. The motion of the edge wave causes the combined wave to have a range of wave heights at a given location due to the movement at the antinodes. This range is rhythmic and is at its maximum height at the shoreline, decreasing seaward. Various features such as rip currents and beach cusps, which are discussed later in the chapter, are attributed to the presence of standing edge waves.

Wave reflection can also create a type of standing wave that is instantaneous in nature. As waves approach a sea wall, steep beach, or other obstacle in a parallel orientation to the shore, the crest is reflected back and immediately increases the height of the next incoming wave.

Wave-Generated Currents

Two important and widespread types of coastal currents are produced by waves—longshore currents and rip currents. Both result from the shoreward progression of waves and both are important in transporting sediment along the surf zone.

Longshore Currents   There is a demonstrable but quite slow, shoreward transport of water produced by the landward progression of gravity waves. The rate at which this occurs is quite slow and is not directly responsible for any sediment transport. The refraction of waves as they move shoreward through shallow water does produce an easily recognizable and measurable current that flows essentially parallel to the shoreline, the longshore current, sometimes called the littoral current.

As the wave refracts during steepening and breaking, there is both a shore-ward and a shore-parallel vector to its direction. This produces a shore-parallel transport of water that is related to the size of the breaking wave and to its angle of approach to the shoreline. The system has an effective seaward boundary at the breaker zone and another at the shoreline. It acts much like a channel with the greatest velocity near the middle. In some circumstances, a shore-parallel wind vector enhances the speed of the longshore current. Longshore currents typically move at speeds of a few tens of centimeters per second but during storm conditions they commonly travel more than a meter per second.

In tandem with the waves, longshore currents transport sediment in large volumes along the shoreline. The waves, through interaction with the bottom during steepening and breaking, cause large amounts of sediment to become temporarily suspended and then transported along the shoreline by longshore currents.

Because waves may approach the coast in different directions depending upon the direction of the wind, the longshore current may flow in either direction along the shoreline. Thus there is considerable sediment transport up and down a particular reach of coast, and the net littoral transport may be only a fraction of the total. We typically speak of littoral transport in terms of the annual flux, for example, it may be 100,000 cubic meters per year. This is the net transport, the total amount may be many times that in each direction.

Longshore currents and littoral transport may occur in any coastal environment where waves refract as they approach the shoreline. Although open ocean beaches are the site of the greatest volume of littoral drift, these currents and resulting sediment transport are also common on bays, estuaries, and lakes.

Rip Currents   The landward transport of water caused by friction of wind and by progressive waves produces a slightly higher water level at the shoreline than exists seaward of the surf zone. This is called the setup and is basically generated in the same fashion as the storm surge but it may extend only a few hundred meters along the shore. The super-elevation of the water in this narrow zone is typically a few centimeters. The setup may be enhanced by edge waves and may be somewhat trapped by longshore sand bars present in the zone of breaking waves. The net result is that water is essentially piled up against the shoreline in an unstable condition that cannot persist.

This condition produces seaward-flowing rip currents that relieve the set-up and provide circulation cells (Fig. 4.24) within the surf zone. Rip currents tend to be narrow and regularly spaced with speeds commonly 10–30 centimeters per second. They can transport sediment and are supplied by feeder currents that are part of the longshore current system. The rip current is the phenomenon that is mistakenly called a *rip tide* (but it is not related to tides) and that can be a

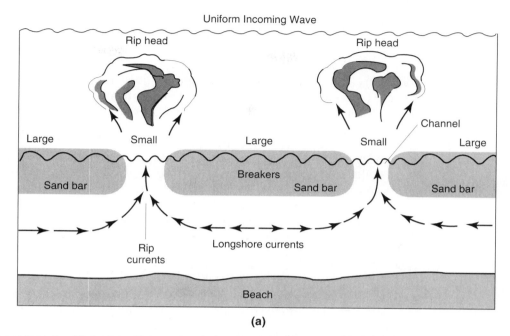

(a)

(b)

FIGURE 4.24
Schematic diagram a) and photograph b) showing a rip current cell along the coast.

danger to swimmers. Because of their narrow width one needs only to swim a short distance along shore to safety rather than to try to swim against the current and risk being carried a few hundred meters out to sea.

Rip current size, orientation, and spacing is commonly related to both wave conditions and nearshore bottom conditions. Along a smooth shoreline and in the absence of longshore sand bars, the rip current spacing is typically tied to the wave length of the standing edge waves present. This is at the antinode positions where breaker height is smallest. Incoming waves that are essentially parallel to the shoreline produce a nearly symmetrical circulation cell with feeder currents coming equally from each direction. Those rip currents that develop as waves approach at an angle tend to be associated with asymmetrical cells and feeder currents.

Rip currents also may develop in a more opportunistic fashion through low places in longshore sand bars. Here the pile of water associated with the shoreline set-up finds a path of least resistance and moves through it.

BIOLOGICAL PROCESSES

In some situations organisms may have a profound influence on the coast but for the most part they are not responsible for the primary morphology we see in the coastal zone. The one exception is coral reefs, which are the dominant coastal feature in many locations, and which are solely the result of specific organisms colonizing under correct environmental conditions.

The processes by which organisms influence coastal morphology can be separated into two distinct categories: one involving the growth and development of communities of specific types of organisms and the other based on how the activities of organisms influence the coast. The first category is dominated by plants such as marsh grasses, sea grasses, and mangroves, but also includes some animals like oysters and tube worms. We will call these the "constructors." In all cases the growth of dense colonies of the organisms results in a specific coastal feature or controls one. The other category deals primarily with the activities of organisms that result in movement of sediment, fixing sediment, breaking rocks into sediment, or making big particles into smaller ones as the organisms search for food and shelter. These will be called the "changers."

Influence of Constructors

A variety of coastal morphology results directly from the growth of certain types of organisms. These are primarily intertidal or subtidal in position but in some cases may reach into the supratidal environment. The plants that provide the most influence are the marsh grasses and the mangrove trees. These organisms occupy at least a part of the intertidal zone. The establishment of salt marshes dominates many coastal areas on both open and protected coasts. They occur either alone or in conjunction with river deltas, barrier islands, and estuaries. Mangrove swamps occur in similar environments, with their primary limitation being winter freeze, therefore they are latitude-controlled.

Sea grasses tend to be subtidal but some, for example, *Zostera,* may extend up into the intertidal zone and help form coastal morphology by both trapping and stabilizing sediment. As they spread, they prevent or inhibit sediment removal. Subaerial vegetation on dunes and other supratidal environments produces a similar effect.

Animals may provide similar, but usually less dramatic, influence in some coastal environments. The constructors here are the reef-forming oysters such as *Crassostrea virginica*, the common edible variety, tube worms such as sabellarids, and vermitid gastropods that build large, resistant reefal colonies (Fig. 4.25). These organisms build mound-shaped structures that may cover several hundred square meters each, and these are properly considered to be reefs. They tend to be located in estuaries, lagoons, or other relatively protected coastal environments.

Both the plants and animals mentioned above contribute to coastal morphology by the extent and nature of their colonization. The biological processes that they contribute to the coast are their reproduction, growth, and development. They interact in various important ways with physical processes such as

FIGURE 4.25
Oyster reefs in an estuary at Beaufort, South Carolina. These features result from biological processes and they form an important morphological element of the coast.

tides, waves, and currents, and thereby are fundamental to a comprehensive understanding of coastal processes.

Changers

Many organisms also contribute to the coast through more direct biological
processes by active involvement in the formation, destruction, or transportation
of sediments and therefore in influencing the characteristics of various coastal
environments. Probably the best place to begin is sediment production. A great
variety and large numbers of organisms produce skeletal material that contributes to the sediment that forms depositional coastal features. It may be mud,
sand, or gravel in particle size, but its composition is generally calcium carbonate.
Only a small volume of sediment is contributed as phosphatic material from
teeth or bones, or as siliceous skeletal material from radiolarians or sponge
spicules. The mollusks, echinoderms, coelenterates, and foraminifera produce
most of the calcium carbonate skeletal sediment but many other groups contribute small quantities.

Breakup of the skeletal material is largely by physical processes such as
waves and currents that provide for multiple rather than violent collisions between particles. Because of the soft nature of calcium carbonate (hardness of 3)
coupled with the delicate construction of some shells, breakage is easy. We
should not, however, overlook the contribution to skeletal breakage and, in fact,
also to the breakage of nonskeletal particles, by the feeding and burrowing
processes of organisms (Fig. 4.26). Some animals, such as starfish, crabs, or birds,
crush living bivalves in the feeding process. Others drill into the shell for the soft
tissues and either break or weaken the shell in the process. Many animals burrow into sediment or bore into rock for food and/or shelter. Both processes cause
breakage of sediments, biogenic and otherwise.

A variety of organisms can erode rock substrates and thereby directly influence coastal morphology. Sea urchins, chitons, and some gastropods and sponges
can bore or scrape rocky surfaces and thereby remove material and cause development of characteristic surfaces. One of the most pronounced is the very rough
surface produced by boring sea urchins, which can occur intertidally or subti-
dally, producing relief on the surface of up to 30 centimeters. Such activity also
weakens the rock and makes it more susceptible to attack by waves. A dramatic
example is the formation of the sea notch near sea level. Sea urchins, chitons,
and boring algae erode limestones in low latitudes, producing a significant over-
hang that commonly collapses.

Another important biological process is pelletization of fine sediment by
suspension and detritus-feeding organisms. These animals ingest considerable
sediment that is taken from suspension in the water column or from bottom
feeding without selectivity. In both cases considerable sediment is undigested
and is passed out through the organism through production of fecal pellets (Fig.

FIGURE 4.26
Numerous burrows in a tidal flat;
an example of small-scale
biological processes that are important on the coast.

4.27). This process plays an important role in the coastal zone. First, it removes much suspended sediment from water and second, the sediment is converted from very fine easily transported particles into sand-sized particles that require more energy to move. Whereas mud particles are typically transported in a suspended mode, fecal pellets are generally in the bed load. The volume may also be quite large. Some estuaries or protected coastal bays may be completely floored with fecal pellets in the form of cohesive mud.

CHEMICAL PROCESSES

Chemical reactions, both destructive and constructive, occur in various coastal environments. Destruction is dominated by the chemical weathering of rocks and sediment particles and construction through the lithification of sediment into rock. The processes are quite slow and tend to be local.

Chemical Weathering

Coastal conditions of chemical weathering of minerals are quite similar to those inland except for the salt water. This difference plays no major role in the weathering of most rocks but is important in precipitation (see later section on Precipitation). The result is that climate and composition of the rocks or sediments will be the important factor under consideration. We can, for practical purposes, for-

FIGURE 4.27
Fecal pellets adjacent to the burrow in which they were formed.
This is another important biological process in coastal environments. Each cylindrical pellet is
about 1–2mm long.

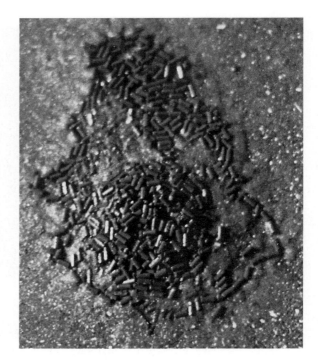

get about the chemical weathering of individual sediment particles because they
are generally moved with enough frequency that physical processes dominate
their deterioration.

The basic ingredient in the chemical weathering process is availability of
moisture. Hot, humid areas such as the tropics experience considerable weathering of various minerals whereas the deserts experience essentially none. The
minerals present also provide an important variable in that they vary greatly in
their susceptibility. For example, calcium carbonate (limestone) is quite soluble
and weathers rapidly (Fig. 4.28) whereas quartz (sandstone) is almost chemically
inert under all climatic conditions. Various igneous rock types like granite and
basalt are relatively easily weathered.

One of the fundamental variables that must be included in the chemical
weathering scheme is time. Other than limestone (calcium carbonate), the time
required for nearly all other rock types is so long that the actual location or environment in which the rocks are present will probably change multiple times during the weathering process. The rocks in question may be in the subsurface, exposed, on a coast, or inland hundreds of kilometers while millions of years pass;
not an unusual period for weathering of many rock types. The point is that the

FIGURE 4.28
Irregular limestone surface along the coast in the Bahamas caused in part by erosion from the activity of sea urchins and other grazing animals.

weathering characteristics one sees in rocks along the coast are most likely inherited from previous geologic settings and did not develop on the coast itself.

The major way that chemical weathering contributes to coastal morphology is through susceptibility to physical erosion. Those rocks that are easily weathered will be physically broken down and removed by waves and currents whereas others will better withstand these processes. This chemical breakdown may occur in the mineral grains of the rock or the cement that binds them together.

Precipitation

The construction of rock typically requires at least millennia and is not a factor in coastal morphology. There are, however, a few exceptions that involve precipitation of evaporite minerals and calcium carbonate. Evaporite minerals, although common in some coastal lagoons, do not provide any morphological characteristics other than flooring salt pans or similar local and restricted environments.

Calcium carbonate precipitation can be important to the morphology and preservation of two related but distinct coastal environments—beaches and coastal dunes. The formation of beachrock can take place in only decades as evidenced by the presence of soda bottles, beer cans, and other datable artifacts (Fig. 4.29). Lithification of coastal dunes into eolianites, literally dune rock, takes longer but in the scheme of geologic time is quite short. In both cases, abundant calcium carbonate grains, typically biogenic skeletal particles, are cemented together by calcium carbonate cement. The beach sand and/or gravel, or the dune sand, needs to be about half calcium carbonate and the remainder of nearly any composition but is typically dominated by quartz. This provides both a source of materials for the calcium carbonate cement and appropriate surfaces on which it can readily precipitate.

In the case of the beach material, the regular spray of the upper beach by breaking waves provides the calcium and carbon dioxide for the cement, and the evaporation of the regularly wetted surfaces enhances the lithification of the sediments. Climate is quite important; beachrock is typically restricted to low-latitude, tropical or semitropical areas like the Caribbean, Bahamas, Pacific Islands, and other similar locations.

Lithified dunes or eolianites are also confined to a similar coastal climate. Although sea spray is not so important, percolation of ground water is the pri-

FIGURE 4.29
Beachrock along the coast at Heron Island, Australia. The formation of this material by chemical processes is an important factor in stabilizing this small island.

mary mechanism for providing the raw materials and their delivery to the grain surfaces for cementation. This is the main reason formation of eolianites takes a longer time.

Both beachrock and eolianite provide special characteristics to a coastal area. Both greatly resist erosion by physical processes as compared to their un-lithified counterparts. In fact, these products of chemical processes commonly provide protection from erosion to other parts of the coastal system. The nature of chemical processes is such that they are most influential in low-latitude, tropical coasts but have essentially no role in temperate and higher latitude areas, except in very long-term weathering of minerals.

SUMMARY

The variety of processes that work along the various coastal environments is broad, but only a few are important in the day-to-day changes that we can observe. The majority of all coastal characteristics, regardless of their specific environment, are either directly or indirectly controlled by waves and tides or the currents that they generate. These processes are essentially universal and rapid in their influence. It is possible to sit on the coast for only a few hours, perhaps even minutes, and see the various effects of both these major parameters. Regular return to the same coastal location over months or years shows major changes.

Biological and chemical processes produce generally slow and small-scale changes on coasts; these are detectable only by the keen observer. Production of pellets or breakage of bivalve shells are typically unnoticed although they are significant. Likewise, observable lithification of dunes, weathering of a granitic bluff, or growth of an oyster reef takes place over time periods beyond one's lifetime. The typical beach visitor is unaware of the occurrence of any of these processes even though they are important in the overall scheme of coastal development.

5
River Deltas

Except for coasts that are dominated by glaciers, most of the sand and mud that is contained in the coastal zone arrived at the coast via a river system. These river-borne sediments are transported to different coastal and marine depositional environments depending upon their size (mass) and the strength of the transporting currents. They may be carried out into deep water and never become involved in the coastal zone, they may be transported along the coast and incorporated in various coastal depositional environments, or they may accumulate at or near the mouth of the river in the form of a delta (Fig. 5.1), the topic of this chapter.

The first known application of the Greek letter delta (Δ) for the accumulation of sediment at the mouth a river was by Herodotus in the fifth century B.C. in connection with the Nile River in Egypt. Our detailed knowledge of deltas as a geologic entity has been acquired in a fairly short time, all within the twentieth century. The first significant mention of the deltas was by G. K. Gilbert (1885) in his famous studies for the U.S. Geological Survey on Lake Bonneville, the present reduced version of which is the Great Salt Lake. It is from his work that the terms *topset, foreset,* and *bottomset* for the parts of the delta were first applied. Up until H. N. Fisk began his extensive work on the Mississippi Delta in the 1940s, there were only two or three additional studies of modern river deltas. The work of Fisk and his colleagues, along with the newly recognized importance of deltas as oil and gas producers, stimulated a great deal of research by the petroleum industry beginning in the 1950s. This started on the Mississippi and moved to the Niger in Africa and the Orinoco in Venezuela—all important oil-producing deltas. Unfortunately, because of the great wealth of information on the Mississippi Delta, it became considered a representative delta

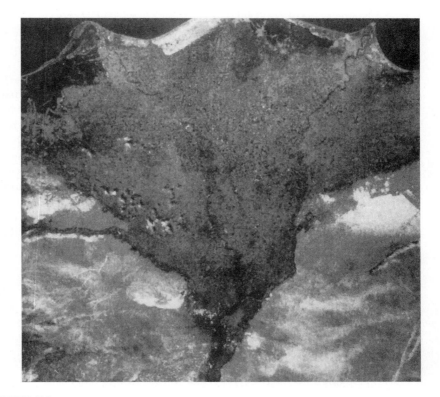

FIGURE 5.1
Satellite photo of the Nile Delta showing the generally triangular shape.
(Courtesy of EROS Data Center)

for global interpretations. In fact, however, the Mississippi is an end member and essentially one of a kind. We will consider this further in the section on delta classification.

The accumulation of sediments in riverine deltas may be quite temporary or may be permanent. Considerable interaction exists between the riverine processes of sedimentation with those of the open marine system, especially waves, longshore currents, and tidal currents. The interaction of these processes, along with the sediment load of the river and the physical setting at and near the river mouth, determine the presence and the nature of the delta. The first and foremost requirement for the formation of a delta is the delivery of sediment in excess of what is removed and redistributed by waves and currents. This varies greatly from location to location. Places characterized by large waves and/or strong tidal currents require considerably more sediment than those locations in which waves and tidal range are small. The other important variable is the physiography of the continental margin adjacent to the coast. The sediments carried to the coast by the river must have a place on which to accumulate if a significant delta is to be built.

Plate tectonic history and the regional geologic setting are quite important in the development of river deltas (Fig. 5.2). Trailing edge or passive margins are conducive to delta development whereas leading edges or active margins are not. Extensive drainage basins typically form in areas in which there is little relief and no major obstacles such as mountain ranges blocking the path to the coast. Consider, for example, the Mississippi River drainage system in the United States and the Amazon River complex in South America. The Mississippi actually includes the Missouri and Ohio river systems and represents a collection of surface water and sediments from most of the area between the divides of the Rocky Mountains and the Appalachian Mountains, more than half of the country. The Amazon River system drains most of South America with the divide in the Andes on

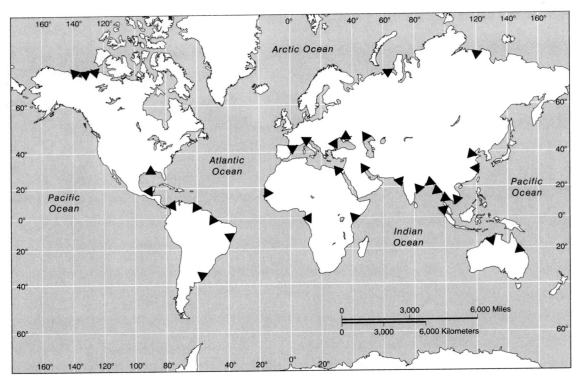

FIGURE 5.2
Map showing the global distribution of major deltas.
(From Wright, L. D., 1978, *Deltas* In Davis, R. A. (ed.) *Coastal Sedimentary Environments*, Springer-Verlag, New York, p. 6, Fig. 1)

the western side of the continent being the western boundary. Both of these river systems drain huge, relatively stable continental regions and debouch onto a stable, trailing edge margin with a broad, relatively gently sloping continental shelf, a setting highly suitable for deltas to develop.

Marginal sea coasts also are well suited for delta formation. The Yangtze and Wang Ho rivers of China form large deltas along the South China Sea. Other examples of similar settings where deltas have developed include the North coast of Alaska and the North coast of the Mediterranean Sea.

By contrast, there are no really large river systems and therefore, large deltas, on the western margins of North or South America (Fig. 5.2). These leading edge, active margins are adjacent to high relief, mountainous areas with nearby divides. The result is that drainage systems are quite limited in their geographic extent, and many of the rivers drain terrain that has thin soil cover. These conditions do not produce enough sediment at the mouths of the rivers to form a delta. Additionally, there is no significant, gently sloping, continental shelf on which the deltaic material can accumulate. Another factor that inhibits delta development is the narrow, steep continental shelf that permits large waves to reach the coast with little attenuation. These waves remove and redistribute sediment brought to the coast by rivers. In summary, large deltas, with rare exceptions, can only develop on trailing edge coasts because it is there that abundant sediment, proper site for accumulation, and appropriate physical conditions for their maintenance exist. Global distribution of the major deltas shows this relationship with plate tectonics quite well (Fig. 5.2). There are none around the Pacific except those in China that border marginal seas. There are also some prominent trailing edge coasts that lack significant deltas. A good example is the Atlantic coast of North America where rivers typically empty into estuaries and do not carry their sediment load to the open coast.

DELTAS AND SEA LEVEL

The deltas of the present coastal system are geologically quite young. The individual deltaic systems tend to be from a few thousand to hundreds of thousands of years old but the presently active deltaic lobe may be much younger. Deltas depend upon rivers for their existence. River discharge is related, in part, to sea level, and the site of the deltaic accumulation is also related to sea level. Because of these factors, we must consider the role of sea level in the formation and maintenance of deltas.

When there were extensive glaciers, and sea level was much lower than it is now, large rivers were flowing across what is now the continental shelf, dumping their sediment load at near the shelf edge. This resulted in extensive turbid currents and other sediment gravity processes carrying most of the sediment load to the continental rise where it accumulated in thick wedge-like deposits. Deltas were not actively being formed, and previously existing deltas near the present position of the coast were being bypassed as rivers flowed across the shelf.

Melting glaciers caused rapid rising sea levels, and the river mouth essentially retreated across the shelf without time for deltas to accumulate. When sea level rise slowed down about 6000 to 7000 years ago, deltas began to develop because there was time enough for large quantities of sediment to accumulate without being dispersed by waves or tidal currents. This is not to say that all deltas are only a few thousand years old. Some have been around for millions of years. These old deltas have not been continuously active because of their abandonment by the shoreline as it moved. The Mississippi Delta and the Niger Delta in Africa are good examples. Both of these present deltas are underlaid by ancestral deltas that are at least 10 million years old.

In the case of the Mississippi Delta, the Holocene portion is only 5000 to 6000 years old but it consists of 16 recognizable lobes. Different lobes are formed when the focus of river deposition shifts due to channel switching, avulsion, or other natural causes. These 16 lobes can be lumped into only a few (Fig. 5.3) based upon radiocarbon dating and location. The present lobe began to form about 600 years ago, not much before the discovery of the New World by Columbus, and the most active portion has developed since the settlement of New Orleans by European settlers (Fig. 5.3). In fact, about one-half of the State of Louisiana has been formed by the Mississippi River during only the past 6000 years.

MAJOR DELTAIC ELEMENTS

Deltas represent what is probably the most transitional of all coastal environments between truly terrestrial and truly marine conditions. There is no easily recognized landward or seaward boundaries for deltas; they grade nearly imperceptibly in both directions. The river commonly splits up its main channel into multiple distributaries that actually distribute the discharge of the river, both water and sediment, across the delta and into the marine basin. This provides a condition of overall progradation of sediment accumulation into the basin of deposition, which could be a lake, estuary, lagoon, or other standing body of water as well as the ocean itself.

As a consequence of this type of setting, the delta includes subaerial, intertidal, and subaqueous sedimentary environments as well as freshwater, brackish, and marine conditions. For the purpose of discussing sedimentary environments and their processes, the delta can be subdivided into three major parts, each of which has its own specific environments. Landward to seaward these are the delta plain, the delta front, and the prodelta. This discussion will emphasize the first two; the prodelta is strictly subtidal and extends into fairly deep water of the outer continental shelf.

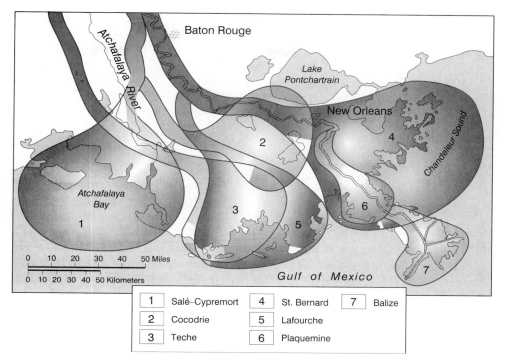

FIGURE 5.3
Holocene deltaic lobes in the Mississippi Delta showing the large number of shifting positions of sediment discharge into the Gulf of Mexico.
(From Kolb, C. R. and Van Lopik, J. R., 1966, In Shirley, M. L. (ed.), *Deltas and their Geologic Framework,* Houston Geological Society, Houston, Texas, pp. 17–61)

The delta plain is primarily influenced by the river and its processes with tides and waves playing less of a role overall. However, the influence of marine processes increases toward the seaward portion of the delta plain. The delta front is dominated by marine processes and tends to be subtidal with a small intertidal portion in some.

Delta Plain

We can think of the delta plain (Fig. 5.4) as basically the coastal extension of a river system. The delta plain is dominated by channels and their deposits, and the associated overbank environments that receive sediment during flooding. This scenario is parallel to that of a typical meandering river system. In fact, all of the specific elements of a meandering river complex are typically present on

FIGURE 5.4
Oblique photo of a typical delta plain environment which contains distributaries, natural levees, splays, and interdistributary marshes and bays.

many deltas. There are some deltas, however, that have only a portion of this environmental spectrum.

The distributary channels on a delta plain contain point bars formed as the channel migrates, forming broad meander loops that may experience cutoff leading to the formation of oxbow lakes. Channels produce scars of their former location as they migrate across the delta plain leaving subtle but recognizable geomorphic and vegetation patterns, another parallel with the fluvial system. Adjacent to the channels are three major types of overbank or flooding deposits: natural levees, cravasse splays, and floodplains, in that order away from the channel.

Natural levees (Fig. 5.5) are produced during flooding when the river overtops its banks and immediately deposits much of its sediment load. The confinement of the channel, coupled with high discharge volume and rate, causes the river to carry considerable sediment. Sudden loss of this confining characteristic when overflow occurs results in a sudden loss of velocity and carrying capacity, causing much sediment to be deposited at the edge of the bank. This condition takes place each time a channel floods, thus causing the levees to build vertically. Although the natural levees may be only a meter or so high, they are important features of the distributary channel system.

Flooding may also cause a natural levee to breach due to a weakness in the accumulated sediment, to perhaps a low area in the levee, or even to a human-induced cut in the levee. Any of these conditions can permit river flood waters to flow through the levee depositing sediment on the floodplain in the form of a

FIGURE 5.5
Natural levee accumulations along a major distributary of a delta plain.

crevasse splay (crevasse refers to the cut in the natural levee). Splays are fan-shaped deposits (Fig. 5.6a) that can cover many square kilometers with a sediment thickness that is typically less than that of the adjacent natural levee. These splays may be reactivated during successive flooding conditions and thereby can grow significantly in elevation and extent (Fig. 5.6b).

The most widespread but thinnest of the overbank accumulations are the foodplain sediments. Even after losing sediment to natural levees and splay deposits, there is substantial fine sediment in suspension during flooding conditions. The spreading of the floodwaters beyond the channel causes important loss of velocity and thus, in capacity, resulting in the deposition of fine and extensive floodplain deposits. Such floodplain sediments commonly are draped over vegetation or other materials that occupy this environment. We have all seen many examples in the media of mud, caused by flooding, that has covered cars, carpets, and furniture in houses (Fig. 5.7). The floodplain in the delta plain may take on a variety of characteristics. These include subtidal environments such as interdistributary bays, intertidal marshes (Fig. 5.8), swamps, and tidal flats, or, in the most landward areas, even subaerial environments of various types.

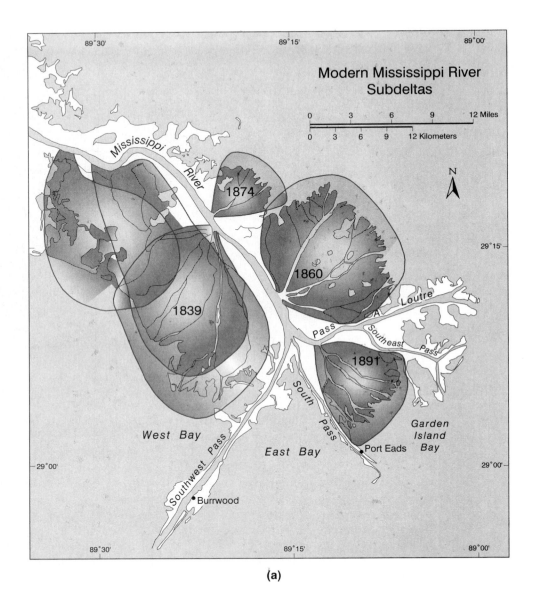

FIGURE 5.6

a) Diagram and b) photograph showing crevasse splay accumulation on a delta plain showing the fan shape and the cut in the natural levee through which the sediment was transported.

(a - From Coleman, J. G. and Gagliano, S. M., 1964, Cyclic sedimentation in the Mississippi River deltaic plain, *Gulf Coast Assoc. Geol. Soc. Trans,* 14, pp. 67–80)

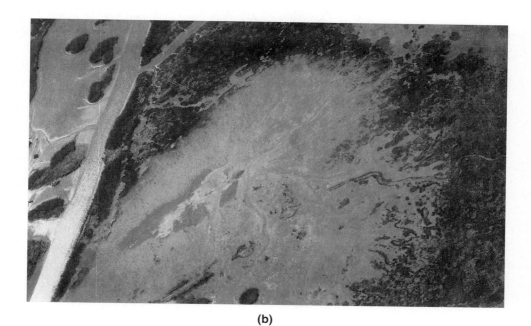

(b)

FIGURE 5.6   (*Cont.*)

The upward and lateral growth of the delta plain portion of the delta depends upon flooding periods for sediment distribution to the overbank environments. The typical situation is that the channel and its associated levee extend seaward at the outer limit of the delta (Fig. 5.9). The levees may even be subaqueous at the most distal end of the channel. The initial subaerial portion of this distributary channel is the natural levee, followed by small splay deposits. Continued flooding will enlarge the splays until at least a portion is subaerial. Continued accumulation of these splays along with the slower but more extensive floodplain deposits will eventually lead to the interdistributary area being filled, producing a continuous delta plain system (Fig. 5.10).

Delta Front

The seaward edge of the delta plain merges with the generally continuous subtidal portion of the delta that is called the *delta front*. It is this part of the delta that is most affected by marine processes, especially the waves. Sediment empties out of the mouth of the distributary channels as both suspended load and bed load. The finer suspended sediments tend to be carried away from the mouth of the channel by currents whereas much of the coarser bed load tends to accumulate near the channel mouth. The vast majority of the coarse sediment is the sand that comprises the delta front system.

FIGURE 5.7
Photo showing water level on building as the result of a flood event.
(Photo courtesy of O.H. Pilkey)

FIGURE 5.8
View of an interdistributary environment where sediment is provided only as the result of a flood event.

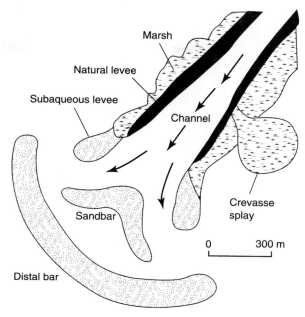

FIGURE 5.9
Diagram of the terminus of a distributary showing the nature of subaqueous levees.
(From Coleman and Gagliano, 1964)

The nature of the sand accumulations in the delta front depends upon the volume of sand transported to the distributary mouth and the relative roles of the interacting river currents with the waves and tidal currents. A common sand body is distributary mouthbars (Fig. 5.9), which accumulate just seaward of the channel mouth and typically cause the channel to bifurcate. The isolated distributary bar with little or no sand on either side is not a common finding because of the influence of waves, which generally spread the sand along the delta front. As the waves approach the shallow part of the delta, they refract and generate longshore currents, in the same fashion as they would along a beach. These currents carry the sand away from the mouth of the channel and distribute it along the outer delta plain, forming a nearly continuous delta front system. The degree to which this takes place depends upon the wave climate.

There is a wide range in the nature of the delta front sand bodies that comprise the outer part of the delta's upper part. In some deltas in which there are several distinct distributaries, as on the Mississippi Delta, the delta front tends to be rather subtle with distinct sandbars near the channels (Fig. 5.11). By contrast, on some river deltas there is considerable redistribution of the sand from the

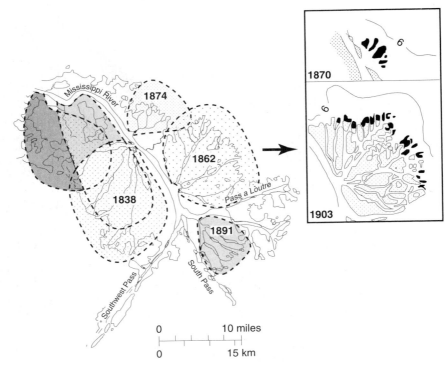

FIGURE 5.10
Growth of the delta along a distributary channel through sequential building of the
crevasse splay deposits.
(Modified from Coleman and Gagliano, 1964)

channel mouths across the outer delta plain margin. In these situations there
may be beaches and dunes on this part of the delta because of the abundance of
sand and the appropriate wave climate to redistribute it (Fig. 5.12). The São
Francisco River in southern Brazil is a good example of this type of delta.

DELTA PROCESSES

The interaction of riverine processes with the wave- and tidal-generated marine
processes is quite complicated and results in a wide variety of deltaic forms and
features. River-generated processes include both confined flow in open channels
and unconfined flow during flood conditions. Wave-generated processes include
the waves themselves in a variety of sizes along with the currents that they gen-

FIGURE 5.11
Photograph of distributary mouth bar during exceptionally low tide and offshore winds on the Mississippi Delta.

erate. Tides produce important currents that not only distribute sediment but also influence the discharge from the delta's distributary channels.

River Processes

The fundamental role of the river in the delta system is to provide the sediment. In doing so, the river is at the mercy of climatic conditions and seasonal changes in discharge. More recently, humans have played an important role in many river systems, causing many problems on the delta. The variables that influence the nature, amount, and rate of sediment delivery include the geology, geomorphology, and climate of the drainage basin. Also involved are the human influences such as agriculture, navigational structures, and dams.

The combination of rock type and climate are major controls on the sediment provided to the river. Rainfall and its distribution over time are the fundamental factors of river discharge and therefore on the sediment provided to the delta. Prolonged periods of drought place serious constraints on delta formation

FIGURE 5.12
Photograph of beach on the wave-dominated portion of a delta.

FIGURE 5.13
Photograph of a flood event on a delta showing widespread submergence of the delta plain. Only the higher parts of the natural levee area are visible above water level.

and maintenance. The typical climatic influence is in the seasonal distribution of temperature and precipitation. There are at least two important aspects to these cycles, including the annual distribution of rainfall. In areas in which monsoon conditions exist during the summer, such as in Southeast Asia, there is tremendous discharge and typically devastating flooding during this 2 to 3 month period. The flooding in Bangladesh of the Ganges–Brahmaputra Delta area is probably the most consistently dramatic case of flooding in the world. Most rivers, however, experience flooding during the rainy season (Fig. 5.13), and in some places this is especially problematic because the spring wet season coincides with the spring melting of snow. The Mississippi River is such an example. Most of the midwestern part of the United States has high rainfall in the spring at the same time that the snow in the Rocky Mountains and northern latitudes in the basin is melting. Flooding can be very severe for the people living along the river, and this is exemplified by the devastation of the 1993 floods. Similar phenomena may take place in the delta area. On the other hand, these floods are highly beneficial to the delta because these conditions provide the highest rate of sediment delivery to the delta, a crucial source of mineral nutrients to the delta. Flooding also washes out soluble salts that have built up in delta sediments.

The annual distribution of sediment to a river delta varies greatly at each river because of the dependency on climatic conditions. Desert rivers tend to have little discharge of water and therefore transport little sediment. However, when there is rainfall, it typically is a large amount in a short time, a condition that delivers considerable sediment to the river, creating essentially a flood condition. Rivers like the Ganges–Brahmaputra that experience monsoon conditions discharge many times the normal rate during this season. Even the Amazon (Fig. 5.14) or Mississippi River shows a marked difference in discharge during the wet season compared with the rest of the year.

Human Influence

As people began to populate drainage basins of major rivers and the banks along the courses of these rivers, they have profoundly influenced the delta in several ways. Most, but not all, of these influences have had detrimental effects on the deltas. In most countries, the earliest important human activity was agriculture and forestry. Both have tended to benefit the growth of the delta even though they produced some important negative effects in the drainage basin. Cultivation and deforestation increase erosion of the soil and provide the river, and therefore the delta, with a high rate of sediment discharge. This has resulted in the accelerated growth of many deltas, the prime examples being the Mississippi Delta in the nineteenth century and the present Amazon River delta. As the rapid diminution of the rain forest in Brazil takes place, vast quantities of sediment are provided to the delta.

The more widespread human influence is the reverse situation, that is, re-

FIGURE 5.14
Aerial photograph of the Amazon River delta area showing the abundant suspended sediment in the water.
(Courtesy of Charles Nittrouer)

ducing the sediment supply and thereby causing the delta to shrink in size. There are three important ways by which this occurs: (1) diverting water from the river, (2) controlling navigation on the river, and (3) damming the river. All reduce the discharge of the river, and the latter two physically trap sediment and keep it from moving down the river.

Several major cities use large percentages of river discharge in their municipal water supply. The southern California area depends on water from various rivers in the Southwest for its water, both for irrigation and for domestic use, including the Colorado River that flows through the Grand Canyon. Both activities greatly decrease the water discharge of the river affected and thereby diminish the sediment provided to maintain the river delta. They also decrease the frequence of flooding across the delta, causing delta sediments to become increasingly salty, which may affect the type of vegetation that grows there.

Locks for navigation on major rivers invariably have dams associated with them. On the navigational portion of the Mississippi River that begins near Minneapolis, Minnesota, there are many such structures. The small amount of water impounded is typically not a big problem but the sediment that is trapped behind the dam is literally stolen from the system and, eventually, from the Mississippi

Delta. More important related impoundments are the huge dams built for reservoirs and/or hydroelectric power. They are extremely good sediment traps and some also serve as sources for water diversion. The bottom line is that the amount of water and sediment that the river has available and can transport is not being delivered to the delta.

Two good examples of this problem are the Colorado River that empties into the Gulf of California and the Nile River in Egypt. The headwaters of the Colorado are in the Rocky Mountains in the state for which it is named. Along the course of over a thousand kilometers there are numerous dams and reservoirs as well as places of diversion. The result is that virtually no water and sediment are provided to the Colorado River Delta, which is rapidly being eroded by strong tidal currents. The case of the Nile River is similar. The Aswan Dam was constructed to make the desert fertile and to a degree it has succeeded in doing that. The dam has been quite successful in trapping virtually all of the sediment being carried by the Nile that was destined for the delta. Thus, the outer margin of the delta is eroding rapidly by waves produced in the eastern Mediterranean (Fig. 5.15).

FIGURE 5.15
Photograph of erosion along the outer portion of the Nile Delta as the result of the presence of the Aswan Dam.
(Courtesy of D. J. Stanley)

We cannot continue to rob our rivers of their water and sediment load without experiencing the consequences that these circumstances produce for the deltas that they feed. At present the most viable alternative appears to be the abandonment of deltas as places of extensive development.

The waves, tides, and their resulting currents interact with the riverine processes to prevent, mold, or destroy the deltas, depending upon the specific local circumstances. At those river mouths where waves and tides carry all the sediment away, there is no delta. At many places the delta is allowed to accumulate and prograde but at some, such as the previously mentioned examples, the processes are now creating overall erosion. The relative role of the waves and the tides is also an important factor in the formation, maintenance, and the overall morphology of deltas.

The primary direct marine processes are the waves, wave-generated currents, and tidal currents; the rise and fall of the tide has little direct effect on the redistribution of deltaic sediment. Waves impart energy along the delta and cause sediment to go into temporary suspension whereas longshore and/or tidal currents transport it. During storms this distribution or removal of sediment reaches its height. The overall influence of the waves ranges from mostly longshore transport along the delta front, which provides sediment to various parts of the delta, to actual offshore or alongshore removal of sediment from the delta proper. Waves and wave-generated processes work to smooth the outer delta shape.

Tidal currents usually have at least a shore-perpendicular component and move in and out of the delta complex as flooding and ebbing occurs. The stronger the current the more sediment that is redistributed in this shore-perpendicular fashion. Some deltas have developed on coasts with high tidal ranges, such as the Colorado Delta in the United States (3.5 meters), the Ganges–Brahmaputra Delta in Pakistan (4.0 meters), and the Ord River Delta in Australia (7.0 meters). In these and similar deltas sediment is being carried inland and deposited by flooding currents, and large volumes of sediment is being carried offshore beyond the delta, such as on the Amazon Delta.

DELTA CLASSIFICATION

Both wave and tidal processes on the delta essentially compete with the riverine processes to leave their imprint on the delta morphology. These competing processes and the resulting configuration of the delta provide a framework for classifying deltas. The three major processes that influence deltas provide convenient end members for a comprehensive organization of deltas by shape. This classification was first presented in published form by William Galloway of The University of Texas, Austin, and has become a standard.

The classification consists of a triangle-shaped diagram with riverine processes, waves, and tides at the three apices (Fig. 5.16). A delta that is clearly dominated by any one of the three processes is placed at the appropriate apex.

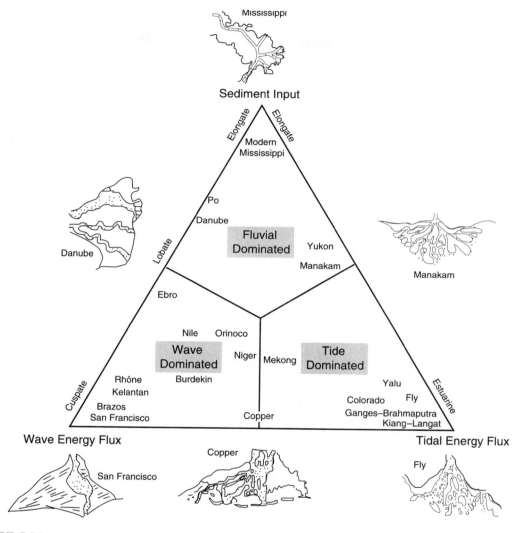

FIGURE 5.16

Classification of river deltas based upon the scheme presented by William Galloway. The many examples included are based on qualitative assessments of the relative influence of river, wave and tide processes. (From Galloway, W. E., 1975, Process framework for describing the morphologic and stratigraphic evolution of deltaic depositional systems, In Broussard, M. L. (ed.) *Deltas: Models of Exploration,* Houston Geological Society, Houston, Texas, p. 92, Fig. 3)

The Mississippi Delta is quite distinctly dominated by river processes in the form of sediment input due to the large volume of sediment discharge and little marine reworking. This gives it its so-called bird's foot configuration. By contrast, the Fly Delta in Papua New Guinea and the Ord Delta in the Cambridge Gulf of northwestern Australia are fine examples of domination by tidal flux. At each site, delta sediment bodies are oriented essentially perpendicular to the trend of the coast. Lastly, the São Francisco Delta in Brazil and the Senegal Delta in Africa show distinct domination by wave processes. Both contain smooth outer margins caused by sediment distribution along the coast that is the result of wave-generated longshore currents.

Most deltas fall somewhere nearer the middle of the classification than do these examples because all deltas experience some influence from all three types of processes (Fig. 5.17). The morphology of each tends to reflect these influences. In general, river influence produces a digitate morphology with a well-developed delta plain having several distributaries. Tide-dominated deltas display a strong shore-perpendicular trend and have extensive tidal flats with little mud. Wave-dominated deltas typically have well-developed beach and dune systems at their outer limits with few distributaries. Neither the absolute values of the processes nor the size of the delta are important in determining the position of a given delta in the overall classification scheme. It is the relative influence of the interactive processes that gives the delta its character.

River-Dominated Deltas

Conditions that foster river-dominated deltas include a high water and sediment discharge with small waves and low tidal ranges in the receiving basin. A broad, gently sloping continental shelf provides the typical resting place for this large volume of sediment. These conditions are best fulfilled by trailing edge and marginal sea situations; both tectonically stable coasts that are sheltered from large waves and have small tidal ranges. The Gulf of Mexico is a perfect setting as it hosts the Mississippi Delta (Fig. 5.17). Other similar settings and their example deltas are the Black Sea with the Danube, the Adriatic Sea with the Po, and the Yellow Sea where the Huang Ho Delta is located. All have good sediment supplies, low tidal ranges, and are sheltered from large waves. The Mississippi Delta does experience exceptional wave energy when hurricanes pass through the area. Some of the most devastating of these storms have eroded large areas of the delta.

Tide-Dominated Deltas

Strong tidal currents in the absence of a substantial wave climate and strong river influence will produce a delta that is tide-dominated. Large tidal channels

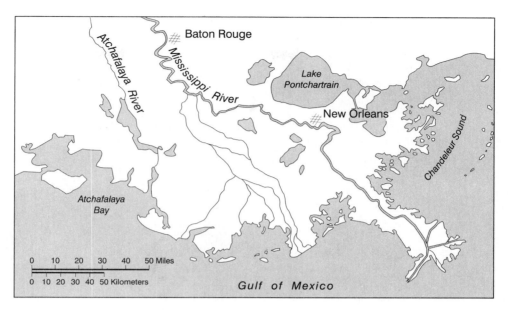

FIGURE 5.17
Mississippi Delta, a good example of a river-dominated delta.
(Modified from Wright, L. D. and Coleman, J. M., 1973, Variations in morphology of river deltas as functions of ocean wave and river discharge regimes. *Amer. Assoc. Petroleum Geol. Bull.,* 57, p. 377, Fig. 2, reprinted by permission)

with intervening tidal sediment bodies dominate the delta and generally are more numerous than the river distributaries. Intertidal environments are widespread and are often partly covered with vegetation such as salt marsh or mangroves.

The Ganges–Brahmaputra Delta is the largest of the tide-dominated deltas and is an area of great interest because of the frequent and devastating floods it experiences (Fig. 5.18). This is a large river system that supplies huge quantities of sediment to a coast where the tidal range exceeds 3 meters and the waves are modest. One of the major factors in this delta's development is the annual variation in discharge. During the monsoon season the amount of sediment delivered to the delta is orders of magnitude greater than during the rest of the year. Strong tidal currents redistribute the sediment in elongate bands that are separated by numerous large tidal channels.

Wave-Dominated Deltas

Some deltas don't really look like deltas because of the strong influence of waves. They may mimic the appearance of barrier island systems with beaches,

FIGURE 5.18
The Ganges-Brahmaputra Delta,
a good example of a tidally
dominated delta.

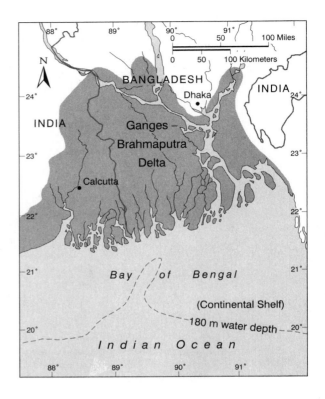

dunes, and wetlands landward of them. These wave-dominated coasts are deltaic in nature because the sediment is supplied directly by the river and then reworked by the waves and wave-generated currents. The distributary channels do not protrude into the basin, thus a smooth outer shoreline exists. Typically, wave-dominated deltas are small, in fact, they grade into conditions of no delta if wave processes are strong enough to carry away all of the sediment supplied by the river.

Wave-dominated deltas may occur in different styles depending upon the nature of the longshore current patterns. The São Francisco Delta in Brazil is fairly symmetrical about a single and centrally located large distributary with a smooth overall cuspate shape (Fig. 5.19). This is due to the absence of a strong littoral drift in either direction caused by the wind patterns and related direction of wave approach. By contrast, the Senegal River in West Africa displays a very strong change in direction of its course due to longshore currents and resulting littoral drift (Fig. 5.20). The river course is shifted over 50 kilometers by the longshore currents. The mouth of the river is marked by a distinct spit that mimics a coastal barrier, and extensive wetlands cover the delta plain.

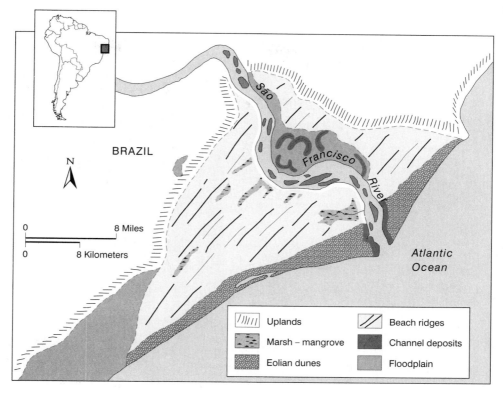

FIGURE 5.19
Sao Francisco Delta in Brazil, a good example of a symmetrical, cuspate wave-dominated delta.
(From Wright and Coleman, 1973, reprinted by permission)

Intermediate Deltas

Intermediate types of deltas display features indicating the influence of both river and marine processes. The Mahakam Delta on the coast of Borneo is small but has a shape that shows the important influence of the river and tidal currents. It has numerous distributaries and a well-developed delta plain with distinct lobes that protrude into the receiving basin. Spring tides range up to 3 meters and have currents of 100 centimeters per second that form distinct tidal channels between the distributary mouths.

The Nile Delta is a good example of a delta that is intermediate between river- and wave-dominated deltas (Fig. 5.1). Tides in the Mediterranean Sea are nominal and waves are modest. River input has historically been fairly high until

FIGURE 5.20
Senegal Delta in Africa, a
classic case of the river mouth
being shifted many kilometers
due to a high rate of littoral
drift.
(From Wright and Coleman, 1973,
reprinted by permission)

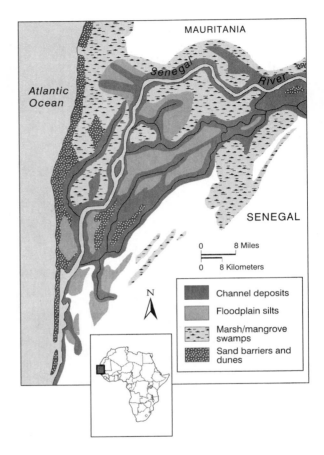

the construction of the Aswân Dam in the 1960s. The delta plain is traversed by a modest number of well-defined distributaries, each protruding into the sea. Between the distributary mouths the delta displays a relatively smooth outline with beaches and other wave-dominated features.

Probably the best example of an intermediate delta is the Niger Delta on the coast of Nigeria (Fig. 5.21). It falls in the middle of the classification, showing equal influence of the river, waves, and tides. It has a well-developed delta plain with a complex network of distributaries, a spring tidal range of up to 2.8 meters, and is exposed to waves of the south Atlantic Ocean. The result is a delta that incorporates some features of each of the major processes that influence deltaic coasts.

FIGURE 5.21
Niger Delta, a delta that is about equally influenced by river, wave, and tidal processes. (Modified from Allen, J. R. L., 1970, In Deltaic Sedimentation, *SEPM Spec. Publ.* No. 15, Tulsa, Oklahoma, pp. 138–151)

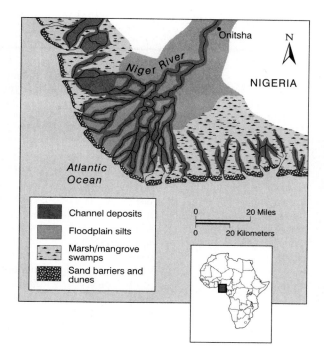

SUMMARY

In some ways river deltas may be considered the most important of all coastal environments because they are the site of sediment introduction for most of the other parts of the coast. On the other hand, people rarely spend any time visiting a delta on vacation or going to and from places of work or play there. Deltas tend to be remote, without traffic arteries, and are generally inhospitable due to insects. Because of their critical role in the overall scheme of the coastal zone it is important that we have an understanding of river deltas and their characteristics.

Deltas are among the most productive and valuable environments in the world. They contain highly productive ecological niches in which a wide variety of both plants and animals thrive. Their marshes are among the most extensive and productive environments anywhere. Deltas represent very important nursery grounds for juvenile fish and marine invertebrates. Their marshes also are important filters that trap contaminants and pollutants during flooding of distributaries.

The size and shape of the delta is a consequence of the interplay between the river and the sediment it provides with the wave and tidal processes of the marine coast. Deltas have developed quite rapidly in the context of geologic

TABLE 5.1
Some large modern deltas.*

River	Landmass	Receiving Basin	Size (km^2)	Annual Sediment Discharge (tons × 10^6)
Amazon	South America	Atlantic	467,000	1,200
Chao Phraya	Asia	Gulf of Siam	25,000	5
Danube	Europe	Black Sea	2,700	67
Ebro	Europe	Mediterranean	600	—
Ganges–Brahmuputra	Asia	Bay of Bengal	106,000	1,670
Huang	Asia	Yellow Sea	36,000	1,080
Irrawaddy	Asia	Bay of Bengal	21,000	285
Mahakam	Borneo	Makassar Strait	5,000	8
Mekong	Asia	South China Sea	94,000	160
Mississippi	North America	Gulf of Mexico	29,000	210 (469)
Niger	Africa	Gulf of Guinea	19,000	40
Nile	Africa	Mediterranean	12,500	0 (54)
Orinoco	South America	Atlantic	21,000	210
Po	Europe	Adriatic Sea	13,400	61
Rio Grande	North America	Gulf of Mexico	8,000	17
São Francisco	South America	Atlantic	700	—
Senegal	Africa	Atlantic	4,300	—
Yangtze	Asia	East China Sea	66,700	478

*Parentheses indicate discharge before major human modification.

time, and they can be destroyed just as rapidly. As we influence our environment more and more, we need to do a better job of considering the long-term consequences of our actions. The role of human intervention is critical to the maintenance of this coastal environment as evidenced by what has happened on the Nile and Colorado deltas as well as on others.

6
Estuaries, Marshes, and Tidal Flats

Most coasts have embayments of various sizes, shapes, and origins. The differences in the nature of the embayments can be for many reasons but most are related to plate tectonics. Bays that have come about through tectonic means are commonly associated with leading edge margins like the West coast of the United States. Here, faults and movement along them may produce bays that are typically long and narrow such as Drakes Estero in California (Fig. 6.1) where the San Andreas Fault system forms the geologic setting for an embayment. Other bays may result from the effects of rising sea level drowning drainage networks producing branching bay systems such as Chesapeake Bay (Fig. 6.2) and Pamlico Sound on the central Atlantic coast of the United States. This common type of coastal bay is typical of trailing edge coasts with broad coastal plains and well-developed river systems. Other varieties include (1) fjords, which are elongate embayments excavated by glaciers, (2) bays formed by barriers such as coral reefs and barrier islands, and (3) embayments constructed by human activity, more commonly called harbors.

This brief list shows the spectrum of origins and related shapes that coastal bays assume. It is not only their size, shape, and origin that give coastal bays their character—hydrology is also important because it tends to control the water chemistry, the biota, and the sediment that forms the substrate. Hydrology provides the best criteria for classifying coastal bays into broad hydrologic categories. Two categories, estuaries and lagoons, account for most of the important bay types. Estuaries are coastal bays that have significant freshwater influx from one or more perennial rivers, regardless of shape. They also experience regular and

FIGURE 6.1
Drakes Estero, California, an example of a fault-generated estuary in the San Andreas
complex north of the San Francisco area.

significant tidal influence. Lagoons are the coastal bays that experience neither of
these processes. Not all coastal bays fall into one or another of these two types,
although the vast majority do. The others are best considered simply as coastal
bays, without any specific type assigned.

In this chapter we will consider the range of estuaries and also the associated tidal flat and coastal marsh environments that are widespread and extremely important in the estuary system. In some low-latitude parts of the world
the coastal marsh is absent and mangrove swamps replace this estuarine environment. The extent and nature of tidal flats are largely controlled by the tidal
range along with the geomorphology of the area affected. The highest tidal
ranges in the world are in an estuary, the Bay of Fundy in Nova Scotia, Canada.

ESTUARIES

Given the above definition for estuaries, one might question how they differ
from river deltas, which also have important freshwater input and experience
tidal influence. The difference is that an estuary is a coastal embayment whereas
a delta is really the opposite—it protrudes into the ocean or whatever the receiving basin may be. In fact, many characteristics are common to these two coastal
systems: (1) both deltas and estuaries typically have tidal flats and marshes or
mangrove swamps, (2) both are influenced by rivers, waves, and tides, (3) both
are important sites of sediment accumulation, and (4) both are young features in
the framework of geologic time.

We typically refer to estuaries as sediment sinks, that is, places where sedi-

FIGURE 6.2
Chesapeake Bay, an example of an estuary formed by the drowning of a complicated fluvial system producing a complex coastline.

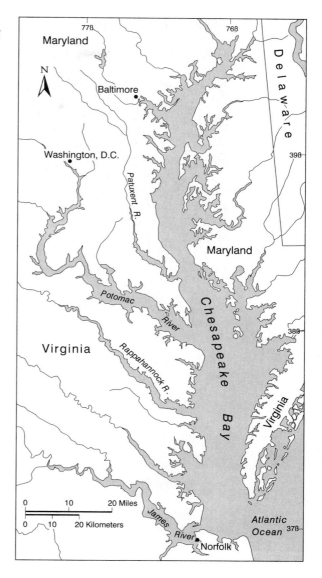

ment tends to accumulate and to stay for long periods of time. In fact, it is because of this characteristic that the geologic lifetime of an estuary is short. The embayment provides a local basin for sediments to come to rest. The runoff from rivers as well as from the tidal fluctuations provides sediment from both the landward and seaward directions. Estuaries tend, therefore, to be filled in toward the middle. If sea level rises during this infilling process, then the accommodation space for sediment continues to increase, whereas if sea level falls, the estuary is left essentially "high and dry."

Estuarine Hydrology

The fact that both rivers and tides influence the estuary means that both fresh-water and seawater mix in this environment. It is this interaction of different water types that gives the estuary one of its most important characteristics along the coast—brackish salinities. Runoff from a river is continuous but there is vari-ation in discharge depending upon seasonality, climate, and other factors, just as there is for deltas. On the other hand, the tidal influence into an estuary is typi-cally regular and predictable. The range changes with spring and neap conditions but the periodicity remains constant.

Seawater has a salinity of about 35 parts per thousand or 3.5 percent, whereas freshwater's salinity is essentially zero. This contrast in composition pro-duces a significant difference in the density of the two fluids; everyone knows how much easier it is to float in saltwater than in a swimming pool of fresh-water. This difference seems small in absolute numbers, 1.000 grams per cen-timeter for freshwater and 1.026 grams per centimeter for saltwater, but it is very important. In the absence of waves or strong currents, these different water types will become stratified, with the lighter freshwater "floating" on the heavier saltwater. We can begin to see the potential complications that this condition presents to the estuary in the form of circulation into and out of the embayment.

Estuarine Classification

A common classification of estuaries is based on the way in which the freshwater and saltwater interact. In the 1950s, Donald Pritchard, a scientist at the Chesa-peake Bay Institute recognized three types of circulation: (1) stratified, (2) par-tially mixed, and (3) mixed (Fig. 6.3). In a stratified estuary there is essentially complete separation between the fresh and saltwater masses due to lack of tur-bulence caused by waves or strong currents. Estuaries dominated by rivers may display stratified water masses such as does the Hudson River estuary in New York where the saltwater wedge extends tens of kilometers up the river. In some estuaries a portion of the saltwater mixes with the freshwater, producing a zone of intermediate salinity between the fresh and saltwater. Places where tidal cur-rents influence part, but not all, of the estuary, such as Chesapeake Bay, display this characteristic. Totally mixed estuaries produce a vertically homogenized water column with a gradient of increasing salinity toward the ocean. This could be the result of waves in a shallow estuary such as in Pamlico Sound, North Car-olina, or Mobile Bay, Alabama, or it could be due to strong tidal currents such as in the Bay of Fundy, Canada, or Delaware Bay on the Atlantic coast of the United States.

Many estuaries move from one type to another depending upon seasonal variations in runoff, wave climate, or other phenomena that lead to variations in the amount of mixing. For example, in a large but shallow estuary such as Mo-

FIGURE 6.3

Pritchard's estuary classification which includes; a) stratified, b) partially mixed, and c) fully mixed categories.

(Modified from Pritchard, D. W., 1955, Estuarine circulation patterns, *Amer. Soc. Civil Engr., Proc.* 81, pp. 1–4, Fig. 2. Reproduced by permission of ASCE.)

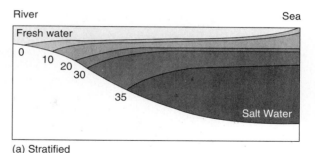

(a) Stratified

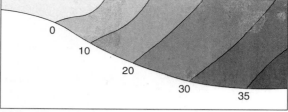

(b) Partially mixed

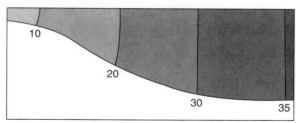

(c) Fully mixed

bile Bay or Pamlico Sound waves may mix the water column thereby destroying any stratification. In the summer, waves are absent or small, conditions that permit stratification. On the other hand, the tidal currents in the Bay of Fundy are always strong enough to completely mix the water in this estuary.

Estuarine Processes

By their nature, estuaries tend to be influenced primarily by river or tidal processes with wave influence depending on the size and depth of the estuarine basin. Rivers provide freshwater and sediment to the estuary. The amount of both and the rate at which they are delivered are critical to the nature and longevity of the estuary. Some estuaries are fed by a single river and therefore the sediment supply is essentially at one point, a bayhead in which where much of the sediment accumulates in the form of a riverine delta (Fig. 6.4). Most of the

FIGURE 6.4
Guadalupe River entering San Antonio Bay on the Gulf Coast of Texas, forming a
bayhead delta.

large estuaries on the Texas coast have this characteristic. San Antonio Bay is fed
by the Guadalupe River, Corpus Christi Bay by the Nueces River, and Galveston
Bay by the Trinity River. Another good example is Mobile Bay in Alabama with
the Tensaw River. These estuaries tend to be river-dominated because of the
strong influence of the debouching stream and the absence of strong tidal currents and big waves. The tidal influence in these Gulf Coast estuaries is damp-
ened by the presence of the barrier islands across the mouth of the bays and is
also limited by the small tidal range; less than a 1-meter spring tide for all of
them.

Other estuaries tend to have numerous rivers emptying into them with little or no development of a bayhead delta. Probably the best example is the
Chesapeake Bay (Fig. 6.2), which receives input from numerous large rivers but
which has no significant delta formation within it. Here the digitate nature of
the river valleys traps most of the relatively coarse sediment in this part of the
estuary. Many of the small West Coast estuaries are similar but typically having
only a single stream feeding them. Although this type of estuary can develop
any of the three hydrologic styles mentioned above, nearly all are stratified or
partially mixed. In addition to the presence of the bayhead deltas, terrigenous
sediment accumulation in these river-dominated estuaries is generally dominated by mud.

The other end of the spectrum is the tide-dominated estuary, which is typically funnel-shaped and has no barrier or other constriction at its mouth. Such a configuration not only eliminates the dampening effect that barriers have on tidal flux but commonly enhances the tidal wave producing macrotidal ranges. Both conditions result in maximizing the influence of tides and create totally mixed hydrologic conditions in the estuary. The combination of high tidal range with strong tidal currents generally results in a sand-dominated estuary floor; the mud tends to be swept out to sea or is trapped at the landward limits of the estuary. Good examples are the Bay of Fundy and the Gironde Estuary on the Northwest coast of France (Fig. 6.5).

The strong tidal currents in these tide-dominated estuaries move great volumes of sediment into the estuary and then move sediment in the estuary back and forth during each tidal cycle. Sand can be transported by currents of as low as 20 to 30 centimeters per second, depending on the size of the sand particles. These conditions are achieved or exceeded for several hours during each flood and ebb tidal cycle. As a result, the tidal currents produce numerous bedforms on the floor of the estuary (Fig. 6.6). These bedforms result from the shear between the bed (sediment) and the water column, and thereby cause turbulence and bedforms ranging in size from ripples to sand waves. The size and shape of these features are controlled by both grain size and the velocity of the tidal currents.

FIGURE 6.5
The Gironde Estuary in France displays a funnel shape common among tide-dominated estuaries.

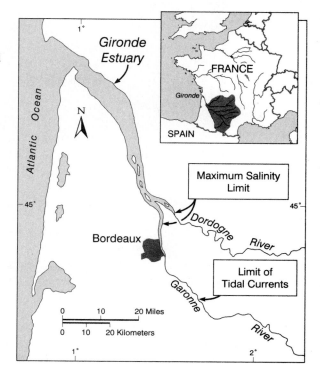

(a)

(b)

FIGURE 6.6
Photos showing a) ripples, b) megaripples, and c) superimposed ripples and megaripples, all are common bedforms in estuaries.

(c)

FIGURE 6.6   (*Cont.*)

Time–Velocity Curves   The record of the rise and fall of the tides produces a plot that shows the change in water level over each tidal cycle; the curve is essentially symmetrical. If we plot the velocity of tidal currents that are produced by this rise and fall of the tides the curve is very different. There is considerable asymmetry to the velocity data, and the duration of flood and ebb may be different. This graph is called a time–velocity curve and the absence of symmetry is called time–velocity asymmetry (Fig. 6.7). That is, the velocity varies with time as the flood and ebb of the tide takes place, and although it is quite systematic and predictable, it is simply not symmetrical.

Each location within an estuary displays its own characteristic time–velocity curve showing its own asymmetry. Changes to the asymmetry will occur within the lunar cycle and if channels or other aspects of the estuary floor and tidal channels are changed, all of which strongly influence the flow of tidal current. As a result, time–velocity curves may show steep slopes or more gradual ones, or, the duration of the flood and ebb portion of the tidal cycle may show distinct differences, more than an hour in many cases. These conditions may produce either flood-dominated or ebb-dominated locations that may be adjacent. For example, it is common for an ebb-dominated channel to be adjacent to flood-dominated tidal flats.

Model Estuary

A good way to conceptualize an estuary is through the use of a simple model. The estuary can be subdivided into three main parts: (1) the landward area of

FIGURE 6.7
Plot of two examples of time–
velocity curves for different
locations in an estuary. These
curves will have different
shapes from one location to
another.
(From Postma, H., 1961, Transport
and accumulation of suspended
matter in the Dutch Wadden
Sea, *Netherlands Jour. Sea Res.* 1,
pp. 148–190)

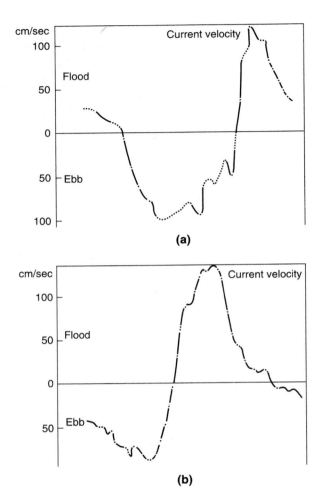

river influence, (2) the middle, truly estuarine area, and (3) the seaward area of marine influence (Fig. 6.8). The relative proportions of each vary with individual estuaries and with the influences of the major processes. Tides are commonly less influential landward from near the mouth; however, there are exceptions in which the shape enhances tidal range, the Bay of Fundy being an example. Wave influence tends to be directly proportional to the size of the estuary or to the fetch of a particular portion of it. Riverine influence is likewise proportional to the amount and rate of river input relative to tidal flux.

There is nearly always significant overlap in the sediment supply from the river and marine sources although the nature of their respective contribution is generally different. River sediments are generally sand and mud whereas marine

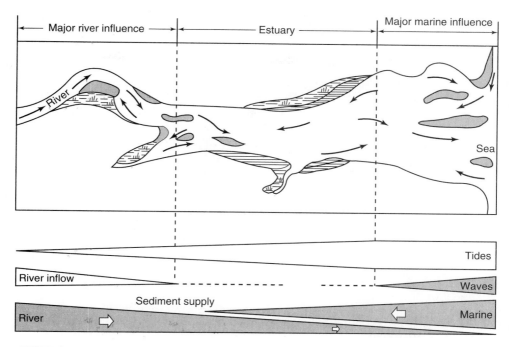

FIGURE 6.8

General diagram of an estuary including the major sections and sediment varieties.
(After Nichols, M. M. and Biggs, R. B., 1985, In *Coastal Sedimentary Environments,* Springer-Verlag,
New York, p. 158, Fig. 2.48)

sediments tend to be dominated by sand with some shell gravel; mud is rare (Fig. 6.9). The estuarine transport of sediments includes both bed load and suspended load. The latter is particularly important in low-energy estuaries in which it forms the bulk of the accumulated sediment; less is carried out into the open marine environment with ebbing tides.

The zone of fresh- and saltwater mixing strongly influences suspended sediments because it is a place in which water density changes significantly. Flocculation of the fine clay mineral particles (less than microns in diameter) takes place here, and floc size may reach up to 30 microns. This is also the zone of the turbidity maximum in both partially and fully mixed estuaries. Here suspended sediment concentrations are highest. This phenomenon is controlled by the mixing of the freshwater with the leading edge of the saltwater. Some of the particles suspended in the overlying freshwater mass settle as currents diminish and are then entrained by the lower, more dense saltwater and carried landward to the turbidity maximum. This process produces the high sediment accumulation rate associated with the turbidity maximum.

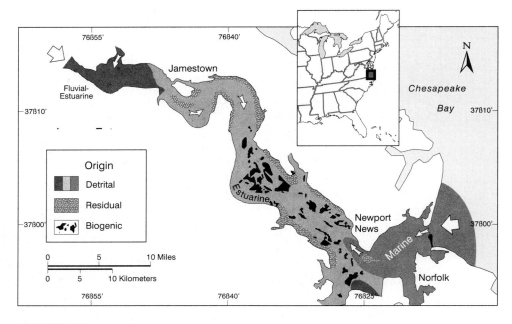

FIGURE 6.9
Map showing major environments within the James River estuary, a branch of
Chesapeake Bay.
(From Nichols, M. M., 1972, Effect of increasing depth on salinity in the James River Estuary, In
Geol. Soc. Amer. Memoir 133, pp. 571–589)

There is a third source of sediment in estuaries; the biogenic material that is
produced or modified in the estuary itself. This sediment tends to be most abundant and accumulates most rapidly in the middle zone (Fig. 6.9). Numerous organisms that thrive on brackish salinities characterize the central portion of most
estuaries. The typical salinity range here is from about 5 to 20 ppt. Ostracods,
foraminifera, various mollusks, and worms are the most common animals, and
algae and some grasses exist on the fringe. Water clarity strongly inhibits photosynthesis in many estuaries. Skeletal carbonate material from many of these organisms makes an important contribution to the sediment of the estuary. Oyster
reefs are particularly large and widespread in many of the low-energy, muddy
estuaries (Fig. 6.10).

The other aspect of the contribution made by benthic organisms is through
pelletization of suspended sediments by filter feeders and to a lesser extent by
grazers. The biggest contributors are the oysters and worms, both of which filter
their nourishment from suspended particles provided by currents. Much of the
suspended material is composed of clay particles and other inorganic debris. The
organisms pass the inorganic particles through their digestive tracts and excrete
pelleted mud in large quantities. Most accumulated estuarine sediment is actu-

FIGURE 6.10
Oyster reefs in an estuary along the South Carolina coast.

ally in the form of pellets that are sand-sized, cohesive aggregates of mud parti-cles. The filter feeders greatly increase the rate of benthic sediment accumulation by taking suspended sediment that might otherwise be carried to sea out of the water column and converting it to larger particles. Many of these pellets are too large and cohesive to be transported by tidal currents, and they become part of the estuarine stratigraphy. In areas of high tidal range, estuarine margins may exhibit significant desiccation.

TIDAL FLATS

The margins of most estuaries are rimmed by unvegetated intertidal zones of sediment accumulation called *tidal flats*. The width and extent of tidal flats are di-rectly related to tidal range and to the morphology of the estuary. In some estu-aries, especially those that experience macrotidal conditions, much of the estuary may be intertidal except for tidal channels that dissect the flats. The Wadden Sea along the Dutch and German coast of the North Sea is such a place.

Tidal flats and their contained channels may be mud, sand, or, more typi-cally, a combination of both. The nature and rigor of the tidal currents and also the waves, tend to be the controlling factors in both the rate and nature of sedi-ment accumulation.

Tidal Flat Processes

Tide-generated processes tend to dominate most sediments that are accumulating on estuarine tidal flats, although waves are locally important. The same currents that distribute sediment throughout the estuary are responsible for its transport onto tidal flats; however, in this environment special conditions occur. For purposes of explanation, the tidal flat is best viewed as a smooth and gently sloping surface. Certain key elevations are noted on this surface based on the position of the water level at given tidal stages. Spring high tide is the highest position of regular and predictable inundation of the sediment surface by water, and spring low tide is the lowest (Fig. 6.11). Wind tides may cause water level to move up to the supratidal environment or below low tide depending upon direction and strength. Neap tidal range may be only about half of the spring range, thereby causing considerable variation in the intertidal zone, depending upon the lunar phase.

Tides   The scheme of sediment transport on tidal flats has been best described in studies of the tidal flats on the Wadden Sea. The model produced shows the effects of the combination of the settling lag and scour lag on the paths of sediment particles as they are transported up onto the tidal flat surface (Fig. 6.12) and how, over a long time, sediment builds up and out into the estuary. The distance–velocity curves are asymmetrical and show where a given particle is entrained, transported, and deposited.

During flooding tides, the sediment particle at location 1 on curve A-A' is picked up at a tidal current velocity shown at point 2 and carried landward until that velocity is again reached at point 3 on the curve. The particle then begins to

FIGURE 6.11
Diagram showing various important tidal levels during a lunar cycle.

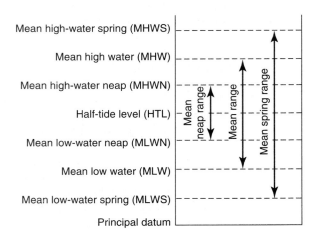

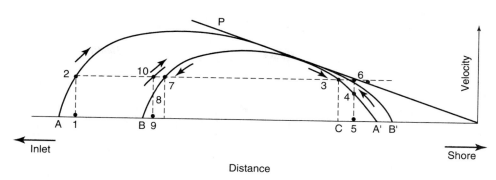

FIGURE 6.12

Postma's diagram for settling lag and scour lag on tidal flats. The numbers reflect the positions of a sediment particle as it moves up the tidal flat as the tide floods and ebbs.
(From Postma, H., 1967, Estuaries, *Amer. Assoc. Adv. Sci. Spec. Publ.* 83, pp. 158–179)

fall and reaches the tidal flat surface at point 5 when the current velocity is at location 4. The difference in the velocity of entrainment, which is greater than at settling, is quite important. This provides the settling lag effect.

Ebbing tidal currents follow curve B-B', which represents a more landward water mass and achieves less of a maximum velocity at this position on the tidal flat. The same particle is picked up at location 5 when the velocity is reached at point 6 on the curve. It is carried until point 7 when it begins to fall and eventually settles to the bottom at point 9. This diagram shows that the net result is movement of a sediment particle from location 1 to location 9 during a single tidal cycle. This is obviously an oversimplified model because there are many pertubations on the tidal flat that interfere with the processes. It does, however, serve to illustrate the basic mechanism by which sediment particles are transported up on to the tidal flats.

Size of the sediment particles is an important variable in the above scheme. Bigger particles will be transported a shorter distance over a given tidal cycle than smaller particles. The more time an area is covered and the deeper the water, the more tidal energy is expended on a given location on the tidal flat. As a consequence, there is a regular decrease in sediment particle size up the tidal flat toward the spring high-tide level (Fig. 6.13).

This scheme of flood and ebb tides, coupled with the grain size range that is typically present in an estuary, produces what is called tidal bedding (Fig. 6.14). This thin and regular type of layering represents the cyclic deposition of sediments produced by the tides. The thickness represented by each tidal cycle may be only a couple of millimeters or more than a centimeter. Spring and neap tidal conditions may also leave a record of relatively thick and thin layers. In some

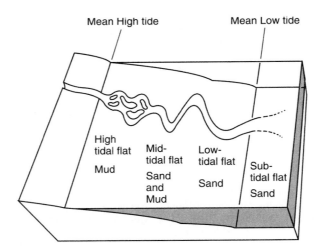

FIGURE 6.13
Diagram of sediment texture distribution across a tidal flat.
(From Klein, G. deV., 1985, Intertidal flats and intertidal sand bodies In *Coastal Sedimentary Environments*, Springer-Verlag, New York, pp. 187–224).

places it is possible to recognize hundreds of these units, and they are an important criterion in recognizing ancient tidal flat deposits in the sediment layers of the geologic record.

Conditions in some areas produce discontinuous mud or sand layers due to some combination of sediment availability and tidal current strength. These can be formed through tidal processes and represent what is essentially discontinuous tidal bedding or alternations in current energies that are not produced by flooding and ebbing tides. This can lead to confusion in interpreting ancient conditions of deposition. Discontinuous mud layers in sand are called *flaser bedding*, which commonly form in the troughs of bedforms (Fig. 6.15). Discontinuous sandy lenses within a mud sequence are referred to as *lenticular bedding*, a feature generally associated with limited sand availability but that may also reflect variations in tidal current velocities.

Another type of tidally produced stratification is tidal bundling, which is typically associated with tidal channels or relatively strong tidal currents and large bedforms. The alternation of flooding and ebbing tides is generally accompanied by significant differences in current velocity as shown by time–velocity asymmetry. This commonly produces pulses in the migration of large bedforms, which are characterized by medium- to large-scale cross-stratification. The dominant current moves the bedform, and the recessive current generally produces a mud drape over the bedform, producing a muddy seam between each sand cross-stratum. In many tide-dominated areas the sequence contains readily distinguishable sets of

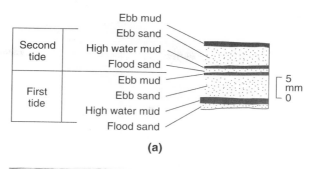

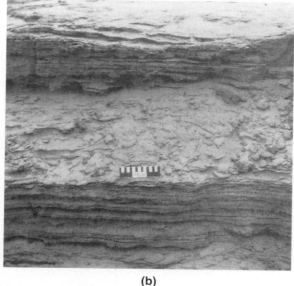

FIGURE 6.14
a) Diagram and photograph b) showing tidal bedding, thin alternating layers of mud and sand that reflect the energy changes during a complete flood and ebb tidal cycle.
(a - From Klein, G. deV., 1977, *Clastic Tidal Facies*, Continuing Education Publication Co., Champaign, Illinois)

cross-strata that change in thickness and sand-mud ratio in bundles of 14. These tidal bundles represent a spring and neap tidal cycle (Fig. 6.16).

Waves   We typically associate tidal processes with tidal flats but there are some locations in which waves play an important role in the dynamics of tidal flats—enough to destroy all of the signatures of tidal processes. In order for this to happen the energy imparted by the waves onto the tidal flat must exceed that

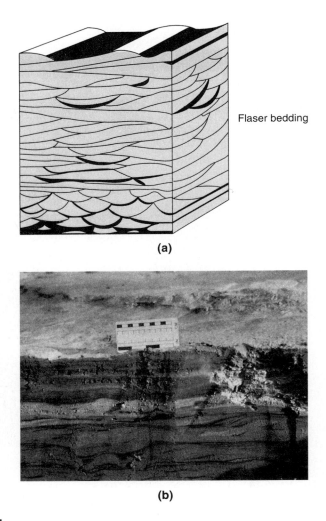

Flaser bedding

(a)

(b)

FIGURE 6.15
Diagram a) and photograph b) showing flaser bedding with small lenses of mud
incorporated in a sandy deposit.
(a - From Reineck, H. E. and Wunderlich, F., 1968, Classification and origin of flaser and lenticular
bedding, *Sedimentology*, 11, p. 100, Fig. 2)

of the tides. The most common conditions under which this can occur are in
places where extensive shallow water covers the tidal flat for long portions of
each tidal cycle. Waves formed in this shallow environment will move large
quantities of sediment through the back and forth motion they produce, thereby
destroying any tidal signature or preventing it from happening in the first place.

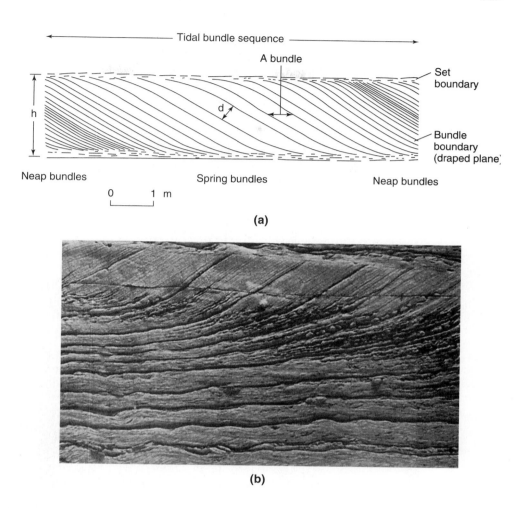

FIGURE 6.16

Diagram a) and photograph b) showing tidal bundles that show the spring and neap tidal conditions as incorporated in cross-stratification.

(a From Yang, C. S. and Nio, S. D., 1985, *Sedimentology*, 32, p. 42, Fig. 1)

The Wadden Sea area on the German coast of the North Sea is a good example of such wave-influenced tidal flats. Here broad, sandy intertidal flats cover most of the area between the barrier islands and the mainland, an area several kilometers wide. The muddy tidal flats are mostly near the mainland. The sandy flats are flooded for 4 to 6 hours of each tidal cycle, and the fetch of several kilometers permits the commonly strong winds to generate modest size waves. This combination of strong wave action coupled with modest tidal currents prevents tidal bedding from forming over much of the tidal flat environment. In contrast, the tidal channels that dissect the tidal flats display tidal bundling, indicating that tidal currents are dominant in this environment.

Bioturbation   Any type of sediment disturbance by organisms is called *bioturbation*. Many of the numerous benthic organisms that live in estuaries are infaunal; they burrow into the sediment both for protection and for feeding. These same animals take in suspended particles and produce most of the pellets that accumulate in estuaries, but the activity of interest here is the actual burrowing process. As a bivalve or worm burrows into and through sediment, it destroys the layering essentially by homogenizing the sediment (Fig. 6.17). This churning of sediment by burrowers (up to thousands per square meter) also destroys the tidal signature of sediments. The extensive tidal flats of the Georgia and South Carolina coasts fall into this category. In fact, in the German Wadden Sea the combination of both waves and bioturbation work to destroy tidal bedding.

It is only in places in which there are few burrowing organisms that tidal bedding is typically preserved. This lack of benthic infaunal organisms can result from a variety of conditions. Exposure and subsequent drying out is a problem, especially for soft-bodied organisms like worms. The higher the position in the

FIGURE 6.17
Photograph of tidal flats that are intensely bioturbated and as a result, no stratification is preserved.

tidal flats, the fewer sessile organisms that will be present because of the exposure factor. Another limiting factor to benthic organisms is an oversupply of suspended sediment particles in the water column. Filter feeders are prone to siphon clogging, and they cannot live under such conditions. The other important limitation is a mobile sediment bed caused by strong tidal currents. Many infaunal organisms, especially sedentary ones, need a reasonably stable sediment base in which to burrow and maintain an existence. It is obvious therefore, that the problems confronting benthic organisms are numerous in estuaries.

SALT MARSHES

It is typical for a portion of the outer margin of an estuary to be covered by a marsh. The proportion of the estuary that supports this environment ranges widely—from essentially all of the estuary except for tidal channels to only a border a few meters wide. The proportion of the estuary that is covered by marsh tends to indicate the maturity of the estuary or the degree to which it has been filled in with sediment. For example, some of the estuaries on the Georgia coast have little open water except near the inlet between the barrier islands. Only tidal creeks dissect the extensive marsh environment in these sedimentologically

FIGURE 6.18
Photograph of an extensive salt marsh along the southeastern coast of the United States.

FIGURE 6.19
Photograph showing a narrow marsh fringe in The Bay of Fundy is considered to be immature in its sediment infilling.

mature estuaries (Fig. 6.18). By contrast, the German Wadden Sea is bordered by a narrow marsh, and the Bay of Fundy supports a narrow and discontinuous marsh environment (Fig. 6.19), evidence of a sedimentologically immature estuary.

Formation of a Coastal Marsh

A marsh is really the vegetated portion of the higher intertidal environment. Above about neap high tide there is little energy to disturb the sediment substrate, and the sediment that accumulates there tends to be relatively fine grained. All of these factors provide support for vegetation, an undisturbed place of fine, organic-rich sediment. Certain opportunistic and tolerant grasses thrive in this environment. There are two that are particularly prone to establish dense stands on such substrates—*Spartina* and *Juncus* (Fig. 6.20). Although they are not the only marsh taxa, these are the most widely distributed in North America.

The specific type of grass that develops a marsh depends upon climate and latitude. In the southern coasts *Spartina alterniflora* is the low marsh grass that is found between neap and spring high tide; in most estuaries this is a narrow

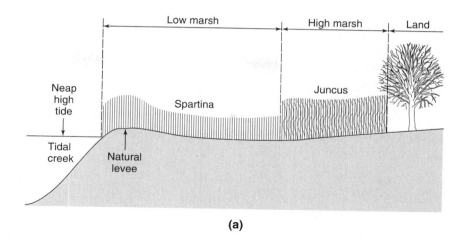

(a)

(b)

FIGURE 6.20

Diagram a) and photo b) showing *Spartina* and *Juncus* zonation along the margin of an estuary.

(a - From Edwards, J. M. and Frey, R. W., 1977, Substrate characteristics within a Holocene salt marsh, Sapelo Island, Georgia, *Senckenbergiana Maritima*, 9, pp. 215–259) range in elevation of a few tens of centimeters, but up to a few meters in estuaries with very large tidal ranges. Individual plants are generally about knee-high but vary greatly depending upon their specific location within the marsh and the availability of nutrients. The highest plants tend to be on the highest elevations, that is, the levees of the channel margins and near spring high tide. The *S. alterniflora* plants at the lowest part of the marsh may be quite small and scattered.

Juncus is the high marsh grass in low to mid-latitudes and is restricted to the elevation at about spring high tide. This plant, also called the *needle rush,* is as tall as a person and has a pointed end that has been known to penetrate shoes. It attains this height throughout the extent of the spring tide position of the estuary margin. In more northern areas the high marsh is characterized by *Spartina patens.*

In high latitudes the high and low marsh are characterized by two species of *Spartina*. In the low marsh this is *S. alterniflora* but here it does not grow very tall. The high marsh is characterized by *S. patens,* which grows taller.

The marsh environment in the estuary is really like the floodplain in the river system: (1) it is typically cut by channels having point bars, (2) it has natural levees, and (3) crevasse splays may breach the levees. The channels display meanders with cutoffs like oxbow lakes. Once sediment accumulation on a tidal flat reaches about the neap high-tide level, colonization by *Spartina* begins to take place. It has the ability to grow on local sites just because they have reached the appropriate elevation. For example, the crest of a large bedform such as a sand wave may have marsh vegetation whereas the trough does not. Eventually the marsh becomes nearly flat or gently sloping and continuously covers the surface.

Marsh vegetation tends to be quite dense and provides an excellent sediment trap in two ways. First, the grass slows the flow of tidal waters to permit settling out of fine suspended sediment particles to the floor of the marsh. Second, considerable fine sediment adheres to the marsh grasses as the turbid water flows past. Both of these mechanisms provide for slow accumulation of generally muddy sediment. Suspension feeders living within the marsh grass produce pellets that accumulate within the marsh and that contribute to its aggradation. After sediment has reached approximately the level of spring high tide the *S. alterniflora* will give way to *Juncus*. Sediment accumulates very slowly in the high marsh because it is only flooded a few days during each lunar tidal cycle and because the sediment-laden water column is quite thin in this area.

A convenient way to consider marsh development is through the relative distribution of the low and high marsh portions of the total vegetated environment (Fig. 6.21). Without using any absolute ages, we can consider young, mature, and old marshes to reflect their progressive development, assuming that sea level has not changed substantially. A young marsh is one that has mostly low marsh vegetation, that is *S. alterniflora,* with perhaps only a fringe of high marsh around the outer edge. Tidal channels are abundant, providing good drainage and sediment supply. This stage of marsh development is present until enough

(a)

(b)

FIGURE 6.21
Photos showing three stages of marsh development: a) youthful with mostly low marsh; b) mature with a nearly even mixture of high and low marsh; and c) old age with mostly high marsh.
(Courtesy of Joe Wadsworth)

(c)

FIGURE 6.21 (*Cont.*)

sediment has been delivered to the upper intertidal area to support an increased upper marsh community.

The intermediate stage of marsh development has a near-equal distribution of high and low vegetation types, and there are fewer tidal channels than in the young marsh. As the sediment continues to be delivered to the upper intertidal area, the marsh becomes quite "old" in its development. *Juncus* or *S. alterniflora* characterizes nearly all of the marsh with a few large tidal creeks interrupting an otherwise continuous stand of this species. Continued sediment accumulation will allow land plants to encroach into the marsh as the estuary becomes smaller.

The end product of this scheme of succession of land plants, marsh, and tidal flats into the estuary will be its complete infilling. Because they are sediment sinks, this is their eventual fate unless sea level changes either enlarge the estuary or abandon it at a high level, in which case, terrestrial vegetation will likely move in.

7
Sandy Coasts

That portion of the coast most familiar to most people is the beach, closely followed by the dunes, which are typically landward of the beach. Although they also occur on the mainland, both of these coastal elements are also typical of barrier islands, quite complicated and dynamic parts of the coast. In addition to the beach and dune environments, these islands include washover fans that commonly become vegetated to form back-island flats (Fig. 7.1). Along the coast, barrier islands are typically interrupted by tidal inlets. The landward portion of the barrier island may also include widespread marshes and tidal flats similar in general character to those that border estuaries. In many barrier island systems, the back-barrier water body is parallel to the island and rather narrow. These water bodies are typically called lagoons, coastal bays that have little or no freshwater input or tidal exchange with the open ocean.

Barrier islands only account for about 12 to 15 percent of the world's coast, but they tend to be the most expensive and most highly developed coastal type. In a cause and effect framework, barriers are the depositional portion of the wave-dominated coast as contrasted to the estuaries that are at least significantly influenced, if not dominated, by tides. The other important aspect of wave-dominated coasts is erosional, typically rocky and will be treated in Chapter 8.

Barrier islands come in a variety of sizes, shapes, and origins (Fig. 7.2). In general, they are elongate accumulations of sand that range from a kilometer or so to over a hundred kilometers in length. Some are barely above high tide, and others have dunes that rise tens of meters above the sea. Barrier islands occur throughout the world, from the north slope of Alaska to the tropics of South America and Australia. They are most prominent on stable, trailing edge and

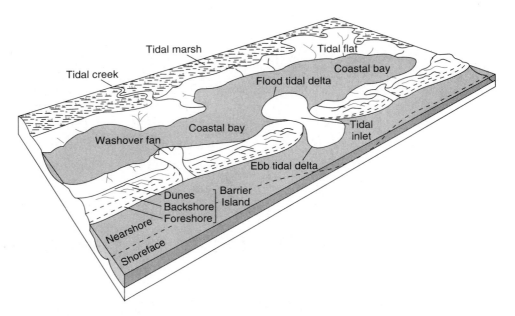

FIGURE 7.1
Schematic diagram of a barrier island system showing major environments.

marginal sea coasts but they are also present on some collision coasts such as on the Pacific coast of the United States, including Alaska.

Barrier islands may occupy virtually any geologic and tectonic setting if there is sediment available, processes to accumulate it, and a place where it can come to rest—a familiar set of requirements for coastal depositional environments. Given these constraints, tectonically active, leading edge coasts are not likely places for well-developed barriers. Even if sediment is available, and it is not always, the wave energy along these coasts tends to remove sediment. Additionally, there is little room for barriers along the generally steep nearshore of an irregular coast. Thus, the only common barriers along tectonically active coasts are short spits. These may, however, be quite common; along the Pacific coast of the United States there are nearly 100 such barrier spits at least a kilometer long.

Most well-developed barrier systems are on trailing edge coasts, where the inner shelf is gently sloping, wave energy is moderate to low, and sediment tends to abound. The Atlantic coast of the United States is essentially one continuous barrier island system from New Hampshire to Miami. Similar conditions may occur along the costs of marginal seas for similar reasons.

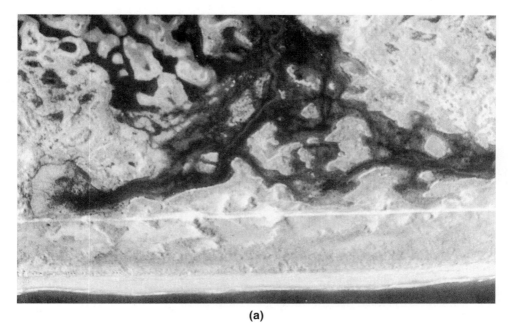

(a)

(b)

FIGURE 7.2
Oblique aerial photos of barrier islands on the a) Texas and b) South Carolina coast.

FORMATION OF BARRIER ISLANDS

The location and configuration of barrier islands give some clues about their origin. They are generally separated from the mainland by open water and are present seaward of a wide variety of coastal environments and morphologies that include estuaries, lagoons, rocky headlands, and gently sloping coastal plains. Apparently the majority of the sediment from which they are made could not have come directly from the landward direction but must have been derived from offshore, alongshore, or some combination thereof.

Another important aspect to be considered in the origin of barrier islands is their age. The present, active barrier islands are all Holocene in age, in fact, they are quite young. Nearly all are less than 7000 years, old and most were formed less than 4000 years ago. The dating part of their origin is rather straightforward; shells, wood, and other carbon-bearing material in the sediments provide radioactive carbon (^{14}C), which can be counted thereby providing a date of origin.

The formation of the barriers is not so straightforward. Three origins for barriers have been presented in the geologic literature, all in the mid- to late-nineteenth century. The first was proposed by a French geomorphologist, Ille de-Beaumont, in 1852. He advocated that waves caused sediment to accumulate in an upward shoaling scheme that eventually led to a supratidal sand bar that continued to accumulate sediment, became vegetated, stabilized, and formed a barrier island. A subsequent theory by McGee in 1890 proposed that coastal dune and beach ridges were drowned by rising water level leaving a strip of sand separated from the mainland by a narrow and shallow water body, also forming a barrier island. The third mode of origin is quite different and applies only to some barriers. In a 1885 publication Gilbert advocated formation of a spit emanating from a headland with eventual breaching at one or more places to form a barrier island with tidal inlets. This mode of occurrence is well documented in some parts of the world but because it requires a headland, most of the barriers of the Gulf of Mexico or of the Atlantic coast could not have formed in this manner. It is most common on the Pacific coast and in New England.

The purpose of this discussion is not to argue about the preferred interpretation of barrier island formation, however, a few comments on the first two modes of origin are warranted. Numerous very young barriers have formed during historical time documented by sequential aerial photography (Fig. 7.3). Many have developed according to the scheme of upward shoaling by wave action, whereas the only ones that have been demonstrated to result from drowning of a coastal beach–dune ridge or mainland detachment are in the Mississippi Delta area where land subsidence is rapid. In other locations it can be argued that sea-level rise has been too slow for any drowning of these ridges to occur in visually recordable history. The key here is that a slow rise in sea level will encourage either destruction or landward migration of the beach–dune ridges, not their drowning.

This brings us back to the question of why we have barrier islands along large sections of the coast. Remembering the discussion of sea-level rise since the

FIGURE 7.3
North Bunces Key, an example of a barrier that was formed on the Florida coast in less than a decade.

melting of the glaciers, for example, the Holocene transgression, provides some important clues. Sea-level rise curves show that the rate of rise was very rapid for several thousand years. This rapid rise probably did not provide a stable shoreline for enough time to develop a barrier island under any of the aforementioned scenarios, although some researchers would disagree.

At about 6000 to 7000 years before present the rate of sea-level rise slowed dramatically. In much of North America sea level was as much as 10 meters below its present position. Regardless of the absolute position of the shoreline relative to now, the rate of sea-level rise slowed to a maximum of about 1.4 millimeters per year, similar to the present rate in much of the United States. The slow rate of sea-level rise permitted enough time for waves and wave-generated currents to mold sediments into coast-parallel barrier islands, and permitted them to persist; some through slow landward migration as sea level rose but others were built vertically or prograded seaward from where they formed.

BEACH AND NEARSHORE

Most people visit or live along the coast to enjoy the beach. The constant change, interesting landscape, fascinating creatures, and the beautiful scenery always have captured peoples' attention. The beach acts as the seaward protection for the coast, whether it be a barrier island or the mainland. Coastal residents commonly observe many aspects of beach dynamics, especially the results of storms and seasonal or long-term changes.

A proper understanding of beaches must include the adjacent shallow marine waters generally called the nearshore environment. It includes the region that extends from the low tide line, the seaward extent of the beach, out across the surf zone and includes the sandbars that are common along most coasts (Fig. 7.4). The width and depth to which the nearshore extends ranges widely depending upon its slope, wave climate, and abundance of sediment. In many places there are rather persistent sandbars that parallel the beach and over which waves break during storms (Fig. 7.5). Although some nearshore areas may be essentially smooth and gently sloping, most are a combination of sand bars and intervening troughs.

The beach itself extends from the low tide line landward across the unvegetated sediment to the beginning of vegetation or to the next geomorphic feature in the landward direction, which may be a dune, a bedrock cliff, or nowadays a seawall (Fig. 7.6). The beach is the most actively changing part of the coast; each wave causes shifts in sediment. It is composed of all kinds and sizes of sediment from mud to large boulders. The typical sandy beach displays two or three different profile configurations. These shapes depend upon the presence and configuration of the major elements that comprise the beach, the foreshore, the backshore, and the storm ridge. The foreshore includes the intertidal zone and extends to the landward break in slope. It is typically gently sloping toward the sea and may display a small, ephemeral bar and trough variously called a ridge and runnel or a swash bar (Fig. 7.7). The foreshore includes the swash zone in which waves rush up and back as they meet the shoreline.

The backshore or backbeach extends from the foreshore across the remainder of the beach and generally is not covered with water. Only during storm surge conditions is the backbeach subjected to wave activity; most of the time it is subjected to wind. This portion of the beach is generally nearly horizontal or

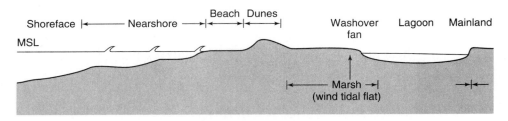

FIGURE 7.4
Profile diagram across the nearshore and barrier showing each of the major environments that are typically represented.
(From Davis, R. A., 1983, *Depositional Systems*, Prentice-Hall, Englewood Cliffs, New Jersey, p. 405)

FIGURE 7.5
Oblique photo of waves
breaking over longshore sand
bars on Mustang Island, Texas.

slightly landward sloping. After major periods of erosion it may be greatly reduced or even absent. Gravel beaches of shell and/or rock fragments commonly include a storm ridge that is just landward of the foreshore. This feature may rise several meters above high tide and can totally replace the typical backbeach. Its composition depends upon the nature of the gravel material in the immediate area, and its size is typically directly related to the rigor of the storms that produce it.

The overall profile of the beach and adjacent nearshore may be steep or gently sloping. This depends upon a variety of factors such as sediment supply, wave climate, overall slope of the inner shelf, and perhaps tidal range. Generally,

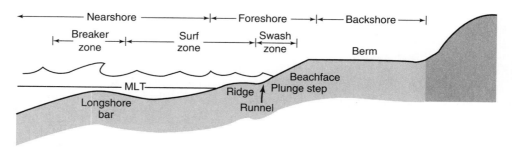

FIGURE 7.6
Beach profile showing major elements of a typical accretional beach.
(From Davis, R. A., 1985, *Coastal Sedimentary Environments,* Springer-Verlag, New York, p. 386)

FIGURE 7.7
Photograph of ridge and runnel adjacent to a beach on the Sand Key, Florida coast.

the steep beach either has poorly developed nearshore sand bars or none at all. Little wave energy is dissipated across the nearshore, thus waves reach the shore with a fair amount of energy. These are the characteristics of reflective beaches. The other end of the spectrum is the gently sloping beach in which energy is gradually lost as the waves move toward the shore. These are dissipative beaches. The intermediate beaches tend to exhibit good development of the nearshore bars and formation of rip channels.

Beach Materials

Nearly anything that can be transported by waves can form a beach (Fig. 7.8). Whatever is available will be incorporated as long as it can be carried to the beach and be at least temporarily stable there. Mud is uncommon because of the wave energy that characterizes beaches, but it does accumulate in large quantities on some beaches, for example, along the coast of Surinam on the northern coast of South America where huge quantities of fine sediment are made available by the Amazon River.

Gravel particles of virtually all sizes and compositions are fairly common on beaches given the correct set of circumstances—a readily available source and

FIGURE 7.8
Example of beach material showing different grain sizes and compositions.

generally a high wave climate. They may range from small pocket beaches between headlands on an otherwise rocky coast to beaches that extend for many kilometers. Those in the northern latitudes are typically composed of rock fragments from glacial deposits or stream accumulations or are directly eroded from bedrock. The gravel beaches that are associated with barrier islands are composed of shell gravel that is especially abundant in low latitudes where there is little other sediment available.

Most beaches are dominated by sand; generally quartz in composition but they may contain nearly any mineral. Some are composed of only one mineral or rock fragment type if that is the only material available. Examples include the black or green beaches of some Pacific Islands and the white, fine shell beaches of the Bahamas and southern Australia.

The interaction of waves and currents with beach sediments produces certain textural characteristics. It is possible to generalize about these characteristics, especially for sandy beaches. As a consequence of wave activity, a given beach or a portion thereof displays a narrow range of particle size (Fig. 7.9). This is called *good*

(a)

FIGURE 7.9
Examples of good sorting in beach sediment comprised of both a) biogenic and b)
terrigenous grains.

sorting. That is, the waves and their related processes arrange the sediment particles
in such a fashion that at any spot, one would expect to find sand grains that are
nearly the same size. The same is true for gravel beaches; they are also well sorted,
even though the absolute particle size is much larger than on sand beaches.

Beach Dynamics

The changes that take place on beaches range from the short-term ones, such as
when individual waves strike the shore, to those that are long-term, taking at
least decades. Likewise, the rate of change covers a very broad spectrum, to the
extreme erosional conditions caused by severe extratropical storms and hurricanes. Regardless of the rate or scope of the changes that take place along
beaches, there is some general level of predictability associated with each level of
change. There are various cycles that beaches experience including those related
to the tides and to the seasons of the year. The following discussion centers on

(b)

FIGURE 7.9 (*Cont.*)

the various levels of change, how they affect the beach, and what causes them. All of these cycles tend to be present on beaches regardless of where they occur—mainland, barrier island, rocky coast, or wave-dominated delta.

Beach Processes   Both waves and tides and the currents that they generate may influence both the sediment and morphology of beaches. The breaking of waves produces obvious interaction with beach sediment (Fig. 7.10); each crash of the wave places sediment in temporary suspension, the amount directly related to the size of the wave. This suspended sediment is then moved by currents, primarily wave-generated longshore currents (see Chapter 4). The role of tides and tidal currents on beaches is more subtle. As the tides cause a rise and fall in the water level, the shoreline moves, causing the influence of waves to move accordingly. The greater the tidal range, the wider the band of change in incident wave energy. Tidal currents themselves do not appear to have a significant effect on beaches because they are so slow in this area. Only at the mouth of tidal inlets are these currents important.

Currents produced by waves are among the most important processes that

FIGURE 7.10
Diagram of the surf zone
showing back and forth sediment
movement under waves.
(From Ingle, J. C., 1966, *The
Movement of Beach Sand*, Elsevier
Publishing Co., Amsterdam p. 53)

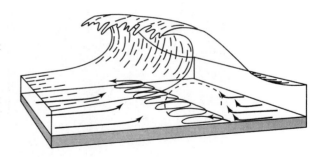

generate change in the beach. These include (1) combined flow currents, (2) longshore currents, (3) rip currents, and (4) the onshore–offshore currents produced in the swash zone. All occur in the surf zone and adjacent beach, and all are responsible or partially responsible for transport of sediment.

As waves propagate shoreward they are refracted, causing a vector of water movement along the shore that generates longshore currents. These currents can move in either direction along the beach, depending on the wave approach, and can range widely in their velocity, depending upon wave height and angle of approach; they may exceed 100 centimeters per second under storm conditions. The combination of waves stirring up sediment and the longshore current transporting it can move thousands of cubic meters of sediment in a day or two.

The shallow nearshore and commonly ephemeral sand bars that parallel the shoreline commonly have saddles or rip channels (Fig. 7.11). Rip currents that flow through these channels can also carry a modest amount of sediment (Fig. 7.12).

The other mechanism for sediment transport in this environment is on the swash zone where the uprush and backwash of the final breaking wave carries sediment across the foreshore. Depending upon wave conditions, slope of the foreshore, and sediment permeability, there may be a significant difference between the amount carried up the beach and that carried off the beach. One of the most important factors is permeability. With each wave a coarse and therefore permeable beach will experience a greater uprush of water than backwash. This is due to a portion of the water contained in the wave swash infiltrating into the sediment, limiting the return flow back in a seaward direction.

Beach Cycles   The general conditions of beach processes and their interaction with beach sediment can be considered in two distinctly different but common scenarios. The most prevalent condition is one in which wave conditions are about equal to or below the mean energy conditions. At most beaches this includes a swell wave with a low wave height (generally less than 1 m) and a period of 8 to 12 seconds. Locally generated sea waves may be superimposed with a similar or smaller height and a period of 3 to 6 seconds. The sum of these condi-

FIGURE 7.11
Oblique photo showing a saddle in a shallow nearshore sand bar; the location of rip
currents.

FIGURE 7.12
Large plume in the nearshore showing sediment transport in a rip current.

tions produces what is commonly called an *accretionary beach* because the dominant condition is one of deposition of sediment or stability; erosion is absent or quite limited (Fig. 7.13). The profile assumed by an accretional beach is one in which the backbeach is well-developed and wide with a relatively narrow foreshore. Nearshore sandbars display a relatively high amount of relief and are well-formed. This is a common configuration on most low-wave climate coasts such as the Gulf of Mexico and the Atlantic coasts of the United States.

The other condition is one of an erosive or storm beach (Fig. 7.14). Storms, although short in duration, are the dominant process along many coasts. During such conditions it is typically the increase in wind wave size that results in this dominance. These relatively steep waves cause considerable entrainment of sediment through combined flow motion and longshore sediment transport. Large quantities of sediment are in suspension, and the currents readily carry this sediment both offshore and alongshore. Additionally, the swash energy is high, and uprush and backwash are more extensive due to the large waves.

The result is removal of enough sediment from the beach to produce an erosional or storm profile. Such a profile is generally flat and featureless and has either a narrow backbeach or none at all, with most or all of the beach being in the foreshore portion. The post-storm beach typically contains a ridge and runnel

FIGURE 7.13
Photograph showing an example of an accretional beach.

FIGURE 7.14
Photograph of an erosional beach profile.

FIGURE 7.15
Photograph of ridge and runnel along a recently eroded beach.

(Fig. 7.15) in the lower foreshore. The nearshore sandbars and related troughs tend to display less relief and move offshore up to a few tens of meters. The beach itself commonly is covered with a veneer of heavy minerals that accumulate as a lag deposit as the result of concentration during removal of the light fraction of the sand. This is really a placer deposit in much the same fashion as gold is concentrated in streams.

The storm beach is a temporary condition and in the absence of successive storms the recovery period begins as the storm starts to wane. This recovery process is initiated by the return to low-energy wave conditions and an absence of strong longshore currents. Along most coasts rip currents tend to develop best during low-wave energy conditions, but the amount of sediment they transport seaward is small compared to wave and longshore current transport. As swell and small wind waves persist there is significant landward transport of sediment. The nearshore sandbars return to their original position and configuration. More obvious is the shoreward migration of the ridge that results from washover during a flooding tide (Fig. 7.16). The original, somewhat symmetrical bar becomes asymmetric with the steep side landward. Over a period that ranges from about two weeks to as much as three months, the ridge repairs the beach, and an accretional profile that resembles the pre-storm situation is created. There may be some net loss, or even some net gain, depending upon how much sediment was lost or gained through longshore transport during the storm.

At some places where beaches are strongly influenced by waves that approach parallel to the coast, rip currents are strong during high-energy conditions, and longshore transport is minimal. This condition is common along the Pacific coast and also occurs in northern New England.

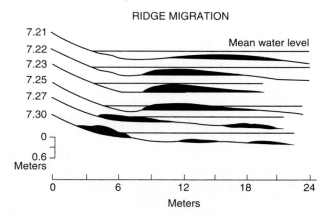

RIDGE MIGRATION

FIGURE 7.16
Diagram showing sequential migration of ridge and runnel as low energy conditions prevail after a storm.
(From Davis, R. A., et al, 1972, *Jour. Sed. Petrology,* 42, p. 416, Fig. 4)

The beach recovery process can be interrupted by storms that return the beach to an erosional condition. The somewhat closely spaced occurrence of these storms during the winter season has led to what is commonly called a *winter beach profile,* the same as a storm profile. If storms are frequent and severe, such as is common along the West Coast of the United States, the entire beach can be removed leaving a bedrock bench that is essentially devoid of sand. This condition may persist for a few months until the lower wave energy conditions of the spring and summer return sediment to the beach and eventually build an accretionary profile (Fig. 7.17). Good examples of this situation take place along the central Oregon coast and also in southern California.

This sequence of beach conditions is quite seasonal and predictable, and produces the most obvious cyclic sequence in the dynamics of the beach environment. Other less pronounced cycles are associated with the diurnal tidal cycles and also with monthly lunar cycles. In each there is slight change in the foreshore beach. As the tide rises and falls, the waves are permitted to impact on different parts of the foreshore. Likewise, during the lunar cycle, the neap tidal range produces a narrower range of wave impact on the swash zone than does the spring tidal range.

Although beaches are quite dynamic by nature, and there is a wide variety of beach locations, sediments, and sizes, there is a predictable pattern to their behavior and to their morphology. Likewise the sediment we find on the beach is typically well-sorted but with a wide range in grain size. We can learn much more about beach dynamics from observing a single beach over an extended period of time than we can from visiting numerous beaches each a single time.

DUNES

Sand dunes are an important part of many, but not all, coastal areas. These dunes are large piles of sand that accumulate from similar processes and in generally similar shapes and patterns as do the dunes on inland deserts. The fundamental prerequisites in both cases are a supply of sediment and the wind to move it. In the case of the coast, the wind is typically not a limiting factor although the sediment supply may be. Nevertheless, we have coasts in which dunes may exceed 100 meters in elevation (Fig. 7.18).

Coastal dunes are not restricted to barrier islands, although nearly all barriers have at least small dunes. Some coasts without barriers have tremendous dune fields. Particularly good examples are the southern coast of Oregon where the dunes extend a few kilometers inland from the coast and the southeastern part of Lake Michigan where dunes over 100 meters high have developed. Among the largest dunes in the world are those on the coast of Namibia in southwest Africa where barriers are absent.

(a)

(b)

FIGURE 7.17
Beach on the Oregon coast a) after sediment is removed in the winter and b) when it returns during the spring.
(Courtesy of William T. Fox)

FIGURE 7.18
Photo showing examples of very large coastal dunes along the eastern coast of Australia.

Dune Formation and Distribution

Any coast where sand accumulates has the potential to develop dunes. On most coasts prevailing winds or diurnal sea breezes provide the transport mechanism. Most areas have prevailing winds with some component that is onshore or shore-parallel, and in many areas the sea breeze may be a major factor, in fact, it is dominant along the southwest coast of Australia near Perth. In some places, such as along the New England coast, the dominant winds are the major factor in eolian sediment transport. Basically any dry part of the beach is subjected to eolian (wind) transport. The backbeach is especially susceptible to such processes because it is rarely wet. In fact, it is common for the backbeach to show various evidences of wind transport including ripples, sand shadows (Fig. 7.19), and heavy minerals or gravel lag concentrates. The sand shadows indicate a recent wind direction and may show scour around a shell or pebble. The gravel lag deposit is caused by wind blowing the fine sand from the beach and leaving the larger particles that cannot be transported. After a while the large particles become quite concentrated and actually form almost a pavement. Such a pavement inhibits further wind erosion and is called *desert armor* because of its importance in protection from wind erosion.

Much of the wind-blown beach sand tends to accumulate just landward of

FIGURE 7.19
Photo showing sand shadows
and shell lag on the backbeach.

the active backbeach. It is stopped from further transport by any type of obstruction that may be present, including bedrock cliffs, vegetation, existing dunes, or even human construction such as buildings or sea walls. Once the accumulation of eolian sediment begins, it continues unless conditions change, such as loss of sediment supply or the destruction of the stabilizing factor.

One of the best and most widespread aids in dune development is vegetation. Any type of plant serves as a focus for anchoring wind-blown sediment. Typically, the relatively inactive backbeach is covered with opportunistic plants such as the beach morning glory, beach *Spinifex*, and marram grass (Fig. 7.20). One of the most effective dune stabilizers on southern dunes, up to the latitude of Virginia, is sea oats (*Uniola*), while the American beach grass (*Ammophila*) extends from Virginia up to Nova Scotia in Canada. It is quite common to see small piles of sand around isolated plants on this part of the beach. After only months, these piles increase in size and the plants spread, thus increasing their effectiveness. In fact, even pieces of wood or any other sizable obstacle can act as a seed for dune development. Eventually small dunes or coppice mounds are present.

Such small incipient dunes are quite vulnerable; even a modest storm can destroy them, requiring the building process to begin again. This is the reason

FIGURE 7.20
Opportunistic backbeach vegetation and small coppice mounds; the precursors to dunes.

that so much attention is paid to preserving vegetation on the backbeach and at the foot of the dunes. Absence of intense storms along with an abundant supply of sand and a regular mechanism for sand delivery eventually produces a dune. Dune size depends largely on the supply of appropriate sediment.

The typical configuration of dunes just landward of the beach is a linear arrangement that is essentially one dune wide. This dune ridge is called the *foredune* because of its location in the seaward or front of the barrier or the mainland as the case may be (Fig. 7.21). Many coasts contain numerous parallel dune ridges, each of which developed immediately landward of the active beach as a foredune ridge. The presence of several dune ridges indicates the portion of the coast that has had a history of growth or progradation toward the sea (Fig. 7.22). This is the desired condition for any coast because it indicates an overall lack of erosion. Dunes are about the best protection we have against severe storms and their related large surges. Some barrier islands contain a complicated assortment of dune ridge arrangements that show sets of ridges at acute angles to one another. This condition indicates periods of erosion that separated periods of dune accumulation and barrier progradation.

Not all barrier island dunes are located adjacent to or are associated with the beach. Like those near the beach, their presence depends on an abundant

FIGURE 7.21
Photo of foredune ridge along 90 Mile Beach on the Victoria coast of Australia.

FIGURE 7.22
Oblique aerial photo of multiple dune ridges formed as the coast prograded seaward, Victoria, Australia.

sand supply and a means to move and accumulate it. In most instances one of two conditions leads to landward dune development on the coast—a tremendous sediment supply or an absence of stabilizing vegetation. Probably the best example of extreme abundance of sand is found along the coast of southern Oregon. Here the strong winds off the Pacific along with great amounts of sand have produced huge mobile dunes that extend 3 to 4 kilometers inland. These coastal dunes have inundated forests of mature trees as they migrate in a southerly direction perpendicular to the coast. Similar conditions exist elsewhere, for example, at Dauphin Island, Alabama, at Kitty Hawk, North Carolina, and Horseneck Beach, Massachusetts.

Generally subarid conditions in addition to abundant sand along the beaches have resulted in an extensive active dune complex in the Padre Island National Seashore, Texas, on the central part of the island. Extensive cattle grazing on the island during the late nineteenth and early twentieth century helped create these conditions. This portion of the Texas coast is one of considerable sediment accumulation and persistent onshore winds. As a result, the island is extremely wide, and the mainland is dominated by an extensive dune complex. The barrier itself contains extensive active dunes that range from being only a meter or so high on the landward side near Laguna Madre, to several meters high in the central island. The limited development of the dunes on the landward part of the island is due to their destruction from storm surge associated with hurricanes. These small dunes are on the wind tidal flats where storm surges of a meter or so are fairly common and can flood the dunes, destroying them by a combination of waves and currents. After the surge subsides, the wind and available sand must start again to construct the dunes.

Dune Dynamics

The existence of dunes is testimony to how sand can be transported by wind on the coast. Attack by waves is an obvious factor in dune stability. Although vegetation is an effective stabilizer of these accumulations, there are conditions in which even vegetated dunes may become mobile (Fig. 7.23) or eroded.

The first and most obvious factor is the attack by waves. Even though dunes are out of the regular influence of waves, they are quite vulnerable even to only modest surge produced by storms. In areas of generally erosive beach conditions, dune retreat is a particular problem because there is no backbeach to protect them. Elevated water level with superimposed storm waves produces swash and in some cases, direct wave attack, at the base of the dune. The sand is easily washed away and carried both offshore and alongshore. Even though a dense dune grass cover is present, the sand is easily removed, commonly leaving a dense root system hanging over the scarp in the dune. Post-storm recovery may occur and return some, or even all, of the sand to the beach. Proper conditions can start the rebuilding process of the dune but it can take many years to

FIGURE 7.23
Large, mobile coastal dunes on the New South Wales coast of Australia.

restore the loss of just a single storm. It is generally rather easy to recognize dunes that have been eroded and then rebuilt by their profile change and perhaps even by their type of vegetation. By providing continual increase in the accessibility of the dunes to wave attack, rising sea level presents another scenario for dune erosion.

The other major aspect of dune dynamics is concerned with the migration of part or all of the dune through eolian processes. The same mechanism that forms the dune also can cause it to move, sometimes great distances. Generally dune mobility is associated with an absence of vegetation. Climatic conditions may reduce or eliminate vegetative cover, or overgrazing may remove much of the vegetation. Regardless of the reason, the result is the same—sediment begins to move.

The most common process for dune migration is called *blowover*. The onshore wind component simply carries sand across the dune surface and permits it to move down the landward side by gravity. This creates a relatively steep slope called the *angle of repose,* generally about 30 degrees (Fig. 7.24). In other words, the sand is able to maintain a slope of this gradient as it migrates landward. This is true for all dunes regardless of their location or direction of migration. The sed-

FIGURE 7.24
Steep landward side of migrating coastal dunes that are transgressing over a forest on the coast of Spain.

iment may move as the result of individual grains rolling down the steep slope or as the result of grain flow. This is a type of sediment gravity process whereby oversteepening of the slope causes an instability that results in large numbers of grains moving down the slope in an avalanche fashion (Fig. 7.24). Anyone who has walked down a dune face has seen this phenomenon take place as the dune is disturbed. Migration of large dunes pays little attention to trees, buildings, or whatever is in its path as long as the dune is larger that the obstruction it will move over. Houses have been buried and then many years later exumed as a result of migrating dunes.

OTHER BARRIER ISLAND COMPONENTS

Although the beach and dune environments are the ones we most commonly associate with barrier islands and the seashore in general, there are other important parts of a barrier system. A look at a profile of a barrier island or at an aerial photograph shows that there is generally a fair amount of area between the dunes and whatever the water body might be on the landward side of the barrier. Most of the landward portion of the barrier area is rather flat and only slightly above sea level. It typically continues with little change in profile across the back part of the island to a marsh and eventually to a tidal flat along the margin of the coastal bay that separates the island from the mainland. This flat, landward portion of the barrier is readily divisible into at least three distinct environments based upon vegetation and elevation relative to mean sea level.

Washover Fans

Virtually all of the sediment on which these environments have developed, however, was originally deposited by one mechanism and accumulated in one type of sediment body—washover fans (Fig. 7.25). Washover fans are thin, individually fan-shaped wedges of sand that are deposited during intense storm conditions when all or part of the beach–dune system is overtopped by waves and storm surge. On some barriers the individual fans coalesce to form a washover apron. The sediment accumulations that represent a single storm range up to about a meter in thickness but are more commonly few tens of centimeters. On narrow islands or under conditions of very high energy, the fans may extend completely across the island and into the adjacent coastal bay (Fig. 7.26). Fan sediments are primarily sand with some shell and are generally well-stratified in near horizontal layers.

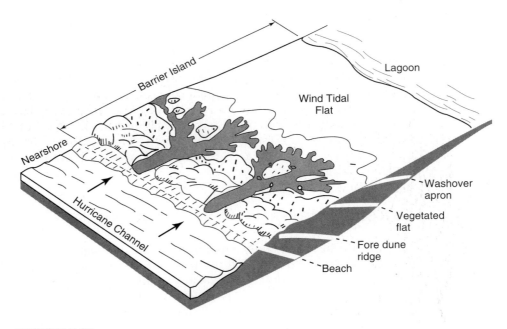

FIGURE 7.25
Diagram showing washover fan and its sub-environments on the back-barrier area.
(From Scott, A. J. et al, 1969, Effects of Hurricane Beulah, 1967, on Texas lagoons and barriers, *UNAM-UNESCO Symposium on Coastal Lagoons,* Mexico City, pp. 221–236)

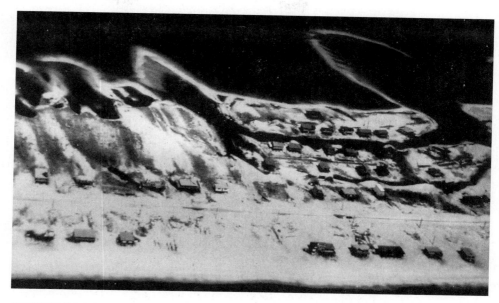

FIGURE 7.26
Aerial photo showing washover fan extending into the back-barrier bay, Dauphin Island, Alabama.
(Courtesy of Dag Nummedal)

The sediment that accumulates in the washovers comes from the surf zone, beach, or even dunes and is carried by the combination of waves and undirectional currents that overtop low barriers and travel relatively low paths. Many barriers have foredune systems that are too high to permit washover to take place. It is this condition that demonstrates dune protection for the more landward portion of the barrier.

The vegetation in the landward part of the barrier tends to be fairly resilient. Complete or partial burial by washover fans typically has only a modest effect, and the upland or marsh grasses that live here grow up through the fan sediment in several weeks to a few months (Fig. 7.27). The very thick fans may completely destroy the underlying plant community but the opportunistic nature of barrier island vegetation colonizes their surfaces in generally less than a year, depending upon climate. Even after the washover fan is completely vegetated, its general shape is detectable from aerial photographs, especially if there has been incursion into the bay on the landward side (Fig. 7.28).

It is the postdepositional phase of the washover fans that is fairly complicated. Once the fan has been deposited, it soon begins to be transformed. Partially buried plants penetrate upward through the fan, and the downward penetration of roots from surface plants causes disruption of the typically well-developed stratification of fan sediments. The part of the fan that extends into

FIGURE 7.27
Photo showing partial burial of vegetation by washover fan. Typically the vegetation is resilient and will grow up through the fan eventually causing it to lose its definition.

FIGURE 7.28
Relict washover fan that extends into the bay on the Delaware coast but is vegetated.
(Courtesy of J. C. Kraft)

the intertidal zone or below is also rapidly occupied by a broad spectrum of benthic organisms that include marsh grasses and burrowing organisms. Bioturbation also destroys the stratification signature of the washover fan and contributes a small amount of fine sediment through the accumulation of fecal pellets. Additionally, the tidal and wave processes that act on the distal end of the fan cause sediment to be reworked. All of these processes may transform the package of sediment that was deposited as a washover fan into environments such as tidal flats, marshes, wind tidal flats, and back-island areas that have little or no resemblance to the original depositional character of a washover fan.

Tidal Inlets and Tidal Deltas

Barrier islands do not continue without interruption. They are cut at various locations by tidal inlets that are the most important link between the open marine environment and the environments landward of barrier islands. After beaches, the tidal inlets are probably the most dynamic part of the barrier island system. Along many coasts where they occur, inlets may range widely in size, stability, and water flux. They owe their origin to a variety of circumstances with storms and human activity among the most important.

Elements of Tidal Inlets There are basically three major parts to a tidal inlet: (1) the inlet throat, the channel between the adjacent barrier islands and through which the tidal flux passes, (2) the ebb tidal delta, and (3) the flood tidal delta (Fig. 7.29). Tidal deltas are accumulations of sand that vary greatly in size and shape and that are located at the landward and seaward end of the inlet channel. They have many similarities to a fluvial delta in that they are caused by a sudden loss of the ability of currents to carry sediment at the end of a channel, resulting in accumulation of sediment. Because of tidal flow, the short inlet channel has a mouth at each end.

The main channel of the inlet is essentially as long as the width of the barrier island through which it cuts. It is deepest at the narrowest part, usually near the middle of its length, and the cross section commonly shows some asymmetry that typically has the deep side in the direction of the net longshore transport. The amount of asymmetry is generally proportional to the stability of the inlet; the more it migrates the more likely the channel is to be asymmetrical. Some quite stable inlets may have nearly symmetrical channels. The size of inlets ranges from only tens of meters to a few kilometers in width and up to depths of more than 30 meters.

Much of our terminology and understanding of the morphodynamics of tidal inlets and especially tidal deltas, comes from the work of Miles O. Hayes and his students who have provided most of the pioneering work on the dynamics of inlet systems in the late 1960s and early 1970s.

The two types of tidal deltas are best considered separately because they are

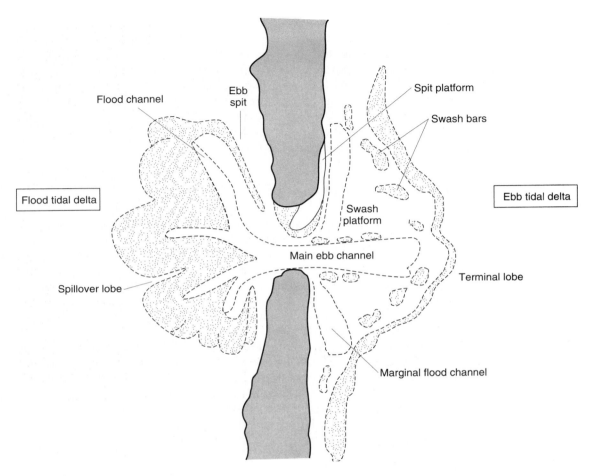

FIGURE 7.29
General diagram of a tidal inlet and its associated tidal deltas.
(From Davis, R. A. and Gibeaut, J. C., 1990, Historical morphodynamics of inlets in Florida; models for coastal zone planning, *Florida Sea Grant College Program, Tech. Paper 55,* Gainesville, Florida, p. 6, fig. 3)

quite different. The flood tidal delta develops on the landward side of the inlet in the coastal bay (Fig. 7.30). Because of location, this tidal delta is protected from significant wave influence; tidal currents are the primary physical process to which it is subjected. The shape of flood deltas varies a fair amount. In general, they are fan- or horseshoe-shaped with a broad ramp that slopes up to the surface on the seaward end. This ramp is a shallowing continuation of the inlet channel and carries sediment to the tidal delta during flood tides.

Tidal range and surface elevation of the flood delta strongly influence the outer shape of the sediment body. Along coasts in which tidal range is about a meter or less, the shape of the flood delta tends to be multi-lobate reflecting its

FIGURE 7.30
Aerial photo of a multilobate flood tidal delta at Chatham Harbor, Massachusetts.
(Courtesy of A. C. Hine)

original configuration, especially for those produced by storms (Fig. 7.30). The sediment bodies that comprise these tidal deltas are typically no more than 2 to 3 meters thick. Because of the low tidal range, tidal currents are not restricted in their flow and generally move back and forth without modifying the tidal delta. Eventually many such flood deltas become vegetated and further stabilized.

In areas in which tidal range is at least 1.5 meters, flood tidal deltas typically have a different appearance because tidal currents are strong and sediment transport is relatively high compared to the areas of lower tidal range (Fig. 7.31). Here the tidal range causes ebbing tidal currents to be deflected around the lobes of the flood delta. This, along with the regular addition of sediment across the flood ramp, produces a sand body with at least a modest amount of relief. The outer part of the tidal delta is smoothed by the ebbing currents, which carry some sediment and deposit it in the form of ebb spits, and breaches may form in the high part of the flood delta forming spillover lobes. The overall configuration of this diagram resembles the outline of a horseshoe crab.

Ebb tidal deltas exhibit greater variation than flood deltas because they are

FIGURE 7.31

Diagram of a mesotidal flood tidal delta, including its major components.
(After Hayes, M. O., 1975, *Estuarine Research*, Academic Press, New York, 2, pp. 3–22)

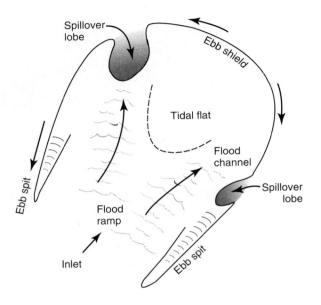

exposed to open water waves (Fig. 7.32). This additional complication provides for great variety in the amounts of physical energy to which the tidal delta is subjected and the directions from which it comes. Assuming that a substantial sediment supply is available, the controlling factors in the size and shape of the ebb tidal delta are the tidal currents and their interaction with wave-generated processes. The tidal currents are largely controlled by the tidal prism, the amount of water that moves in and out of the inlet during each flood, and the ebb cycle of the tide. This water volume is based on the product of the tidal range and the area of open water in the back-barrier area served by the inlet. The time period involved is restricted to a little over 6 hours for flood and ebb if tides are semidiurnal, but the amount of water entering and leaving (the tidal prism) varies greatly. The more water that must move through the inlet in the given time period, the faster it has to flow.

The three general types of ebb deltas are tide-dominated, mixed energy, and wave-dominated (Fig. 7.33). The tide-dominated ones tend to protrude into the sea at essentially right angles with well-developed sandbars along the margins. The mixed energy ebb deltas have a generally smoothed and arcuate sandbar, and the wave-dominated ebb deltas have very little sediment accumulated at all.

Any one of these conditions can develop over a rather broad spectrum of tidal ranges because the tidal prism is the key factor here. For example, the western Gulf Coast of Florida experiences less than 1 meter of tidal range throughout yet it contains all types of ebb tidal deltas. The reason is that some of these inlets

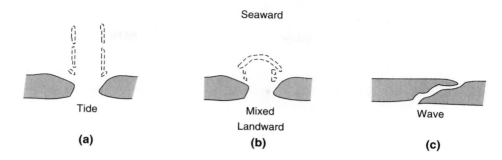

FIGURE 7.32
Diagrams of each of the three main types of ebb tidal deltas: a) tide-dominated, b) mixed energy, and c) wave-dominated.

serve very large bays that provide large prisms, whereas others interact with only small bays or even share the prism of a bay with other inlets.

Inlet Dynamics   There is far more to tidal inlets than tidal currents simply moving in and out carrying a bit of sediment. Typically, a large amount of sediment is transported in the littoral system on the open coast by longshore currents. When this sediment reaches the inlet mouth, it may bypass the inlet, it may be deposited in the ebb tidal delta, or flood currents may carry it into the inlet and deposit the sediment on the flood delta. The size, shape, and location of the inlet experience changes that result from these conditions and also from variation in the amount of water that flows through the inlet during tidal exchange. Intense storms may also cause quite severe changes that can take place in only hours or a few days. All of these phenomena bring about change, typically in a time frame that is geologically short, days to decades.

We can categorize the mechanisms of inlet change into three areas— storms, tidal prism, and littoral sediment transport. Each is important and worthy of some consideration but typically at least two of these processes work together to bring about inlet changes. Because storms are the most rapid mechanism for change we will start there.

Storms   Many tidal inlets owe their origin to intense storms and others have been greatly modified by these events (Fig. 7.34). Low and narrow barriers are quite vulnerable to washover that might lead to excavation of a channel and eventually to a permanent tidal inlet. Several examples are present on the peninsular Gulf Coast of Florida where both hurricanes and low barriers are common. The most severe hurricanes in historical time on this coast occurred in 1848 and 1921; both breached barriers to form permanent inlets. Johns Pass, which separates the southern end of Sand Key from Treasure Island near St. Petersburg, was formed by the hurricane of 1848 and has remained a relatively stable inlet.

(a)

(b)

FIGURE 7.33
Photos of a) tide-dominated, b) mixed energy, and c) wave-dominated ebb tidal deltas.

190

(c)

FIGURE 7.33   (*Cont.*)

Redfish Pass near Ft. Myers, and Hurricane Pass near Clearwater, were both formed during the hurricane in October 1921. Both are naturally stabilized and carry rather large tidal prisms.

Probably the best documentation of the formation and development of a storm-generated tidal inlet was gained by Hurricane Elena, which occurred on Labor Day weekend in 1985. This was a modest storm that did not have landfall along the peninsular Gulf Coast of Florida although it passed close enough to have some influence. Wave size peaked at a height of 2.5 meters and a 13-second period with a storm surge of about 1.5 meters. This was enough to over-wash several areas along the coast in the Tampa Bay area, and in particular, the narrow, northern end of Caladesi Island near Clearwater. The island here was only about 1 meter above high tide and less that 50 meters wide. A huge washover fan was produced that extended hundreds of meters into St. Joseph Sound behind the barrier (Fig. 7.35). Initially only a small tidal flow was able to pass through the washover channel, but it grew rapidly. In three months there was a channel a meter deep and about 30 meters wide. By the end of a year it was over 2 meters deep and nearly 80 meters wide but asymmetrical toward the north. Subsequently the prism of this new inlet was reduced by the formation of another nearby inlet, and it closed in 1991.

FIGURE 7.34
Photo of storm-generated inlet, Redfish Pass, between North Captiva and Captiva Islands, Florida.

Storms can also open inlets from the landward side of the barrier in a seaward direction. A very high storm surge causes the bays to fill far above their normal capacity—commonly meters above normal high tide. Low places in barriers, especially closed former inlets, provide a path of least resistance for the escape of some of this water. A good example took place at Corpus Christi Pass near the boundary between Mustang and Padre Islands on the Texas coast during Hurricane Beulah in 1967. The inlet has been closed for several years, with sediment filling more than half of the length of the old inlet. This storm flushed the sediment into the Gulf of Mexico, producing a straight inlet with a channel nearly 2 meters deep. In less than 10 years the channel was filled to essentially its pre-storm configuration.

The depth of the inlet may be restricted by the geology of the underlying strata. Resistant bedrock will not permit further downcutting. Another factor that often comes into play is the armoring of the channel floor by large gravel clasts or shells. These large particles accumulate as lag deposits similar to those on the backbeach. In the inlet, currents carry the mud, sand and fine gravel away, but the large particles remain, either because of their mass, or in the case of some bivalve shells, because their shape provides stability. Once the inlet floor is paved with these large particles, further downcutting is not possible.

Tidal Prism   The flux of water through the inlet is the primary factor in its maintenance. The interaction of waves with tides at the seaward end of the inlet is the controlling factor in determining the size and stability of the inlet. For pur-

(a)

(b)

FIGURE 7.35
Aerial photos of a) pre- and b) post-Elena conditions showing initiation of a tidal inlet, Willy's Cut, located on Caladesi Island, Florida.

poses of discussion, we will assume that wave conditions do not change greatly and that the primary variable in the inlet processes is tidal prism. Generally, large tidal prisms produce stable inlets (Fig. 7.36a), and small prisms lead to unstable inlets that migrate (Fig. 7.36b) and sometimes close.

Large prisms create strong currents that flow essentially perpendicular to the coast. These strong currents may erode the channel, increasing its size until equilibrium between tidal flux and inlet size is achieved. As long as the inlet cross-section increases or remains essentially constant, the inlet generally will not migrate and will remain stable in its location. Under some conditions when constant tidal prism inlets maintain their cross-sectional area, they do migrate due to a persistent longshore transport of sediment.

If the prism is small, tidal currents are generally weak. Longshore currents can carry sediment along the barrier and deposit it as a spit at the end of the barrier adjacent to the inlet. Continued and rapid accumulation of sediment by this process will lead to migration of the inlet, in some cases more than a kilometer. These unstable conditions can lead to eventual closure of the inlet. The composition of the inlet banks and the net rate of longshore sediment transport are the major factors in the rate of inlet migration.

It is the tidal prism that exerts ultimate control on inlet stability. Although tidal range generally does not change, other factors can cause either an increase or decrease in tidal prism at a given inlet but a decrease in prism is most common. It may be caused by human activities such as construction or by natural changes and can be either quite slow or rapid. If the bay being served by the inlet is an estuary with significant sediment influx from numerous sources, it will decrease in area slowly as the estuary fills in. The effect on the inlet will be quite slow, as long as centuries. The more drastic natural change in inlet stability is caused by closing or opening adjacent tidal inlets. Many barrier island systems along trailing edge coasts have multiple inlets connected through the back-barrier water bodies. In fact, some adjacent inlets share the tidal prism, with one being more flood-dominated and the other being more ebb-dominated in tidal flux. In other words, what goes in during a flood cycle of a particular inlet does not necessarily come out during the subsequent ebb cycle. If a new inlet is opened on a barrier by a storm, the tidal prism carried by the inlet must come from somewhere. In fact, it is captured from the previously existing adjacent inlet or inlets (Fig. 7.37). In the event that the amount of prism taken by the new inlet is sufficient to maintain a channel, the inlet will be stable and persist. Most such storm-generated inlets tend to have only small prism and are commonly unstable and ephemeral. Hurricane Allen in 1980 cut over 50 channels through Padre Island in Texas but none remained open for more than a year.

The opposite condition can also occur. When an inlet is closed, the prism that it was carrying is transferred to an adjacent inlet. Most inlet closure is fairly gradual so that this transfer is slow and unnoticed. In the event that an inlet is closed by a storm, the transfer of tidal prism is more abrupt and may cause the associated inlet to expand fairly rapidly.

(a)

(b)

FIGURE 7.36
Photo showing examples of a) a stable tidal inlet and b) an unstable, migrating tidal inlet.

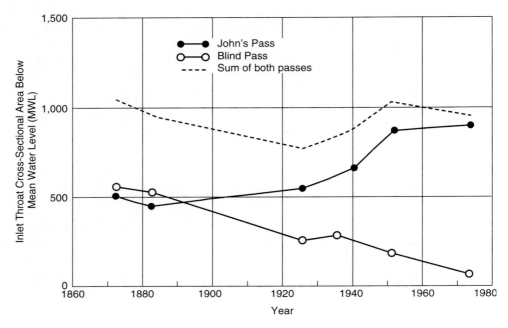

FIGURE 7.37
Graph showing changes in cross-section of Johns Pass and Blind Pass through time.
(From Mehta, A. H. et al, 1976, Johns Pass and Blind Pass, *Glossary of Inlets Rept., Florida Sea Grant Program, Rept 18,* Gainseville, Florida)

Littoral Sediment Transport

Wave-generated longshore currents may carry a large volume of sediment in the littoral system, especially under elevated wave conditions during a storm. Storms cause the volume and rate of transport to increase thereby making it difficult for the tidal inlet to adjust to the volume of sediment that passes by the mouth of the inlet. Changes in tidal prism provide the inlet with either the greater or lesser ability to do so.

Under conditions of a large tidal prism, the increase in sediment flux along the coast will accumulate near the mouth of the inlet in the ebb tidal delta. Continuation of this scenario will mean that the tidal delta will become larger and larger, eventually bypassing some of the sediment around the mouth of the inlet. If the rate of sediment flux decreases, the ebb delta will decrease in size as long as the wave climate remains the same. Under similar conditions of littoral sediment supply, inlets with small tidal prism will migrate and close with the rate of closure dependent upon the rate of sediment supply. In this scenario little sediment will be incorporated into the ebb tidal delta and will bypass the inlet or be incorporated in the spit as it moves to close the inlet.

In some cases, there is a balance between sediment supply and tidal prism that permits the inlet to maintain essentially its same cross-sectional area but to migrate along the coast. In fact, some inlets may move great distances under these conditions. Midnight Pass near Sarasota, Florida, moved in this fashion for 3 kilometers, mostly during the nineteenth century. What generally happens under this condition is that the narrow spit that forms on the seaward side of the barrier is breached by a storm and the inlet follows a new path (Fig. 7.38). This occurred at Midnight Pass as the result of the 1921 hurricane, the same one that formed the inlets mentioned previously.

BARRIER ISLAND DYNAMICS

To really understand the dynamic nature of various components of a barrier island, it is necessary to consider how the entire system works rather than to look at each major element. This is especially important now that there is great concern about the increase in the rate of sea-level rise. Such increases will have dramatic effects on all coasts, but especially on barrier islands.

Like previously discussed parts of the coast, the systematic study of barriers is a fairly recent phenomenon. One of the first papers that considered their dynamics appeared in 1934 and dealt with the New Jersey coast. Since the 1950s there has been an explosion of research into the nature and morphodynamics of barrier islands. The majority of this research initially was conducted by oil companies for use in developing exploration strategies in the ancient stratigraphic record. More recently, there has been considerable attention from the science and engineering community for purposes of coastal management.

Moving Barriers

From the earlier discussion about beaches, dunes, and washover fans, it is evident that considerable sediment is carried from beaches and dunes to the back of the barrier and deposited as washover fans. If this scenario continues over an extended period of time we will have a landward displacement of the barrier in a conveyor belt type of condition. It is this broad condition that causes great concern about a rapid rise in sea level. Such a sea-level rise will make barriers ever more vulnerable to this type of landward movement. The more rapid sea level rises, the easier it is for storms to overtop the barrier and carry sediment landward.

This overall condition of landward-moving barrier islands is called transgression; the island is transgressing over back-barrier environments in its landward movement. We can see evidence of barrier transgression by looking at the beach and surf zone in many areas. The presence of peat, tree stumps, oyster shells, layers of fine-grained organic mud (Fig. 7.39), and other features are all

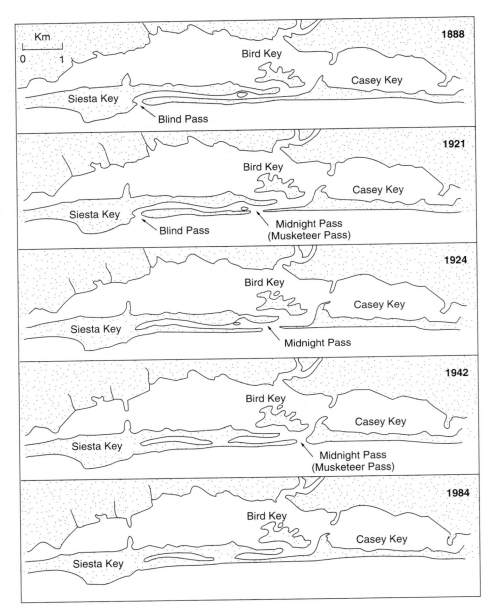

FIGURE 7.38
Diagrams showing long migration of Midnight Pass on the Florida Gulf Coast during the 19th century.
(From Davis, R. A. et al, 1987, Midnight Pass, Florida: inlet instability due to man-related activities in Little Sarasota Bay, Coastal Sediments '87, *Amer. Soc. Civil Engr.*)

FIGURE 7.39
Photo of a transgressive barrier showing marsh deposits in the surf zone.
(Reproduced by permission of ASCE.)

representative of deposition in a quiet water, protected, back-barrier environment such as a marsh. We can be certain that they did not accumulate in the surf zone in which they are now found. This is proof that the sandy environments of beaches, dunes, and washovers are moving landward over older, back-barrier environments.

As the barrier transgresses it may lose some of the sand-sized sediment by leaving it behind in the nearshore or inner shelf, particularly if sea level is rising. Unless more sand is made available, largely through longshore transport, the barrier is likely to be destroyed before it reaches the mainland. If it does reach the mainland, it will merge much like the migration and welding to the beach that takes place in a ridge and runnel system after a storm. There will, of course, be a major difference in scale. Examples of this condition include the eastern shore of Virginia, some locations in the Georgia Bight area of South Carolina and Georgia, and on the West coast of Florida.

There is at least one good example of barrier coasts in which sea level is already rising quite fast—the Mississippi Delta area. Conditions there and the plight of the barriers can be used to learn a great deal about how a rapidly rising sea level will affect barriers in other areas. To this end, a cooperative study of these barriers has been completed by the U.S. Geological Survey and the Louisiana Geological Survey. They have found that some of the barriers developed on abandoned lobes of the Mississippi Delta are transgressing landward at rates of meters per year due to the combination of low elevations, rapidly rising sea level, and frequent washover from storms. They are also becoming smaller as they transgress. In fact, many of these barriers are fragmenting through over-wash more than they are moving landward due to the rapid rate of local sea-level rise. A good example of this situation is the Chandeleur Islands off the Louisiana coast.

Barriers also may grow in a seaward direction by the addition of sediment. This condition is called *progradation* and is quite different than transgression in that the barrier does not move as a whole. The addition of sediment causes multiple beach/dune ridge systems to develop and the open water shoreline actually moves seaward; the landward, back-barrier shoreline remains in place. Conditions that produce a prograding barrier must include an abundant supply of sediment. Sea level can rise, fall, or remain static, the important factor is the more sediment is delivered to the beach and dune system than can be carried away either alongshore or over the barrier.

An individual barrier island can actually experience both conditions of transgression and progradation at the same time. This requires that sediment made available to the barrier is not uniformly delivered along its extent by waves and longshore currents. Most of the sediment is trapped at one end of the island, and the other end suffers a deficit of sediment. The result is that the end of the island receiving sediment progrades (Fig. 7.40) and the sediment-starved end transgresses. Good examples are Caladesi Island and Cayo Costa Island on the Florida Gulf Coast.

FIGURE 7.40
Progradational barrier with parallel prograding beach ridges.

Resulting Types

The interaction of the various coastal processes with the sediment available produces variety in the shape of barrier islands. The development of barriers depends upon a prominent, if not dominating, influence of waves over tides. Regardless of the specifics on the origin of barriers, their presence depends upon waves and wave-generated currents to produce the linear accumulation of sediments that comprise barriers. When tides become the dominant process along a coast, barrier islands give way to tidal flats and coastal marshes. These are the conditions that exist in the corner of the German Bight on the North Sea Coast of Europe and also on the open coast of the Florida peninsula north of the Tampa Bay Area and near the Everglades.

There are two general forms that barrier islands take. One is a long and generally narrow barrier that owes its shape to distinctly wave-dominated conditions (Fig. 7.41). The other type is a relatively short barrier having one end much wider than the other. This configuration results from a combination of both and wave- and tide-generated processes. Wave-dominated barriers are long and narrow, inlets are small and typically unstable, and washover fans are abundant. These are likely to be transgressive in nature, however, if abundant sediment is

FIGURE 7.41
Aerial photograph of an example of a wave-dominated barrier island showing the typical long and narrow shape.

available, multiple and essentially parallel dune ridges may develop. The Outer Banks of North Carolina and the barriers of the Texas coast are good examples of wave-dominated barriers.

The longshore currents produced by refracting waves carry great quantities of sediment along the coast. This factor, in combination with a typically low tidal prism in the inlets, causes inlet migration through spit development at the end of the barriers. It is possible that over a long period of time, centuries at least, the direction of littoral drift may change. This produces inlets that move back and forth, filling in behind them as they migrate. The unstable nature of the inlets also means that some will close. Storms may breach the low and narrow barriers creating new tidal inlets.

Mixed energy barriers have been named "drumstick barriers" by Miles Hayes because of their resemblance to the drumstick piece of a chicken (Fig. 7.42). The range in sediment supply and width of the barrier results from the interaction of the inlet and the barrier. In mixed energy inlets there is generally a

FIGURE 7.42
Diagram showing the morphodynamics of drumstick barriers.
(After Hayes, M. O., 1979, In *Barrier Islands, from the Gulf of Mexico to the St. Lawrence Seaway,* Academic Press, New York, p. 17, fig. 12A)

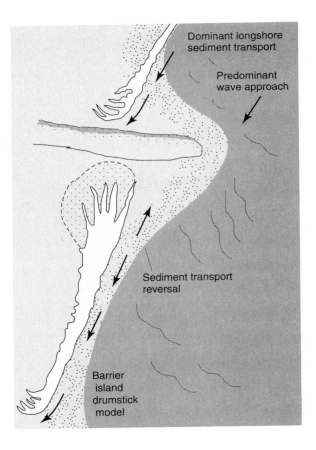

Dominant longshore sediment transport

Predominant wave approach

Sediment transport reversal

Barrier island drumstick model

modest and arcuate ebb tidal delta that protrudes into the sea. As waves approach this shallow accumulation of sediment, they are refracted around it. This refraction pattern actually causes a local reversal in the longshore current and thus in sediment transport. It is this mechanism that traps sediment at one end of the island while essentially starving the other. The sediment is generally in the form of intertidal swash bars that migrate landward and eventually weld to the beach in a series of prograding ridges. The result is progradation at the updrift end of the island adjacent to the tidal inlet and transgression at the narrow, low-lying downdrift end (Fig. 7.43). This combination of progradation and transgression can change the shoreline orientation of a barrier. During only a century Caladesi Island on the Florida Gulf Coast has experienced a change in shoreline orientation of 15 degrees. Examples of mixed energy barrier systems are found in the German Bight, the Georgia Bight, and the west Gulf Coast of Florida.

There is another important result of this tidal inlet and barrier island inter-

FIGURE 7.43
Oblique photo of Caladesi Island, Florida, an excellent example of a drumstick barrier island.

action. The continuation of this scenario will produce barrier shorelines that are markedly offset on each side of the tidal inlet. This downdrift offset as it is called, is an important feature of mixed energy barrier island systems (Fig. 7.44).

It is easy to see, therefore, that barrier islands are complicated, fragile, and dynamic. The ones we have are geologically quite young and with the forecast for rapid global sea-level rise, they might not become much older.

FIGURE 7.44
Oblique photo of a downdrift offset of the barriers at an inlet, Big Sarasota Pass, Florida.

8
Rocky Coasts

The greatest variety of coastal types are depositional in nature—such as deltas, estuaries, and barrier islands—however, there are also many coastal reaches that are and have been dominated by erosion. Although there is great variety in the general morphology and in the geologic character of these consistently eroding coasts, they tend to be dominated by bedrock and are characterized by modest to high relief that is accompanied by high-energy wave conditions (Fig. 8.1).

On a global scale, the extent of rocky coasts is much greater than that of barrier coasts, up to 75 percent of the global total. Much of the northern half of North America, southern and eastern Australia, the West coasts of North and South America, the East coast of Asia, the northern Mediterranean, the Antarctic, and most of the island coasts of the world are dominated by rocky cliffs (Fig. 8.2). The nature and age of the rocks cover a wide spectrum as do their origins. Tectonic and geologic settings play a large role in the development of this coastal scenario as does the wave climate of the adjacent sea.

ORIGINS OF ROCKY COASTS

The global perspective of the crustal plates and their movement provides the largest scale for consideration of the origin of rocky coasts. From this level, down to the individual bluff, there is a spectrum of conditions involved in producing the rocky coast. Chapter 2 discussed how collision coasts are tectonically active and thereby produce high relief and a narrow or absent continental margin. The best example of this condition is the present western coastal area of North and

FIGURE 8.1
Photo of wave breaking on a cliffed rocky coast.

South America where nearly all the coastal region is a plate margin under which another plate is descending. The mountainous area along the edge of the continents continues beneath sea level to produce no typical continental shelf and a steep slope or the structurally complex borderland along southern California.

The resulting geology is a combination of various rock types in structurally complicated settings of faults, folds, and igneous intrusion and extrusion. The topography is dominated by steep slopes both on land and beneath the adjacent sea. These conditions provide the ideal setting for the development of rocky coasts. They are supplemented by a huge basin, the Pacific Ocean, in which large waves can develop and move essentially unhindered to the coast. The combination of the proper geologic setting and an energetic wave climate is perfect for producing the spectacular cliffed coast that dominates this type of plate margin.

Other geologic situations that are not tectonically related may also produce cliffed coasts. Some are composed of various sedimentary strata that are horizontal or that dip at low angles. The adjacent continental shelf is very wide and only modestly steep. Waves are generally quite large because of great fetch. Good examples of this condition are on the South and East coast of Australia (Fig. 8.3) and the West coast of New Zealand. In some places bluffs well over 50 meters ex-

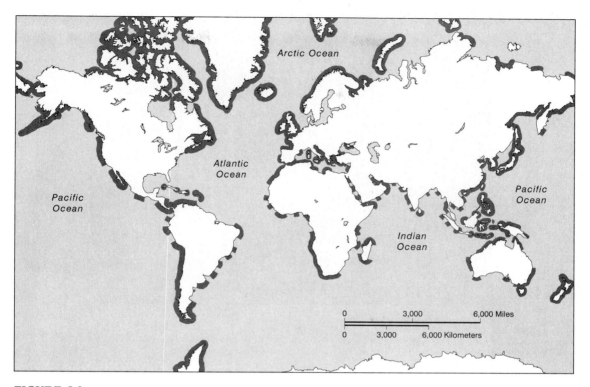

FIGURE 8.2
World map showing the distribution of rocky coasts.
(From Trenhaile, A. S., 1988, *The Geomorphology of Rocky Coasts*, Oxford University Press, Oxford, United Kingdom, p. 169)

tend for hundreds of kilometers along the Nullabor Plain on the southern coast of Australia. Part of the reason for this condition is that these coasts have been exposed to wave attack for many thousands of years. This plus the energetic wave climate produces the spectacular and rugged rocky coasts.

Large waves and cliffed coasts are an obvious association although we do not really know the extent to which these cliffs are produced directly by the waves. The sea bed typically slopes away from these coasts at a high gradient thereby providing little or no influence on incoming waves. During storm conditions, the waves are relatively short and steep, and in calm conditions the long swell waves increase in height as they approach the coast. The typical 10- to 14-second period of the swell represents waves that are very long and which will begin to feel bottom and steepen even on the inclined sea bed near the cliffed coast. This produces large and energetic waves as they crash onto the rocky shore.

Glaciers have also had a hand in producing cliffed coasts; some are rocky and others are not, although their morphology is similar. These moving ice masses have removed large volumes of rock and sediment from coastal areas. In

FIGURE 8.3
Near-vertical cliffs rising high above sea level along the Nullabor Plain in Western
Australia.
(Courtesy of A. D. Short)

some places rock strata have been stripped bare of sediment and in others the
rock itself has been eroded. This erosion has gouged out deep valleys that subsequently drowned after the glaciers melted. The spectacular fjords of Scandinavia,
Greenland, and other high latitude areas have resulted from such erosion during
the Pleistocene glaciation (Fig. 8.4). Low but widespread rocky coasts dominate
some shield areas such as the northern coast of Canada and parts of Scandinavia.

Another aspect of glacial activity has resulted in local cliffed coasts composed
of glacial drift, not bedrock. This is the material that is deposited by the glaciers
and it may be very thick, over 100 meters in some places. Drift may be composed
of nearly any type of material ranging from stiff muds to sand and gravel. Some is
well-layered and some is massive with essentially no internal organization. The
thick accumulations of drift known as end moraines tend to be linear and thick.
Many are present at the coast where waves have sculpted steep cliffs. One of the
most spectacular of these cliffed areas in glacial outwash is at Cape Cod National
Seashore in Massachusetts (Fig. 8.5). Most of the outer portion of Cape Cod that
faces the Atlantic Ocean is an outwash plain. Similar but less impressive bluffs are
present around large sections of the Great Lakes coast, such as Scarborough Bluffs
west of Toronto, and on the southeastern part of Lake Michigan.

An additional variety of rocky and commonly cliffed coast is associated with

FIGURE 8.4
Fjord carved into bedrock by a glacier along the Alaska coast.

FIGURE 8.5
Bluff of glacial drift at Cape Cod National Seashore, Massachusetts.

areas in which the continental shelf and adjacent coast is dominated by skeletal shell debris. This is very common in low latitude areas such as the Caribbean, Bahamas, and the Mediterranean coast, but also along the southern coast of the Australian continent and South Africa where dunes have become lithified. This situation is most common in tropical areas in which there is generally a high rate of calcium carbonate production from organisms and physicochemical processes. There is no fluvially delivered terrigenous or land-derived sediment available. The continental shelf of southern Australia borders the Southern Ocean, hardly a tropical system. The high latitude area is quite productive, and there is no river of any significance emptying into it, a combination that provides abundant carbonate shell debris from the shelf communities, which is diluted only by the small amount of terrigenous sediment that is eroded from the coast.

The abundant carbonate sediment in these contrasting areas produces a similar type of shell-rich beach with strong and persistent onshore winds that blow the sediment landward and accumulate dunes. The combination of the sea spray, percolating ground water, arid climate, and the calcium carbonate sediment results in rapid cementation that converts the dunes to rock called eolianite (Fig. 8.6). Extensive Pleistocene eolianite sequences form rocky and cliffed coasts

FIGURE 8.6
Eolianites that are lithified dunes as they appear along the coast of Australia.

that display spectacular large-scale cross-stratification and soil horizons, indicating periods of weathering in between periods of sediment accumulation.

PROCESSES

On one hand, the processes that operate along rocky coasts are the same as those along any other type of coast. On the other, there are important differences in their nature and, therefore, on their effect on rocky coasts. Waves and tides are the basic forces that occur, although they operate somewhat differently on rocky coasts and certainly have different influences. Like all coasts, the weather is an important aspect of rocky coasts, but for more reasons than the generation of wind and storm effects. Temperature and rainfall may be quite significant factors in the development of cliffs and bluffs by their influence on rock weathering. Biological and chemical processes are also factors in the dynamics of rocky coasts. These are typically at a very slow rate as compared to most physical processes.

Physical Processes

Wave energy is generally high on rocky coasts, at least relative to adjacent beaches and other nonlithified coastal environments. The size of the waves reaching the coast is related to nearshore bathymetry and to the resulting refraction patterns taken by the waves. Aerial photographs show this well, with waves bending around the headlands and into adjacent embayments where the beaches accumulate (Fig. 8.7). The distribution of wave energy can be shown by constructing lines perpendicular to the wave crests called orthogonals that show where wave energy is directed. This energy is focused on the headlands and spreads out in the embayments. This is the reason there is erosion on headlands while sediment accumulates in the intervening embayments under the same open water wave climate.

Many waves reaching the rocky headland, especially those with steep subtidal gradients, are reflected from the cliff with little or no loss of energy. If you watch closely as a given wave hits the base of the cliff, you can see it reflect and reinforce the next incoming wave to produce clapotis (Fig. 8.8). This interaction produces an instantaneous standing wave that is larger than the incoming waves. It appears as a vertical jet of water alternately rising and collapsing. Because these waves do not break, their energy is not dissipated. The shallowing of the water near the cliff causes some energy dissipation of the incoming wave, and the reflected wave is smaller than the incoming wave producing a partial clapotis. This condition is characterized by waves that travel both landward and seaward of the collapsing clapotis.

Air is trapped under pressure as the wave hits the steep rock surface providing a type of cushion for the water hammer, the impact between the water

FIGURE 8.7
Aerial photo of wave refraction
around a headland.
(Courtesy of U.S. Air Force,
Cambridge Research Laboratories)

and a solid (Fig. 8.9). We are still trying to understand the mechanisms whereby waves erode rocky surfaces. Various schemes have been proposed but the details are still a mystery. We do know from various measurements and models that the greatest pressure exerted by waves on a surface are at, or slightly above, the still water level. This is reflected in the presence of numerous notches and surfaces of erosion at this elevation.

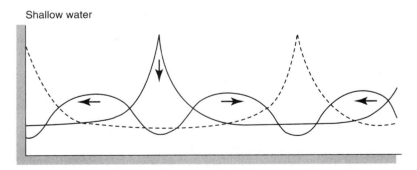

FIGURE 8.8
Diagram showing clapotis as a wave reflects from a vertical surface.
(From Bagnold, R. A., 1939, Interim report on wave pressure research, *Jour. Inst. Civil Engr.*, 12, pp. 202–226)

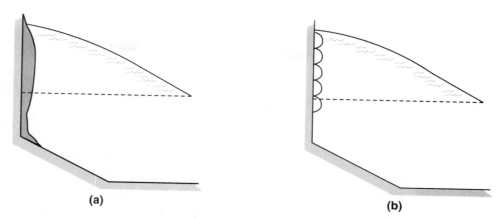

FIGURE 8.9
Diagram showing how air is trapped against a cliff as the wave strikes it.
(From Bagnold, 1939)

Abrasion of rocky coasts by wave-borne particles has been suggested as perhaps the most important process of physical erosion in this setting. The rapid transport of sediment, ranging in size from sand to large gravel particles across the rocky surface, produces considerable impact and abrasion. Researchers in the British Isles, where gravel beaches commonly front rocky coasts, have attributed most cliff erosion to this mechanism. Unfortunately, there are numerous parts of the world, such as the East coast of New South Wales and much of Tasmania in Australia in which erosional features are widespread, but where these gravel clasts are absent. Sand can also be an abrasive agent where a supply is present. Virtually any hard objects that are being transported in the energetic wave zone can be agents of erosion on a rocky coast.

Tidal range on rocky coasts covers the complete spectrum. In fact, a significant part of the Bay of Fundy, the area of the world's greatest tidal range, is a rocky coast. Tides have a somewhat benign influence on these coasts, similar to that on beaches, in that they play a largely indirect role. Tidal range and the gradient of the intertidal zone distribute the effects of waves. Steep or vertical cliffs tend to have wave energy focused in a narrow intertidal area (Fig. 8.10) whereas a gently sloping rocky coast spreads the wave energy over a relatively wide zone. Tidal range is obviously an important factor in combination with the slope of the rocky intertidal zone.

The combination of tidal characteristics, especially tidal range, with wave action is important for erosion and development of landforms on a rocky coast. It makes sense that the place on the coast at which waves can work the longest would experience the greatest wear, all other factors being equal. That means that the zone near mean water level should receive the greatest wave energy on a given reach of coast. Furthermore, the smaller the tidal range, the narrower

FIGURE 8.10
Narrow intertidal rocky coast in the Bay of Fundy, Nova Scotia, Canada where tidal range is very large.

will be the zone in which wave attack occurs. This means that macrotidal coasts experience wave energy over a relatively wide zone compared to microtidal coasts where wave attach is focused in a narrow zone. The erosional notches in cliffs is further testimony to this relationship because they are more common along microtidal coasts than macrotidal coasts (Fig. 8.11).

Unlike depositional coasts, storm events do not appear to have important short-term effects on rocky coasts. Whereas a beach may experience changes several orders of magnitude faster during a storm than during ambient conditions, the rock cliffs are not similarly affected by storms. Erosional features that are elevated above sea level due to storm surge levels do not appear along rocky coasts.

Other more subtle physical processes contribute to change along rocky coasts. They are typically temperature-dependent and involve volume changes or even changes such as freezing and thawing. Basically two styles of this phenomenon can influence rocky coasts. In one, the water invades cracks, crevasses, joints, or other places of entry and then freezes. This can cause the breakage of rocks but the water must be frozen under some confinement for it to have any significant effect. The freezing of pore waters offers more potential for destruction of the rocks. It requires that the host rocks have porosity and some permeability but it

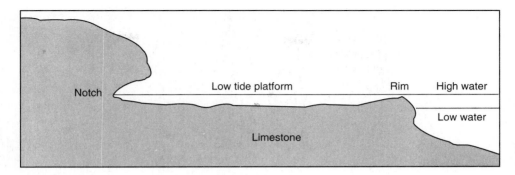

FIGURE 8.11
Notch on a cliff along a microtidal rocky coast.

provides the appropriate confinement for them to break when frozen. As pore water turns to ice, the increased volume forces fractures in the rocks. Such rock destruction is strongly related to climate and therefore to high latitudes.

This water has basically two sources: groundwater may percolate from the land through the cliffs, or waves and aerosols from the sea can invade the rocks. Groundwater or rainfall only may be a factor locally or at specific times. Sea water is always present throughout the shore zone. Although freezing temperatures of sea water are depressed nearly two degrees Celsius by salinity, freezing commonly occurs in high latitudes. The intertidal zone tends to be the area most affected because freezing and thawing can occur with each tidal cycle. It is this repetition that results in the physical deterioration of the rocks and leads to erosion. Rock type appears also to be a factor, especially because a significant amount of water must be absorbed for the process to occur. Those rocks that are thinly layered or foliated are among the most likely to fail in the process of freezing and thawing whereas massive and fine-grained rocks are relatively stable.

Although less effective as an erosion agent, temperature change also causes the mineral grains and rock fragments to expand and contract slightly. For example, halite, which is common salt, expands more than twice the rate of granite. This means that the salt crystals that precipitate in the surface layer of the rock along the shore can cause the rock to deteriorate by heating and cooling alone. The actual crystallization of the halite will also contribute because of the pressures created as it is transformed from a liquid to a solid.

Biological and Chemical Processes

While not as rapid as most physical processes or at the same geographic scope, organisms and chemical reactions have important long-term impacts on rocky coasts. Some of these effects are readily visible and recognizable but others go

FIGURE 8.12
Boring characteristics on rocky
surfaces, and examples of
boring organisms in situ.

unnoticed. The combination of biological and/or chemical processes can weaken
the rocks and make them more susceptible to erosion by waves. In some areas
this is the primary factor in much coastal erosion.

The energetic and rigorous nature of the rocky coast environment requires
that most of the organisms that live there have some means of attachment to the
hard surface or are well-protected from the crash of the waves, both for protection and for food acquisition. The obvious contributors to erosion are the single-
celled, plant-like organisms called monerans and animals that bore into the rock
surface (Fig. 8.12). It may come as a shock to see single-celled organisms listed in
this category but there are many species of microscopic boring algae from three
phyla. These organisms, in fact, comprise the most effective and widespread
group of bioeroders found on rocky surfaces. They penetrate up to 1 millimeter
into the rock and extend from supratidal levels to well below low tide. The major
factor in their effectiveness is their population density—up to 1,000,000 per
square centimeter! Their effect is related to rock type. They are relatively scarce
on granites but are very abundant and can penetrate limestones and other carbonate rocks the deepest. Rocks bored by algae can be eroded rapidly in a grain
by grain fashion as the waves impact on these surfaces.

Macro-invertebrates, including a variety of bivalves, sponges, worms, and sea urchins, are also important borers of rocky coasts. Their activities typically result in penetration of several centimeters for purposes of shelter. For example, sea urchins and abalones penetrate several centimeters into the sandstone and siltstone found on San Nicolas Island off the California coast. This weakens the rock and makes it susceptible to wave attack, especially if the borings are closely spaced.

Grazing animals are also important erosional agents. The most common feeding style of these grazers on rocky coasts is to slowly move along the rocky surface scraping the surface for nourishment (Fig. 8.13). Included in this group are chitons, limpets and snails, some sea urchins, starfish, and parrot fish. The nourishment they seek may be in the form of lichens, fungi, or blue-green algae (cyanobacteria). The algae are a favorite food source because they are abundant, and the combination of the weakened rock surface with the scraping of the grazing animal produces slow but significant erosion.

Chemical erosion of rocky cliffs is basically a weathering process that dissolves or weakens rocks so that waves can break and remove it. Rock type is an important variable in this process as is weather. Some minerals such as carbonates (e.g., limestone) are quite soluble at surface temperatures and pressures. The rate of dissolution may be high, producing small-scale karstic surfaces (Fig. 8.14), which are the very irregular and craggy limestone surfaces of low-latitude coasts such as seen on many islands in the Bahamas and on the Yucatán peninsula of Mexico. Other minerals, such as most silicates (e.g., quartz and feldspar), are very slow to show change. Some silicates will weather, however, and soils will develop. These can then be easily removed by waves, by runoff of surface water, or even by wind.

Chemical weathering also produces interesting surface features and patterns on rocky coasts. Although they are actually small-scale geomorphic features, they will be included here because of their chemical origin. One such fea-

FIGURE 8.13
Chitons and snails grazing along a rocky surface feeding on various encrusted and boring organisms.

FIGURE 8.14
Microkarst surface on limestone due to weathering in the surf zone.

ture is the abundant and somewhat spherical hollows that characterize a range of rock types in many parts of the world. These are called *tafoni* (Fig. 8.15), a term that originated in the Mediterranean where this feature is very common. The actual mode of formation is unknown but relationships with climate, especially moisture, suggest some chemical process must play a role. Honeycombs are another somewhat related feature. Their appearance is as the name suggests, and they commonly occur in association with tafoni. Some are related to small-scale fracturing in the host rock but others occur in apparently homogenous rocks. Both of these features are common in the upper intertidal zone.

Zonation of Erosion on Rocky Coasts

It is important to consider spatial distribution of the processes that control the morphology of rocky coasts before the geomorphology of these spectacular coasts is discussed (Fig. 8.16). The most obvious place in which great energy is imparted is where the wave energy strikes the coast. This phenomenon is typically viewed at the surface, and beautiful photos of the spectacular crash of waves are com-

FIGURE 8.15
Tafoni surface on a rocky coast.

mon, but there is much more going on, even in the realm of the waves. The intertidal zone and the near supratidal area are easily viewed as waves attack and as the biological and chemical processes take place. It is very difficult to see what is going on below that.

None of the processes that affect rocky coasts are restricted to that portion of the coast that we can see; they also have an important subtidal influence. Weathering is more pronounced above sea level, and certainly freezing and thawing are by far more important above low tide. By contrast, the biological processes and wave influence are very important in the subtidal part of rocky coasts. Unfortunately, we know very little about this part of the dynamics of these high-energy coasts because they are just that—high energy—making it both difficult and dangerous to make observations or to place instruments underwater at the base of a rocky cliff or under a bedrock ledge. It is, however, this part of the rocky coast that receives most and sometimes all of the wave energy. It is also the zone in which abundant life exists, with all of the same problems that occur above low tide except for the need for protection from exposure to the

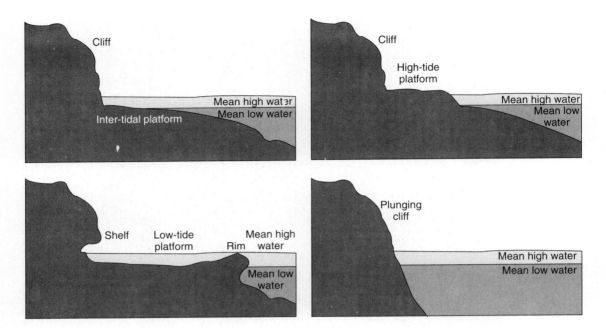

FIGURE 8.16
Diagram showing various types of shore platforms and terraces.
(After Bird, E. C. F., 1976, *Coasts: An Introduction to Systematic Geomorphology*, Australian National Univ. Press, Canberra, Australia, p. 59)

atmosphere. Numerous geomorphic features that are discussed in the following section are present below low tide as well as above, providing validation of the work being done at this horizon.

GEOMORPHOLOGY

The nature of cliffed or rocky coasts is both simple and yet complex. Like fingerprints, no two reaches of rocky coast are alike. The broad range in rock type, structural configuration, and wave climate ensures this variation. Some are steep and others are not, some are smooth and others are rough, some are stable and others are not—the variety is endless. Although there is breadth in the appearance of rocky coasts, some fairly common styles are displayed and specific landforms tend to develop. We will consider some of these and take a look at a few examples.

The most noticeable landforms of rocky coasts are the steep cliffs or bluffs

(a)

(b)

FIGURE 8.17
Photos showing a) a high rocky cliff and b) a low rocky coast.

that dominate the landscape (Fig. 8.17). There is considerable range in the height and also in the steepness of the surface. Some rocky coasts have cliffs that rise over 100 meters above the water surface and are nearly vertical. Examples include the White Cliffs of Dover in England, the southwest coast of Victoria in Australia, and near the mouth of the Columbia River in the state of Washington. Each is composed of different rock types but all have a comparable shape and scale.

Near the other end of the spectrum are the rocky coasts that owe their origin to beach rock. Here tropical conditions interact with waves to lithify beach deposits. The profile of these rocky areas is similar to that of a standard beach with low, seaward dipping layers and an elevation that tends to be intertidal or just above high tide. These present quite a contrast to the high cliffs we generally associate with rocky coasts but still properly belong in the same broad category. Most Caribbean coasts and tropical Pacific Islands have extensive beach rock areas. In many locations they are associated with coastal dunes that have similar lithology. These will be considered later in this chapter.

Because of this range in scales and slopes, it is not practical, or necessary, to adopt a comprehensive classification of rocky coasts. As long as the coast in question has some type of rocky or even resistant material that produces a steep profile, it is worthy of consideration here.

Cliffs and Bluffs

The spectacular scenery that generates the crashing waves along most rocky coasts owes much of its character to the steep cliffs or bluffs that dominate the coast at or just landward of the shoreline. Although most of these features are nearly vertical and are composed of bedrock, there is a range of materials and scales that span the globe (Fig. 8.17).

The presence of rocky shores and/or steep prominences along the coast does not preclude the absence of beaches. They may occur at the foot of the cliffs or in the relatively quiet wave conditions between headlands (Fig. 8.18). The presence or absence of a beach does not significantly influence the cliff or bluff other than to provide some amount of protection from waves. These beaches display the same morphology and experience the same dynamic conditions as beaches on sandy coasts. In many of these settings the presence of sandy beaches is ephemeral, coming and going with the seasons due to changing wave energy conditions. Gravel beaches tend to persist and show changes only during intense storms.

If we consider the distribution and size of cliffed coasts on a global scale, we find that there is a concentration of high elevations above sea level in the mid-latitudes with relatively low cliffs in the low and high latitudes. This is the result of the distribution of high wave energy that is greatest in the mid-latitudes. In high latitudes there is a period of inactivity due to ice along the coast. Tropical areas experience less intense winds than mid-latitudes and tend to have coral

FIGURE 8.18
Rocky coast with a well-developed pocket beach where sediment accumulates due to the combination of decreased wave energy and inability of longshore currents to carry it away.

reefs offshore that buffer wave energy. Another factor in the distribution of bluff size is that glacial erosion has reduced the relief in the high latitudes. In the low latitudes many rocky coasts are dominated by eolianites that are somewhat limited in their elevation. Be assured that there are numerous exceptions to these general patterns, depending upon local conditions of geology and wave climate.

Probably the most important variables associated with the nature of cliffed coasts is their geology. Not only is the lithology important but the stratigraphy, structures present, and the attitude of the rocks is important as well. Various geologic attributes can produce a wide range of coastal configurations under the same environmental conditions. Massive rocks such as granite will erode in a fairly uniform fashion because of the general uniformity of the material. By contrast, layered sedimentary rocks will generally display some heterogeneity between layers and will respond accordingly to various processes. Erosion of alternating sandstones and shales will produce an irregular cliff with resistant sandstones forming ledges between the softer, more rapidly eroded shale beds. Thick-bedded sedimentary rocks present another variation, depending upon where the softer unit is positioned relative to sea level. If the shale layer is in the zone of direct wave attack, the rate of erosion will be much higher than if this zone is occupied by a resistant sandstone. Large overhanging ledges of sandstone can collapse and cause pulses of rapid cliff retreat. An additional factor in this scenario is that boring macro-invertebrates preferentially inhabit the softer shales, further weakening them and increasing the rate of erosion.

Additional influences on cliff erosion are caused by jointing or other fractures in the rock. These weakened surfaces will enhance erosion and result in irregular, step-like faces on cliffs. Even more variation can be caused by the rocks being deformed from horizontal; virtually all orientations are possible. Folding the strata further complicates the picture. All of these geologic parameters produce cliffed coasts that vary greatly in size and shape; in reality, no two are alike.

The steepness of the cliffs is also related to their geologic characteristics and the processes to which they are subjected. Generally the resistant and homogenous rock types produce the steepest rock faces. This tends to be the case if wave processes are distinctly dominant. If, on the other hand, the subaerial weathering processes are important and waves are small, the surface will be sloping.

There are some areas containing very high and steep bluffs that are comprised of unconsolidated sediments (Fig. 8.19). They need to be included even though they are not truly part of a rocky coast because they present a morphology that is similar to many rocky coasts. Typically formed by the erosion of glacial sediments and older coastal deposits such as dunes, they tend to be fronted by beaches that develop from a combination of lag material as the cliff erodes and wave action. This type of cliffed coast has high erosion rates.

FIGURE 8.19
Steep bluff in unconsolidated sediment.

Rates of cliff or bluff retreat range from nearly zero to many meters per year. The combination of resistant rock, such as quartzite, and low to modest wave energy produces no measurable retreat. Quartzite is essentially inert chemically and is too hard for most boring organisms. By contrast, where eruptions place soft volcanic material along the coast, rates of several meters of recession per year can occur. The more common range of cliff retreat is from about a millimeter per year in resistant homogenous rocks to a meter or two on soft shales or friable sandstones.

Platforms, Benches, and Terraces

Rocky coasts, especially those characterized by fairly high and steep cliffs, tend to have surfaces that are flat and essentially horizontal (Fig. 8.20). These surfaces are attributed primarily to the action of waves crashing on the coast for extended periods of time. In fact, they used to be called wave-cut platforms; however, it is now recognized that other phenomena have also contributed to their origin. The term *shore platform* is used for these features with no implication about their origin.

FIGURE 8.20
Photo of a shore platform that has been planed off by waves.

Although bedrock is very resistant to erosion, waves can do considerable work given extended periods of time. This generally requires that sea level be fairly stable to permit the same portion of the coast to be exposed to the work of waves. Some parts of the world, like Australia and New Zealand, have experienced about 6000 years of sea level stability.

There are two major categories of these features: those that are essentially horizontal and those that have seaward sloping surfaces. Sloping platforms typically have gradients of less than five degrees, however they may be as much as thirty degrees, depending upon rock type and orientation. The width of these sloping platforms ranges greatly but their position relative to sea level is typically from about mean tide to just above high tide.

Most people ascribe the origin of these platforms to a combination of wave action and a type of weathering called water layer leveling. This weathering is due to chemical action within the small pools of standing water on a rocky surface during exposure at low tide. In many locations of shallow pools, a variety of sizes and densities is exhibited, depending upon rock type and structural conditions. Some show a distinct pattern with various types of chemical precipitates along joints and other fractures. These linings may stand up in relief due to their relative resistance and thereby create the shallow pools in which weathering can take place.

There are also subtidal platforms or terraces that generally receive little attention because of their position below the visible coast. These features are wave-formed and are positioned at the depth to which waves can do considerable work, which may range from only a few to about 10 meters depending on wave climate and rock type. They are particularly common in less resistant rocks such as limestones, especially in the forereef environment.

Sloping shore platforms can be attributed partly to rock type or inclination of strata but many examples do not show this relationship. It has also been suggested that a better correspondence exists between the gradient of the shore platform and the tidal range. The rationale being, that as the tide rises and falls over a greater range, it provides a mechanism for spreading out the influence of waves. The greatest wave energy is at the seaward edge of the platform because that is where waves spend the most time doing work. Conversely, the least amount of wave energy is expended at high tide. A plot of this relationship, using data from several areas, shows a trend that supports this contention. It should be noted, however, that at several of the areas, there is considerable spread in the gradient which could be the result of overall wave climate.

Rocky coasts in areas of tectonic activity or in areas in which sea level has been considerably above its present position may show terraces. These range widely in size and elevation. Some coastal areas may have several, such as along the California coast where tectonic activity associated with the plate boundary has left multiple terraces well above present sea level (Fig. 8.21). These features are shore platforms that have been moved above the shoreline. The reverse can also occur, drowning similar platforms, which can partially or completely bury the platforms with sediment, thereby obscuring their presence.

FIGURE 8.21
Uplifted terrace on a rocky coast.
(Courtesy of G. Griggs)

Arches, Stacks, and Other Erosional Remnants

The Twelve Apostles along the southern coast of Victoria, Australia, is probably the most photographed rocky coast in the world; certainly it is on every Australian tourist poster. These and other erosional remnants along rocky coasts provide spectacular, but commonly temporary, additions to the already impressive scenery along rocky coasts. The variety is great and their origins are well-known. Like the cliffs and other attributes of this coastal type, the wave climate and the geology are the primary factors in the formation of sea stacks (Fig. 8.22).

Like most erosional remnants, these features result from a combination of varied distribution of wave energy along with differences in resistance of the rock to erosion. The latter may occur due to structural weakness in the rock caused by fracturing, from layering of various rock types, or from different levels of cementation. The one feature that all of these erosional structures have in common is some type of vertical character, which is that characteristic that makes them interesting and photogenic.

FIGURE 8.22
Example of a sea stack formed by differential erosion.

One of the ways by which sea stacks originate is from a remaining resistant rock after the surrounding less-resistant material has been eroded. A volcanic neck composed of relatively tough basalt may remain after the surrounding volcano of tuff, ash, and other relatively soft material has been eroded by wave activity. In many cases a well-formed shore platform will surround the stack. Stacks of volcanic origin may result from differential erosion of basalt that has columnar jointing developed during its cooling history.

A typical setting for sea stack formation is in layered sedimentary rocks that are essentially horizontal. Here variation in wave energy, generally in combination with jointing in the rocks, results in differential erosion. This condition produces narrow arms that form headlands with intervening narrow embayments along the fracture paths. Incident wave energy erodes the headlands, preferentially along the sides, eventually leaving the outer portion stranded as a stack.

Isolated sea stacks are the most typical occurrence; some locations, however, contain numerous examples. One of the most spectacular is the Twelve Apostles on the Great Ocean Highway in western Victoria, Australia (Fig. 8.23). This family of sea stacks ranges in size and distance from the present coast but forms a cluster of stacks that is beautiful when viewed from almost any angle. The overall coast here is quite spectacular with cliffs of Miocene limestone rising about 50 to 60 meters above the ocean for about 100 kilometers. Jointing in the bedrock triggers the production of a wide variety of stacks, arches, and caves. This is a must visit area for anyone who travels to Victoria.

Sea arches are commonly associated with sea stacks and in many cases

FIGURE 8.23
Twelve Apostles, sea stacks on the western Victoria coast, Australia.

may, in fact, be their precursors. These features are, as their name suggests, arch configurations of rock that are also the result of differential wave attack and variation in rock resistance. Essentially the same geologic setting exists as for stack formation. The difference is that the rock layers themselves erode in such a way that there is greater wave erosion at the water level than above. This produces a breach in the narrow headland at the water surface between the outermost part and the mainland. The arch is then formed. It is easy to see how an arch can be the precursor to sea stacks. Some have been documented to do so by photos and old records. Unfortunately, there is nothing in the geologic record that can tell us about the origin of a given sea stack because it is an erosional feature.

Some sea arches are rather rectangular due to structural characteristics in the rocks. A good example is the Tasman Arch on the island of Tasmania in Australia. This huge feature is formed in distinctly jointed but very resistant sandstone. The arch developed at and below sea level and rises about 10 meters above it. Its roof is almost at right angles to the sides because of the jointing. More commonly, the arches are formed by wave erosion, wearing away the material near sea level and below, forming a somewhat curved arch because of the uniform nature of the rock.

The lifetime of sea arches is limited because the erosion that formed them

(a)

(b)

FIGURE 8.24
Before a) and after b) photos of collapsed London Bridge on the Victoria coast, Australia.

continues and will eventually destroy them. A good example of this took place at London Bridge, a popular tourist stop on the western coast of Victoria in Australia. This arch in limestone is only a few kilometers from the Twelve Apostles and had been there in apparently stable condition as long as anyone knows. In February 1989 the arch collapsed suddenly, leaving two people stranded on the seaward buttress; fortunately no one was on the arch itself (Fig. 8.24). A helicopter rescued the marooned visitors.

The West Coast of the United States also has a large number and a wide variety of stacks and arches formed in a range of rock types. Historical changes in several of these erosional features have been studied near LaJolla in southern California. Using primarily photographs, supplemented by ship records and newspaper accounts, a century-long history of information on sea stacks and arches was pieced together. These changes are slow relative to one's lifetime but are very rapid considering geologic time. Rocky coasts are relatively slow to respond to coastal processes as compared to coasts dominated by sand and other unlithified sediments. They do, however, exhibit important change.

9
Human Intervention in Coastal Environments

The previous sections of this book have described various characteristics of a variety of coastal environments. These discussions have emphasized the natural state of the environments and have demonstrated their fragile nature. We have also noted that a large portion of the world's population lives along or near the coast (Fig. 9.1). This is especially true in the United States. The combination of fragile environments and dense population has produced many problems that are growing in number and becoming more severe every year. Domestic and industrial use of the coast tends to produce considerable unnatural alterations that have long-term deleterious effects.

The majority of the problems associated with human occupation of the coast are directly or indirectly associated with construction of some kind (Fig. 9.2). The other major type of problem concerns water and sediment quality. In some circumstances the two are related in a cause and effect fashion. The following discussion will concentrate on these two areas of problems with the natural coastal system. Emphasis will be on problems in the United States, although these problems are common throughout the world.

CONSTRUCTION ON THE COAST

The original coastal settlements were located to take advantage of various attributes of a particular location. Perhaps it was a natural harbor, protection from ad-

FIGURE 9.1
Photo of Sydney Harbor, a very developed estuary in Australia.

FIGURE 9.2
Photo of a highly-developed portion of a barrier on the Florida Gulf coast.

versaries, a desirable food supply, or some other benefit to the population that attracted the first residents to a particular coastal location. These coastal settlements utilized natural conditions without significantly modifying them, even when those areas were densely populated. Eventually the pressures of increasing populations, larger vessels, industrialization, and other factors, resulted in our modifying the coastal environment to better suit our needs. Most of these modifications were undertaken without regard for their impact on the natural coastal system. Surprisingly, this attitude continued into the twentieth century and only beginning in the 1970s has our approach toward coastal construction experienced major changes in philosophy. It is important that we understand how various types of construction interferes with coastal dynamics and as a result, how problems are generated. We also need to know about alternative methods of coastal construction. This understanding will permit us to make proper coastal management decisions in the future, whether it be as a private citizen or as a representative of various governmental units.

Materials

Attempts to protect or stabilize the coast have utilized nearly any type of imaginable material. Some have been successful and some not, and some are legal and others are not. Regardless of material, it is generally the design of the structure(s) and the location that determines success or failure. As might be expected, cost is a major factor in design, scale, and materials used for this type of construction.

Poured concrete, metal sheet piling, and wood are all needed in various ways to provide essentially impermeable types of construction (Fig. 9.3). This approach is termed *hard construction* and is generally for wave protection. Concrete is used in coastal protection in much the same way as it is in buildings or other large structures. Reinforcing rods and tie-downs are added for both strength and stability. Major factors in this type of construction are the thickness of the structure, the depth to which it is placed, and its upper elevation. Sheet piling can be utilized similarly but it has an advantage of being able to be driven or jetted many meters beneath the sediment surface, thereby protected from wave action. Wood is the least expensive and can also be driven or jetted into the sediment but it has a low strength.

Concrete is also fabricated into large elements called *dolos* or *tetrapods* that are composed of four appendages with a common origin (Fig. 9.4). They range in size and are placed in interlocking positions to provide the greatest stability for protection. Probably the largest in the world are used in Japan where individual tetrapods are over 10 meters in diameter and weigh many tons each. *Rip-rap* is a term applied to a range of boulders that are commonly used in various arrangements alone or in combination with other structural material to provide protection (Fig. 9.5). The basic approach is to build structures of blocks of various types

FIGURE 9.3
Example of wood used in coastal construction to protect from erosion.

of rock. Generally each one is cubic in shape but they may have irregular shapes also. The rock may be limestone, granite, or generally whatever is environmentally acceptable, available, and of reasonable strength. Typically the design of the structure will call for blocks of specific sizes placed in designated parts of the structure. Properly done, this is a sophisticated type of construction with each piece of rock placed individually. Some types of coastal construction use smaller rock pieces, generally large cobbles or small boulders that are placed in large wire baskets called *gabions*. These rectangular containers are then placed in various configurations and locations to protect the coast from wave attack.

All of the above described materials have been used in coastal construction for over a century. More recently the development of synthetic fabrics has provided additional materials for this purpose. One of the most widely used is in the form of large, somewhat sausage-shaped, slightly porous plastic bags (Fig. 9.6).

FIGURE 9.4
Photo of concrete tetrapods
used in coastal protection.
(Courtesy of O. H. Pilkey)

These are filled with sand and placed strategically for protection in somewhat the same way as are gabions. Other bags have been filled with a mixture of cement and aggregate and are placed along the shore. The water mixes naturally with the dry contents of the bag and hardens to form a concrete mass to protect the coast.

The least expensive type of protection is also the most aesthetically unpleasing and typically ineffective, that is, the dumping of scrap debris from construction in areas in which erosion is a problem. Broken concrete, asphalt, bricks, and similar other rubble have been used. In some areas old car bodies have also been a popular material (Fig. 9.7). This casual and environmentally unacceptable approach to coastal protection is illegal and has all but ceased.

Fencing is also used in coastal stabilization, primarily to prevent or retard the movement of windblown sediment in much the same way as fences keep snow from roads in the winter. In fact, the original approach to the problem used the same type of wooden lath fence that is used for snow. It is now more common for a plastic mesh or even biodegradable material to be used for the fencing. The posts are sometimes still metal, but wood, which will biodegrade, is also used and is preferable.

Some other synthetic materials that provide a soft or indirect approach to

FIGURE 9.5
Rip-rap material which is composed of large blocks of rock.

coastal stabilization have also been tried. A rubberized material that is sprayed on the sediment surface has been used for dune stabilization with the expectation that it will hold the sediment until vegetation can become established. This approach is similar to that used along roadways and other areas where erosion or construction has exposed the soil to potential mass wasting. Another material that has been tried is a synthetic sea grass designed to dissipate wave energy and thereby permit sediment to accumulate. Although installed at a number of locations, it has yet to be demonstrated as effective.

Many types of material are still in use and are permitted for coastal protection. In nearly all cases, it is not the type of material used but the design and location of the construction that determines its success. Cost is generally the limiting factor in these considerations and that is certainly a consideration for the materials chosen.

Hard Coastal Protection

Probably the most common types of protection along the coast are within the spectrum of structures that are designed for that purpose. This general procedure is typically referred to as hardening the coast. The construction itself may be

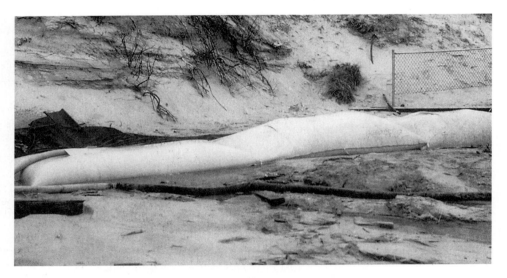

FIGURE 9.6
Sand-filled plastic bags used for low-cost protection from erosion.

FIGURE 9.7
Old car bodies placed along the coast to reduce the rate of coastal erosion.

poured concrete, metal sheet piling, wooden timbers, various sizes of boulders, or anything else that someone believes will stabilize a threatened shoreline. All of these approaches are attempts at keeping waves and currents from moving sediment or eroding rock from its present location at or near the shoreline. Various types of structures have been designed and constructed including seawalls, groins, jetties, and breakwaters.

Seawalls   The landward movement of the shoreline is a normal and natural process along many coasts. Limited sediment supply, rising sea level, or simply the washing over of a barrier during storms all may cause shoreline retreat. Is this type of shoreline retreat really erosion? These processes only become a problem when there are obstacles in the path of the moving shoreline. When these obstacles are expensive buildings or roads, they need protection and in most situations, they get it.

Anyone who has been to the shore has seen some type of seawall. These vertical or sloping structures are generally placed parallel to the shoreline in an attempt to stop, or at least retard, erosion. The need for seawalls is brought about by the landward movement of the shoreline and the presence of buildings, roads, or other man-made structures that are deemed to require protection. Seawalls may be constructed of virtually any type of material, ranging from plastic bags filled with sand to poured concrete armored with large rip-rap boulders. They are one of the most controversial of all coastal structures but nonetheless are still being built in many areas. The problems caused by seawalls include scour from wave attack and eventual loss of beach, reflection of wave energy that may cause problems elsewhere, and their generally unsightly appearance. Seawalls are typically limited in their extent. Even if the structure is successful in holding the shoreline position, the adjacent shoreline beyond the seawall will continue to retreat. This dislocation in the coast can also cause problems, especially with the continual longshore supply of beach sediment.

Vertical and impermeable seawalls cause the greatest problems along a coast because they must withstand the full impact of waves (Fig. 9.8). Permeable structures such as slotted walls or rip-rap walls permit some wave energy to be absorbed through the structure, and sloping walls will dissipate some of the wave energy. The problem is that while these structures are in place, waves scour at their base, eventually resulting in failure of the structure (Fig. 9.8). A good example is a seawall constructed in front of a high-rise condominium along the central Gulf Coast of Florida. After less than 10 years the water was nearly 3 meters deep at the seawall where there was a beach before the seawall was constructed a few years previously. Extreme storm conditions will produce similar results and will also overtop the walls causing erosion behind or landward of them. Modern poured seawalls have tie-downs that anchor them at an angle to the shore but these also commonly fail (Fig. 9.9). The bottom line is that seawalls are very expensive, typically temporary, asthetically unpleasing, and seem to cause as many problems as they solve. There are places where seawalls are required, however, because expensive

FIGURE 9.8
Vertical concrete sea wall that has failed during an intense storm.

property, such as hotels, is in jeopardy. That being the case, then the structures need to be designed and located properly. Large and expensive or historical buildings, even entire towns, deserve protection. One of the best examples of a qualified success in this type of construction is the famous Galveston seawall in Texas (Fig. 9.10). This structure was initially built after a severe hurricane in 1900 killed over 6000 people and nearly destroyed the town. The wall was constructed in sections, with its upper elevation 5.2 meters above mean low water. The basic construction included wooden pilings, sheet piling, and rip-rap with the bulk of the wall a curved poured concrete surface. It is impermeable, but rip-rap at the base and the curved face absorb some of the wave energy. In one of the most remarkable engineering and construction projects of its time much of the town was raised up to the surface of the crest of the wall. Thousands of buildings, including large stone churches, were raised an average of over 2 meters to accommodate it. Although the Galveston sea wall experienced significant damage from a hurricane in 1915 with a storm surge of 3.96 meters, there have been no subsequent major problems during numerous hurricanes. The structure supports a six-lane highway and is also the focal point for waterfront activities in the community. It is limited in its length, however, and has caused a large offset in the coast (Fig. 9.11) because of shoreline retreat at the end where there is no stabilization.

Breakwaters   Some structures that are similar in configuration to seawalls are placed beyond the shoreline itself. These are called breakwaters because they

FIGURE 9.9
Vertical concrete seawall with tie downs on the landward side. Excavation by storms has removed the material from the back of the wall exposing the tie downs that are anchored by concrete.

are designed to break up the wave energy and to prevent it from reaching the shoreline and causing erosion. These offshore structures may have a variety of configurations and locations depending upon the need. The simplest is a linear and shore-parallel structure that is designed to protect a beach or other coastal feature from wave attack (Fig. 9.12a). This type of breakwater is used to help build up beaches for both recreation and coastal protection. It is fairly widespread in Japan but uncommon in the United States. The Five Sisters breakwater in Winthrop, Massachusetts, and a similar structure at Erie, Pennsylvania, on Lake Erie are examples.

Some breakwaters are attached to the shore, and may be designed to form a protective harbor for mooring vessels (Fig. 9.12b). This type of construction is

FIGURE 9.10
Galveston sea wall, one of the oldest and most successful coastal protection projects, showing a close-up of the design and construction.

FIGURE 9.11
End effect of the Galveston sea wall showing shoreward movement of the adjacent unprotected coast where erosion is rapid.
(Courtesy of University of Texas, Bureau of Economic Geology)

fairly common in southern California and also along the Great Lakes, such as the waterfronts of Chicago, Cleveland, and Toronto where natural harbors are absent. Because of their position in at least moderately deep water, breakwaters must be large to withstand attack by waves. They generally have vertical walls of poured concrete but some also have large rip-rap or dolos. Unlike seawalls, most breakwaters withstand the rigors of intense storms.

There are problems associated with breakwaters, especially given the littoral transport system of sediment along the coast. Virtually all breakwaters interfere with this system and limit or prevent sediment movement along the shoreline (Fig. 9.13). In the case of detached breakwaters that are more or less parallel to the coast, the result is the "breakwater effect." By design, the breakwater limits wave energy from reaching the shoreline. Away from the breakwater at either end there is no influence and waves approach the shore without hinderance, producing longshore currents that carry sediment along the surf zone depending upon the direction of wave approach. Landward of the breakwater this phenomenon is absent or limited. The result is that the littoral transport system carries sediment to the sheltered area landward of the breakwater but cannot carry it beyond. This produces a large bulge in the shoreline behind the breakwater. Accumulation of sediment is, of course, in many cases, the objective of the structure, especially if the protected shoreline is a recreational beach. Problems can arise because the trapped sediment may cause erosion downdrift from the breakwater by failing to keep the littoral drift system operating without interruption. Additional problems result from the shoreline prograding all the way to the breakwater, thereby creating a safety hazard for beachgoers. If multiple breakwaters are present, deep holes can develop from wave action between them.

Attached breakwaters produce similar but typically more severe problems. The attachment of a structure to the shore is essentially like building a dam along the shoreline. It interferes with the littoral system and causes large volumes of sediment to accumulate updrift from the "dam" (breakwater) (Fig. 9.13). The biggest problems are downdrift of the structure where the combination of wave activity and sediment being prevented from accumulating causes erosion. In the past few decades this problem has been somewhat alleviated by the installation of sediment bypassing systems where attached breakwaters are located. Attached breakwaters are generally associated with some type of harbor, and the harbor itself commonly receives much of the sediment that would be transported in the littoral system. The bypassing systems may be a permanently installed dredge and pump operation or simply a regular dredging program. These systems are logistically difficult to keep operational because of both the stress of operating pumps in a saltwater environment, and legal challenges from adjacent landowners affected by the sand bypassing activity.

Groins and Jetties   Along with seawalls, groins are the most common types of construction used to stabilize the coast. These are typically short struc-

(a)

FIGURE 9.12
Examples of a) an offshore breakwater and b) an attached breakwater.

tures that are attached perpendicular to the shoreline. They commonly extend across at least part of the beach and out into the surf zone. Construction can be of essentially the same variety of materials as seawalls. Groins are typically grouped along the coast in what are termed *groin fields* (Fig. 9.14).

The basic idea is that the groins will trap the sediment that moves through the littoral transport system and thus will maintain a beach in areas that would otherwise experience erosion. In theory this scheme makes some sense, in practice, however, it rarely accomplishes the goal. The typical result of groin installation includes a small-scale version of the attached breakwater problem—updrift accumulation and downdrift erosion. In some situations, erosion proceeds and the groins become detached from the beach where they have no positive effect.

(b)

FIGURE 9.12 *(Cont.)*

The problem with groins is primarily with their design. At any given location proper design length, elevation, and spacing will permit sediment to accumulate and eventually bypass the buried groin without causing significant downdrift erosion. The ideal groin field would become buried and out of sight except perhaps after a major storm that caused some temporary erosion. In reality, this condition is rarely achieved because detailed localized data on wave climate and longshore transport rates are lacking.

The best examples of apparently proper design and construction of groins tend to be along the North Sea coasts of The Netherlands and Germany where coastal protection has been ongoing for over a thousand years. Here the severe winter storms and the fairly high rate of littoral drift require that the groins be large. Many are hundreds of meters long and stand several meters high. Testimony to their success is the fact that many have become buried, there is little asymmetry to the sediment accumulation on each side (Fig. 9.15), and many have lasted for nearly a century without major maintenance.

In all respects jetties are much like groins except that they are typically larger and are located at tidal inlets (Fig. 9.16). They are for purposes of stabilizing one or both sides of the inlet from shifting its position and preventing large volumes of sediment from filling in the inlet. Jetties are constructed to stabilize

FIGURE 9.13
Accumulation of sand from the littoral drift system at an attached breakwater at Santa
Barbara, California.
(From Anikouchine, W. A. and Sternberg, R. W., 1981, *The World Ocean: An Introduction to
Oceanography,* Prentice-Hall, Inc., Englewood Cliffs, New Jersey, p. 303)

the inlet and to permit its continued navigation. In some cases when jetties are
constructed, the inlet is deepened to accommodate passage of deep draft vessels.

Like groins, jetties cause problems by interrupting the littoral drift system.
Sediment accumulates on the updrift side and is prevented from reaching the
downdrift side of the inlet, thus inducing erosion (Fig. 9.17), the same pattern
seen with groins. Because jetties tend to be quite long, perhaps a kilometer or
more, the amount accumulating on the updrift side may be tremendous. In some
cases the accumulation becomes so large that it extends into the inlet through
the seaward end of the jetties. Sediment bypassing is becoming a part of many
jettied inlet maintenance programs. A good example of this problem is illustrated
by the inlet south of Ocean City, Maryland, that was cut by a hurricane in 1933.
Jetties were constructed shortly thereafter to stabilize the inlet in light of a littoral drift rate of about 140,000 cubic meters per year. No bypass system was installed and as a result the shoreline on Assateague Island, the downdrift part of

FIGURE 9.14
Groin field along a beach. Notice that there is accumulation on the updrift side and erosion on the downdrift side.
(Courtesy of J. C. Kraft)

the system, has retreated about a kilometer through washover and blowover of the barrier island.

Another type of inlet problem requiring construction of a jetty to prevent spit growth into the inlet occurred at Clearwater Pass on the central Gulf coast of Florida, where Sand Key was growing northward and causing the inlet to narrow (Fig. 9.18). In this situation the encroachment of the barrier spit on the inlet did not produce navigational problems but it did cause problems for an existing draw bridge over the inlet. The amount of tidal prism in Clearwater Pass remained fairly consistent over a few decades up to the early 1970s meaning that the inlet cross section should remain constant. If the barrier spit is growing into the inlet causing it to narrow, then it must deepen in order to maintain a constant cross-sectional area. Such deepening occurred and caused undermining of the pilings that support the bridge. A long jetty was constructed to stabilize the inlet width and to keep the bridge from collapsing. Unfortunately, although the jetty stabilized the inlet and the accumulation on the updrift side has provided an excellent park, the bridge stability problem has not been resolved. A somewhat similar condition existed but without a bridge at Masonboro Inlet, North Carolina.

FIGURE 9.15
Large groin in the North Sea showing burial and a symmetrical sand accumulation on both sides.

Soft Coastal Protection

During the past few decades there has been a growing trend away from hard construction and toward a so-called soft means of coastal protection. This approach avoids as much as possible the use of foreign material in the coastal environment that is being protected and does not incorporate any of the traditional types of hard construction. The advantages are the aesthetic appearance of the natural materials used and their compatibility with natural coastal processes. In many cases the cost of soft protection is below hard construction; however, longevity is sometimes a problem. Using some of the more successful examples, we will consider a few of the increasing variety of options for this approach to coastal protection.

Beaches   One of the first approaches to soft construction was to place nourishment sand on eroding beaches (Fig. 9.19). This practice has been used since

FIGURE 9.16
Jettied inlet to prevent movement and infilling of the inlet.

FIGURE 9.17
Inlet jetties showing extensive accumulation of littoral sand on the updrift side (foreground) and erosion on the downdrift side (background) where no sand is being supplied.

(a)

(b)

FIGURE 9.18
Photos showing Clearwater Pass, Florida, a) before jetty construction (1974) and b) a few years after construction (1979). Arrows indicate the same buildings on both photos.

(a)

(b)

FIGURE 9.19
Construction of a beach nourishment project includes a) pumping sand onto the beach in a slurry and b) grading it to the design specifications.

about the turn of the century but has only become widespread with sophisticated design since the 1970s. The first nourishment efforts were typically local and without real planning. Generally an eroding beach was supplied with the closest available sand. It might come from an adjacent dune, just offshore, or from a shoaling inlet. Generally little attention was paid to environmental damage, to the texture of the nourishment material, or to the design of the nourished area. The result was commonly environmental damage, rapid removal of the nourishment sand, and an overall waste of money. This led to a general lack of confidence in this approach to beach protection.

More recently an increasingly sophisticated approach to beach nourishment has been taken and the environmental damage during the process is being minimized. Engineers design the size and shape of the beach to be compatible with the adjacent bathymetry and wave conditions. Borrow material the same grain size or larger than ambient beach material is selected. The borrow site must be located where removal will cause minimal damage to benthic environments. This approach has greatly increased the cost of beach nourishment but has also provided a better product—one that has more longevity and a good appearance. There have, however, been several nourishment projects that have not lasted very long. In some cases nearly all of the sand placed on the beach was removed in only a couple of years when the design called for a lifetime of about ten years. Examples include a nourishment of the beaches south of Port Canaveral on the East coast of Florida where the nourishment material was too fine grained and most was eroded away in less than two years. Another situation of early removal of much nourishment material took place at Myrtle Beach, South Carolina, as the result of Hurricane Hugo in 1989. This was just a matter of bad timing that shortened the project lifetime; though hurricanes are expected along this coast it is not possible to predict when hurricanes will pass a particular coast and when nourishment projects will experience significant sediment loss from this type of storm.

On the other hand, some projects have been quite successful and cost-effective. Probably the best example is Miami Beach where for several years there was essentially no beach in front of the many luxury hotels along this famous tourist coast (Fig. 9.20). A multi-year project of nourishing over 15 kilometers of beach with millions of cubic meters of sand at a cost of $65 million was completed in 1980. The borrow area was the shallow offshore area where the sediment was extracted by a suction dredge and pumped onshore. Here the sediment was placed carefully by earthmovers and bulldozers to conform to the design criteria. Today the beach is still almost as wide as when the project was completed with stabilizing vegetation now present on the backbeach area. It is without a doubt one of the most successful of all such projects. Other smaller but similar projects on Captiva Island and Sand Key on the Gulf Coast of Florida have performed in a similar fashion. This approach to beach protection has almost totally replaced seawalls and other hard measures of protection, partly because of legislation, but also because they are cost-effective.

FIGURE 9.20
Oblique aerial photos of Miami Beach a) before nourishment and b) several years after nourishment.
(Courtesy of U.S. Army, Corps of Engineers)

A major problem associated with beach nourishment is the source material—its texture, location, and cost. The sediment must be essentially free of mud and organic matter in order to avoid problems of turbidity and fine sediment blanketing benthic communities. It must be coarse grained enough to be stable under the existing wave climate but cannot be dominated by coarse shell, which limits the recreational value of the beach. This has been a problem at Mullet Key near the mouth of Tampa Bay and at Marco Island in Florida. Proximity to the nourishment site is always a consideration due to its effect on cost. One of the best sources of borrow material is from the ebb tidal deltas of inlets that contain large mud-free accumulations of sand and shell. The dynamic nature of their surface is typically unvegetated and contains few types of benthic organisms. Current costs for beach nourishment projects including all aspects of design and construction range from $2 to $10 per cubic meter. Depending upon the volume of sediment required per linear meter of beach, the cost ranges from about 0.5 to 3.0 million dollars per kilometer of beach.

Dunes   Dunes are also commonly protected by soft means. Wind activity causes migration, and wave attack produces erosion of the seaward side. Protection and stabilization of dunes can reduce erosion and prevent their landward movement or destruction (Fig. 9.21). Various active measures to solve these problems have been used at least since the 1960s, and since then there has been an evolution in techniques and environmental compatibility that has proven to be successful.

Dunes have always been recognized as a critical factor in protection of the coast. Maintaining them and facilitating their growth is a primary objective of coastal management. This is made difficult because of the extremely fragile nature of dunes, especially their stability. A look at a well-worn foot path or a blowout shows how unvegetated dune sand can be mobilized, even in a small space.

The twofold objective of the dune management effort is simple—build dunes and protect them from destruction. Initial efforts at dune building used various types of fence to trap wind-blown sand (Fig. 9.21). The type and placement of fence varied, with the simplest configuration being one line of fencing at the back of the beach just in front of the dune. Many other more complicated

FIGURE 9.21
Eolian sand being trapped by fencing. Eventually the fences will be buried.

arrangements including boxwork fences have also been used. If successful, the dune grows and is at least partially held in place by the fencing. In some cases the fence is buried and a second-level fence is installed to try to increase the dune height. This activity is not without problems, even though it does produce important dunes. The anchoring provided by the fences prevents any dune migration during washover, and the result may cause accelerated erosion and removal of the sediment by wave attack.

Vegetation by itself and in concert with fencing has proven to be the best dune stabilizer and is also a means of producing the dunes. The combination of root structures, which hold sediment, and the leaves, grass blades and other structures of the plants baffle winds to trap sediment and hold it in place, is effective in keeping dunes from eroding. Well-planned dune building has become widespread along many coastal areas. One of the most simple but effective techniques is practiced along the Texas coast where residents use their old Christmas trees as sand trapping agents in front of the existing dunes. This approach is very low cost and effective, and the trees are biodegradable after several years of burial.

Another effective and inexpensive approach to dune stabilization is practiced along the European coast of the North Sea, especially in The Netherlands. Here, where coastal protection and control has been developed into an art form, the Dutch use an important natural resource, pensioners, to help protect and build dunes. Extensive dune protection is carried out by placing small fence-like structures of shrub twigs and branches in shallow ditches that are dug in various patterns at the base of and throughout the foredunes (Fig. 9.22). Retired coastal residents provide the bulk of the labor force and for it they receive a supplement to their pensions—everyone gains! The short fences are quite effective in trapping sand and also in stabilizing existing dunes.

There is also some important prevention and maintenance that need to be incorporated into dune stabilization. It is one thing to build a dune and stabilize it with vegetation. We must also be concerned with maintaining that stability. Included in this scheme is the construction of boardwalks to prevent destruction of vegetation (Fig. 9.23). Where boardwalks or walkovers are impractical, use of wooden planking along the footpath protects the surface from wind erosion even in the absence of plants. When dunes are built, the paths for people should be oriented at an angle to the dominant wind direction to prevent erosion, and not just perpendicular to the beach as is so often the case.

Back-Barrier and Estuarine Construction

The coastal environments that are protected from open marine conditions tend to experience only small waves and tidal currents. These back-barrier and estuarine environments tend to be characterized by low physical energy except for those such as the Bay of Fundy where tidal currents are very strong. In general, such environments are at or near equilibrium; any changes that take place tend

FIGURE 9.22
Use of brush rows along The Netherlands coast to trap wind blown sand.

to be modest in scope and at a slow rate. Construction in back-barrier or estuar-ine areas tends to be for either of two purposes: to provide transportation or for construction of buildings and related structures. Both of these can cause tremen-dous problems for the natural coast but both can take place in harmony with the environment if done properly.

Causeways   Most coastal metropolitan areas include the need to transport large numbers of people across coastal bays or tidal wetlands for purposes of commuting to work or accessing recreational areas on barrier islands. Whether this be roads or railways, the thoroughfare is typically in the form of causeways over the water surface. Tunnels are very expensive and are only used where the bay is too deep to make causeways cost-effective.

The easiest and least expensive construction approach is by building a roadbed through emplacement of fill on the shallow coastal aquatic environ-ment. Bridges for boat traffic and short overpasses for circulation are commonly provided as breaks in the otherwise solid construction. Additional bridges may be

FIGURE 9.23
Board walk over fragile, vegetated coastal dunes.

built in the event a local area is too deep for fill-type construction. This approach to causeway construction is replete with problems. It directly affects benthic communities by burying some organisms and by destroying others through the dredging required to obtain the fill material for the causeway.

These effects are actually minor compared to the problems the causeway causes to tidal circulation. The causeway itself acts much like a dam and greatly inhibits tidal flushing. This limitation generates two major problems for the coastal bay: (1) the restricted circulation produces problems of water quality, and (2) the tidal prism is reduced, which can cause changes in inlets.

Most coastal bays are quite productive and are high in nutrients. They also commonly receive considerable chemical pollution from the adjacent populated areas through surface runoff and, in some areas, industrial waste. Restrictions in circulation caused by a fill-type causeway cutting across such a bay produce important deleterious changes in water quality. Eutrophication takes place due to an inability to remove decaying organic material and replace oxygen deficient water with well-oxygenated water. Inability to disperse pollutants results in decreased habitat quality, causing death, inability to reproduce, or stunting in the various taxa in the bay.

These effects are direct and obvious. The changes in tidal prism brought about by the causeway's partitioning of the bay may cause indirect responses to the inlets served by the tidal flow into and out of the bay. A reduction in prism upsets the equilibrium condition that controls inlet cross section and stability. What commonly occurs is a decrease in inlet size, migration of the inlet, and in extreme cases, the inlet is closed.

This scenario has taken place at multiple places on the Gulf Coast of Florida where both inlets and fill causeways that connect the mainland to barrier islands are abundant. Dunedin Pass deteriorated from a width of over 150 meters and a maximum depth of 6 meters to instability and near closure during a 60-year period. The problem began after completion of the Clearwater Causeway south of the inlet in 1922 when the inlet cross section decreased greatly. After another causeway on the other side of the inlet was constructed about 15 kilometers north of the first causeway, there was an increase in the rate of inlet instability and a decrease in cross section (Fig. 9.24). Similar conditions have taken place at other Florida locations and in New Jersey, Texas, and other northern Gulf coast locations. Most of the potentially affected inlets in these areas have been stabilized by jetties, making the response, typically an increase in sediment accumulation in the affected inlet, more subtle. Placing causeways on pilings, which is now required construction practice, or cutting additional tidal relief channels in fill causeways, may reduce or eliminate the negative impacts of these common structures.

Dredging

There are many places within the coast that are dredged as part of our attempt to modify the environment to better suit our needs (Fig. 9.25). Most dredging is related to the need to deepen or construct channels to permit boat traffic or to permit an increase in the draft of boats. This is nearly always associated with estuaries and tidal inlets and, in some cases with coastal lagoons. Other dredging is associated with harbor and marine construction and maintenance, mining of shell or sand for construction, and also for increasing upland areas for development. Some of these dredging activities have only modest effects on the coastal environment in which they occur but others cause some serious problems. We will consider some of each category.

There are three primary concerns with channel dredging, especially in coastal bays such as estuaries: (1) the impact on the benthic community, (2) turbidity and suspended sediment caused by the dredging, and (3) disposal of the dredged material. Before the late 1960s and early 1970s there was little or nothing done to address these problems. Dredging destroys some of the benthic community and changes its environment, severely disturbing an area equivalent to that covered by the channel or the part of the channel that is being dredged. Most coastal bays support a diverse and abundant benthic community that can be disturbed or destroyed by the dredging process. Some recent studies have demonstrated the resilience of the benthic organisms where the initial destruction of the community recovers quite rapidly. In less than a year the environ-

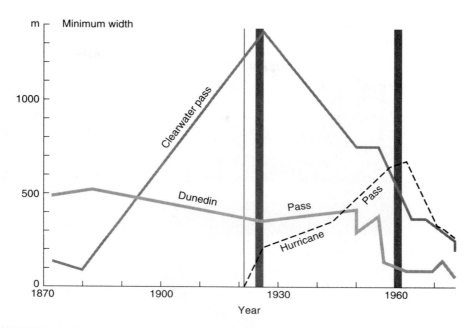

FIGURE 9.24
Graph showing the influence of the construction of two fill-type causeways (heavy vertical lines) on the size of Dunedin Pass on the Florida Gulf coast.

ment returns to its original character; in fact, some benthic organisms become more dense after than before the dredging.

The second major problem with dredging is the turbidity and suspended sediments that are produced during the dredging process (Fig. 9.26) in estuaries or harbors with significant mud content. This is a twofold problem in that turbidity reduces sunlight to photosynthetic organisms both in the water column and on the bottom. Often this is only a temporary problem lasting as long as the dredging activity, typically weeks or months. The eventual settling of the suspended sediment that produced the turbidity is another matter. This fine clay and mud-sized sediment will accumulate on the floor of the estuary or other locations near the dredging process. It may bury some benthic organisms, and it may clog the filtering system of others.

Another aspect of the dredging process is the disturbance of sediments that may contain material harmful to the environment. In industrial areas it may include various toxic pollutants that have accumulated on the floor of the bay. Disturbance by dredging may oxidize and mobilize certain pollutants that were stabilized or bound to clays during their undisturbed reduced state. More commonly, the problem is that the disturbed sediments contain abundant organic matter. Releasing this into the water column places high oxygen demand on the

(a)

(b)

FIGURE 9.25
Photos showing a a) dredge in operation and b) a close up of the rotating cutter head that cuts through the sediment and sucks it up to the dredge or on to a barge for transport.

environment in order to oxidize the organics. This process causes depletion of oxygen in the water and can lead to the death of animals including fish. Fortunately, all of these kinds of problems associated with dredging tend to be short in duration, generally days to weeks.

The third and most problematic negative aspect of dredging is the disposal of the dredged material. Millions of cubic meters of material are commonly re-

FIGURE 9.26
Aerial photo showing plume of sediment turbidity due to dredging.

moved during a single project. This material must be placed somewhere and it cannot have a negative impact on the environment. Before the development of environmental awareness and restrictions, the dredge spoil was placed in upland areas or on low wetland areas for land reclamation, causing pollution and destroying wetland environments (Fig. 9.27). Now dredge spoil may be used to create islands within the bay or is dumped offshore in deep water. The offshore dumping option can present problems for benthic communities, and it is costly. Creation of islands may be a viable alternative. Dikes are constructed and filled with the dredged spoil. This creates another wetland area and attracts abundant wildlife, especially birds. These impoundment islands can become important new habitats and recreational areas for picnicking, fishing, and beach activities. However, drainage of the turbid water from these impoundment sites, and wave erosion of containment dikes, can re-introduce easily suspended muds to a coastal bay. Such sediment pollution can be a chronic problem as is the case along the Intracoastal Waterway in Laguna Madre, Texas.

Dredge and Fill Construction   Waterfront property along coastal bays is scarce and very expensive. For many years it was practice to dredge from inter-

FIGURE 9.27
Placing dredge spoil in an environmentally sensitive location such as a salt marsh.

tidal or shallow bay environments and dispose of the material nearby to create upland areas for development of residential or even industrial property (Fig. 9.28). Many industrial complexes near metropolitan harbors have been constructed on this type of fill material. Included are the metropolitan areas of San Francisco, Miami, and Boston. Residential areas constructed in this scenario are generally characterized by narrow filled areas separated by finger canals. These not only destroy considerable natural bay environment but also create pollution problems in the bays because poor circulation is accompanied by increased influx of products from human development.

An additional problem associated with the dredge and fill practice of construction is that it reduces the area of the coastal bay and therefore reduces the tidal prism for inlets serving the bay. Such a condition of reduced tidal prism causes tidal inlets to become unstable and may even lead to their closure. At the least, the inlet instability has required structures to stabilize its migration and maintain a tidal flow. This has happened in a number of locations along the Florida Gulf coast. These practices of dredging and construction are no longer permitted; however, there are many coastal areas that retain extensive areas of finger canals.

Poor water quality often develops within these canals. Most such construction is in coastal bay settings where tidal range is low. Virtually all the canals have a single opening, therefore no through tidal circulation can take place. The problem is compounded by a high rate of nutrient and pollution influx from lawns, gardens, storm-water runoff, and other products of human occupation. These conditions lead to anoxic conditions and greatly reduce the number of fish, crabs, clams, and other animals that can live in the canal environment. In some cases, phytoplankton blooms flourish in these canals due to

FIGURE 9.28
Dredge and fill construction producing finger canals for residential development.

their stagnant, nutrient-rich water. Although the practice of constructing finger canals has essentially been stopped in most states in the United States, it is still practiced in other parts of the world, such as in Australia and New Zealand.

MINING THE COAST

The term mining generally calls to mind gold mines, open pit coal mines, or the removal of other valuable earth resources. The definition of the term includes removal of any earth material for consumption while making a profit. Some of the materials and rocks of the coastal zone are currently being mined; a few on a large scale. The products that are or have been taken include sand, gravel, heavy minerals, shell, beach rock, and salt.

Sand is the most important commodity currently being mined on the coast and is taken for a wide range of uses, especially for beach nourishment and for construction (Fig. 9.29). Initially, nourishment material was taken from any close place in which high quality sand was available, typically dunes and nearby

FIGURE 9.29
Mining the beach for sand in Puerto Rico.
(Courtesy D. Bush)

beaches. Due to increasing recognition that dunes protect adjacent development from storm damage, coastal dunes are tightly protected from alteration. Thus, virtually all of beach nourishment sand now comes from one of three sources: offshore beyond the zone of regular wave action, ebb tidal deltas off inlets, and upland sources away from the active coastal zone.

Glass and foundry sand for industry is taken from dunes in many parts of the world. These uses require very pure quartz sand, especially for the glass industry. There are still many locations in which sand is taken directly from the foredunes but most mining is restricted to the landward inactive dunes. Less and less of this activity is taking place as coastal management regulations are adopted and enforced, although some mining is still being conducted on the active beach. This is generally limited in volume and is still permitted because of old long-term agreements. Most common sites are at fillets of sand near structures or headlands and at the end of prograding spits. These locations minimize the problems to the beach area but the result is the removal of a valuable resource from that environment.

In some areas sand is very scarce, causing great problems for construction. This is particularly the case in some developing island countries that lack a major river system that can provide a sand source. This situation has led to the mining of the active beach or any other available and accessible sand source. One bizarre example is on the north coast of Puerto Rico where sand is scarce and construction is booming. The beaches are having their sand being "rustled" in the dark of night by end-loaders working in tandem with trucks to remove sand. Authorities are now patrolling the beach to prevent this illegal mining operation.

Heavy minerals commonly accumulate as lag deposits in backbeach areas as erosion occurs. Many of these minerals are valuable commodities such as ilmenite, rutile, zircon, garnet, and magnetite. Concentrations of only a percent or two by volume can be economic and typically are found in old backbeach and beach ridge deposits along the coast. These deposits are currently being mined using dredges and the desirable minerals are separated by hydraulic processes, a mining activity that produces temporary damage to the environment in the form of long shallow pits. Typically less than 3 percent of the sand volume is removed, which permits backfilling with no significant loss of sediment. Strict reclamation regulations require the companies to return the mined area to its pre-excavation condition. The most extensive accumulations of heavy minerals are along the west coast of the North Island of New Zealand where black sands nearly 90 percent magnetite (iron oxide) comprise beaches and dunes (Fig. 9.30). Dredges separate this economic commodity, which is pumped in a slurry onto ships for transport to Japan, where it is processed in the steel industry. Here the large volumes of sand removed create lakes along the coast.

Salt has been an important commodity since the beginning of civilization. It is typically produced in various evaporite areas, in interior desert environments, and also in coastal environments. Conditions necessary for formation of halite,

FIGURE 9.30
Black iron-rich sand on the west coast of the North Island in New Zealand.

common salt, include a high rate of evaporation as compared to precipitation, and a source of sodium and chlorine. Both elements are abundant in sea water, and many coastal lagoons provide an evaporitic environment.

Economic deposits of halite occur in natural settings and also in evaporite ponds constructed along the coast (Fig. 9.31). Most of these halite-forming areas are in low latitudes, for example, along coastal areas of the Persian Gulf and the southern Mediterranean Sea. Some of the constructed ponds are also located in the mid-latitudes such as are found along the southern part of San Francisco Bay in California.

Some of the rocky coasts provide important materials for quarrying. Uses range from crushed stone for aggregate or road metal to dimension stone that is used in various types of construction. In most cases, use of coastal sources of rock is uneconomic because of logistics or distances to area of use. Typically this type of quarrying is done only in areas in which no other source is available. Examples would be small islands. Probably the most extensive quarrying of the coast was carried out in the Caribbean during the early Spanish occupation. Many of these islands as well as the East coast of Florida have abundant beachrock and eolianite as their only available rock. Many of the original fortifications on these islands were built from this type of limestone. The fort at St. Augustine, Florida, the oldest city in the United States, is made from local beachrock.

FIGURE 9.31
Salt ponds for producing commercial products on the southern coast of Spain.

WATER QUALITY

Humans have a history of viewing aquatic environments as being a place in which waste can be disposed without problems; basically "out of sight, out of mind" or "dilution is the solution" approaches. Unfortunately these practices have been quite prevalent in coastal waters and in the ocean as a whole. Problems of water quality caused by these attitudes are not new; they have been around at least since the industrial revolution. With increasing human populations and waste production, coastal waters have been less capable of diluting human and industrial waste. In addition, some wastes simply accumulate, reaching toxic levels after years of input. Environmental awareness, along with the new ordinances and regulations that have followed, have changed our attitudes toward the water environment. Unfortunately, we are still overcoming some of the attitudes and practices of the past but progress has been made.

Nutrient Loading

Coastal waters tend to be shallow, especially in bays. Most of these coastal waters are naturally productive because of their high nutrient content. These nutrients encourage photosynthesis by diatoms, various algae, and sea grasses. Animals that feed on this plant matter are thus also abundant. Nutrients come from the chemical weathering of rocks and soil and are carried by streams to estuaries in which they support a dense and generally diverse community of organisms. These nutrients are a primary reason for estuaries being nurseries for the open marine environment.

As humans began to occupy the coast, especially the margins of coastal bays, the natural system began to change and water quality deteriorated. Domestic waste has always been a problem in coastal waters because of nutrient loading and also because of coliform bacteria and other potentially dangerous pollutants. As agricultural endeavors began to utilize fertilizers, the runoff also contributed considerable amounts of nutrients (nitrogen and phosphorus) to the coast. The same is true for runoff from residential areas around coastal bays.

Around many highly populated coastal areas in which the adjacent waters are overloaded with nutrient materials, extreme rates of productivity and algal blooms exist. The shallow bays become choked with vegetation. As this vegetation dies and decays, oxygen is consumed, thus creating problems for animals that take their oxygen from the water. The process keeps getting worse because the decay makes more and more nutrients available as raw materials for photosynthesis. This snowballing effect eventually stifles all life in the estuary except for huge quantities of plant material.

The only solution to this condition is to restrict use of nutrient-bearing compounds and materials and to better control the runoff discharge into coastal waters. Use regulation is a difficult problem to solve unless the availability of certain levels of fertilizers is restricted. The better way to solve the problem is by discontinuing the practice of discharging runoff via storm drains into coastal bays. Retention ponds can capture the nutrients and put them to good use by irrigating with the retention waters. This practice also helps recharge the groundwater supply. These approaches are being followed in scattered coastal areas; however, costs are high. Future infrastructure plans will include some portions of this scheme but it will be some time before it is a widespread method of addressing storm water runoff.

The other primary type of nutrient loading has been a problem for much longer. Sewage discharge, ranging from untreated to tertiary treated, is now entering coastal waters in varying amounts. In the undeveloped parts of the world like Southeast Asia, raw sewage enters coastal waters on a regular and large scale basis. In most developed countries only tertiary treated waters are discharged unless problems exist with the volume of sewage being directed to the treatment plants. As coastal development continues to grow, the overloading of these facilities is becoming a regular occurrence.

Industrial pollution is another major source of coastal pollution although present regulations have stopped blatant dumping. Many industries use toxic chemicals that until recently were simply dumped into storm sewers or were buried without regard to their ultimate destination. Various heavy metals, acids, organic compounds, and other pollutants may be dumped in this fashion. These chemicals may find their way into sediments, become concentrated in certain organisms, or may be distributed to other areas by tidal currents.

Although the presence of such pollutants in any coastal environment is harmful to the environment, it is a temporary condition that can be corrected, sometimes surprisingly quickly. The shallow coastal waters of the western end of Lake Erie are about midway between Detroit, Michigan, and Toledo, Ohio, two cities dominated by heavy industry. Tremendous pollution from the auto and glass industries among others resulted in this coast becoming essentially a biological desert during the 1960s. Strict regulations for waste disposal brought about the gradual cleaning of the lake's coastal waters and various organisms including game fish returned. After a period of less than ten years, the environment returned to its pre-industrial quality.

Another example occurred in Tampa Bay, one of the largest estuaries in Florida. A phosphate plant was disposing of considerable sulphuric acid into the bay resulting in water quality deteriorating to a pH of 3, with virtually all life gone. Even exotic minerals such as fluorite were precipitating on the estuary floor (Fig. 9.32). After the discharge of acid was stopped the water quality began to improve and within three years the affected area had returned to its natural state with a typical estuarine community. There is presently little evidence of the acidic condition of this part of Tampa Bay.

FIGURE 9.32
Fluorite crust precipitate in inner tidal zone, Tampa Bay, Florida. The result of byproducts from the phosphate industry.

CONCLUDING REMARKS

The coast is complex, dynamic, and fragile. We have occupied it for millenia generally with little or no major modifications. Exceptions to this relationship include Venice, Italy, or the coast of The Netherlands but for the most part people lived in harmony with the coast without major changes. This relationship changed dramatically in two distinctly different times for somewhat related reasons. Firstly, the Industrial Revolution caused great expansion of occupation, industrialization, and shipping, all of which utilized the coast. Much more recently, basically after World War II, use of the coast for residential and recreational purposes expanded greatly. Some of these activities have been in harmony with the dynamics of the coast but others have not.

We have overbuilt the coast, especially with hard construction, interfered with many of the natural processes that characterize these environments, such as littoral drift and tidal flow, removed natural features and replaced them with buildings, roads, and other structures, and have dumped various unnatural materials in coastal waters. Fortunately, the coast and its natural systems are quite resilient. Correcting our mistakes can return much of the natural environments to near their original condition. At this stage, we have reached the level of recognizing the problems that have been created—the future must include not only stopping them but also correcting past mistakes.

Index